Yorktown's Captive Fleet

GREAT JOY
TO THE
DAY.

WASHINGTON
AND
COUNT DE GRASSE:
A NEW SONG,

Designed to add Mirth to the Day of General Thankſgiving, Rejoicing and Illumi-
nation, on Account of the late great and glorious News of the taking York-Town, in
Virginia, in which were Lord Cornwallis and a large Knot of Britiſh troops, &c. ſaid
to be 0000 in the whole; with a 40 gun ſhip, a frigate, an arm'd ſloop and 100 tranſports.

[☞ Tune of WASHINGTON, or any one of the merrieſt Tunes you can find.]

COME jolly brave AMERICANS, and toſs the glaſs around,
Unto thoſe worthy PATRIOTS who rule in Camp or Town;
Unto our Great Commander brave glorious WASHINGTON,
To COUNT DE GRASSE and General GREENE and ev'ry Patriot Son.

GOD bleſs our valiant WASHINGTON! and may he long ſurvive,
Till he compleats a victory o'er all his foes alive;
May Heaven's bleſſings each deſcend, unitedly engage
To crown his life with happineſs unto a good old age.

Let all who love AMERICA, in all their ſonnets ſing
The late exploits of COUNT DE GRASSE and warlike General GREENE
And may each true AMERICAN thoſe valiant SONS adore,
For all their brave heroic deeds 'till time ſhall be no more.

O what a noble capture 'twas! muſt ev'ry one confeſs,
Of valiant COUNT DE GRASSE of late, and each the Hero bleſs;
His conqu'ring pow'r by ſea diſplay'd, forc'd Britiſh ſhips to ſtrike,
One hundred ſail of tranſports yield to the Blue and White:

Beſides three Britiſh men of war were captur'd by his hand,
Struck to this noble ADMIRAL's flag, and bow'd at his command.
Nine thouſand of their armed troops were conquer'd all in one,
Huzza! for Admiral COUNT DE GRASSE and glorious WASHINGTON.

GOD bleſs our noble GOVERNOR! long may he yet ſurvive,
A ſcourge to all baſe Tories who wickedly connive
To undermine fair FREEDOM's walls, with all her noble train;
Huzza! for all our PATRIOT SONS, let FREEDOM ever reign.

Sold at RUSSELL's Printing-Office, near Liberty-Stump. (Pr. 4 Cop.) ☞ At the ſame Place may be
had, cheap to Travelling-traders, &c. BICKERSTAFF's BOSTON ALMANACK for 1782.

Yorktown's Captive Fleet

JOHN O. SANDS

Published for The Mariners' Museum
Newport News, Virginia
by the University Press of Virginia
Charlottesville

Frontispiece: A broadside printed soon after the
victory at Yorktown in celebration of the event.
It is one of the few printed items of the period to ac-
knowledge the presence of the captive fleet. (Courtesy,
The Henry Francis du Pont Winterthur Museum)

THE UNIVERSITY PRESS OF VIRGINIA
Copyright © 1983 by The Mariners' Museum
Newport News, Virginia

First published in 1983
Mariners' Museum publication no. 41

Library of Congress Cataloging in Publication Data

Sands, John O.
  Yorktown's captive fleet.

  Bibliography: p. 255
  Includes index.
  1. Yorktown (Va.)—Siege, 1781.   2. Underwater
archaeology—Virginia—Yorktown Region.   3.   Shipwrecks
—Virginia—Yorktown Region.   4. Yorktown, Region (Va.)
—Antiquities.   5. Virginia—Antiquities.   I. Title.
E241.Y6S26   1983   973.3"37   82-23799
ISBN 0-917376-38-2

Printed in the United States of America

Contents

~~~~~~~~~~

Preface

~~~~~~~~~~~~~~~~

As it so often is with underwater archaeology, the cart was before the horse. The early 1970s saw renewed interest in investigating the shipwrecks at Yorktown, Virginia. The existence in the York River of a group of wrecks dating to the American Revolution was well-known to local historians and to local divers as well, but there was no specific information as to locations, identities, or historical background. Lacking in provenance, the artifacts recovered before that time were little more than curiosities. Alexander C. Brown had done some pioneering research for Homer L. Ferguson's "Salvaging Relics from the York River," but by his own admission he had barely begun. With the certain knowledge that at least several vessels of the eighteenth century, and perhaps a large number, lay at the bottom of the river, it seemed highly likely that some sort of investigation would take place during the period of the bicentennial. It was against this background that I began this study.

This work is an analysis of the role of sea power in the Yorktown campaign. The strategic background is described, the logistical problems are explored, and the tactical consequences of both are studied. The intention is to present a thorough review of the role of the captive fleet in the battle of Yorktown, within the larger context of the southern campaign. Having thus established the background, it is possible to consider the archaeological site within its proper context, to flesh out the detailed history of the captive fleet, and to assess the archaeological significance of the surviving shipwrecks. Through a consideration of both the historical and the archaeological information, a fuller interpretation of the events of 1781 than has previously been made is possible.

The nature of the inquiry resulted in several methodological decisions that affected both the research plan and the finished product. In contrast to most archaeological sites, Yorktown is immensely well documented; if anything, there are perhaps too many records. The overwhelming quantity of the surviving written, pictorial, and cartographic material made it necessary to devote substantial time to a review of the extant records. Though by the nature of the project much of this research was devoted to the discovery of the minute details of shipping, an effort was made to broaden the inquiry so that the events might be viewed in perspective. In consequence, considerable attention was paid to the overall British strategy in the South and to the actions that preceded the Battle of Yorktown. Because of the wealth of original material, it was decided that the story should be told, as much as possible, directly from the primary record. The use of secondary sources has been intentionally excluded so that the picture as it appeared to contemporaries might be painted. It was that picture, after all, which was the basis for the decisions the British had to make.

It should be noted that most of the sources examined in the preparation of this study were seen in reproduction form. Most of the overseas materials and those from anywhere in the United States except Virginia and Washington, D.C., were examined at the Department of Research and Record, Colonial Williamsburg Foundation, Williamsburg, Virginia. A vast collection of documentary material for the study of the history of colonial Virginia has been assembled in that repository. The most significant group is that material gathered by the Virginia Colonial Records Project, a cooperative survey of European archives undertaken in conjunction with the Virginia State Library and the University of Virginia. In addition, however, many records from American libraries have also been copied, most importantly those of the William L. Clements Library of the University of Michigan, Ann Arbor. Suffice it to say that this single repository is necessarily the focal point for any study of the Battle of Yorktown or the Revolution in Virginia. Although many items were examined in reproduction form, I had the pleasure of working for two weeks in repositories in England. A number of the items seen there were not yet available in this country, though some microfilm had been ordered. In view of the rapidly changing contents of the growing collections of the Virginia Colonial Records Project, it has not seemed productive to attempt to distinguish those items seen overseas from those seen here. Because the location and translation of certain of the French archival materials has been difficult in the extreme, they have been used only in translation. It seemed that much was to be lost and little gained by the presentation of these historical documents in their original language, and they have therefore been translated as literally as was consistent with readability. Further, it cannot be said that a full review of the material available in French collections has been possible, due to limitations of both time and funding. It is felt, however, that the bulk of the readily available material has been located.

While the record is detailed in comparison to most archaeological sites, it is by no means comprehensive. As George Washington wrote in 1788: "Your desire of obtaining truth is very laudable. . . . Many circumstances will unavoidably be misconceived & misrepresented.—Notwithstanding most of the Papers which may properly be deemed official are preserved yet the knowledge of innumerable things, of a more delicate and secret nature, is confined to the perishable remembrance of some few of the present generation."[1] In consequence of these lacunae, considerable effort has had to be devoted to the location and preliminary study of the York River wrecks, using archaeological survey techniques. Two magnetometer surveys were undertaken through the cooperation of the U.S. Navy and the Virginia Institute of Marine Science. A side-scanning sonar survey was also made, using a Klein Associates sonar, again with the help of the Virginia Institute of Marine Science. In both instances much of the support and organization was the result of the work of the staff of the Virginia Research Center for Archaeology and other agencies. This was the first time that these shipwrecks had been studied in a comprehensive fashion, and it is one of the earlier attempts at such systematic surveying to have been made in this country. The results indicate that, with a minimum of funds and a cooperative program, significant information can be gathered about a site on a remote basis. It is an important feature of the work that an effort has been made to integrate the technical data into the historical narrative; the two aspects suggest more together than either would separately.

The study demonstrates that sea power played a significant and continuing role in the Battle of Yorktown and, more broadly, in the American Revolution. The strategic and logistical policies of the home government were directly responsible for the choice of Yorktown as a post, for the approach taken toward its defense, and for its eventual loss. The strategic role of the naval forces involved dictated the tactical role of the shipping under Cornwallis at Yorktown. It was a critical element in the battle, a trump card that was never played successfully. The study examines the ways in which this shipping was brought into play, the possible alternatives, and the consequences. Last, the use of modern archaeological survey techniques, in tandem with historical evidence, confirms many expectations suggested by the written record and opens new avenues of inquiry for the future.

Since this project was first suggested to me in December 1971 by Ivor Noël Hume, director of the Department of Archaeology, Colonial Williamsburg, a host of people have assisted with it. First among these is Mr. Noël Hume himself, who has provided constant encouragement both to me and to others working to establish an underwater archaeology program in Virginia. The assistance of Colonial Williamsburg must further be acknowledged in that the resources of the Department of Research and Record were shared so generously with an outsider.

A number of agencies have been of great assistance in the furtherance of this enterprise. The Virginia Research Center for Archaeology, then under the direction of William M. Kelso, has been actively involved with the project since 1976. The institutional support, as well as the freely given assistance of many of the staff members, often on their own time, helped to make the survey efforts possible. John Broadwater, who has been in charge of the center's nautical archaeology program since 1978, has been immensely cooperative and helpful. The Virginia Institute of Marine Science, then under the direction of William J. Hargis, Jr., has been most cooperative in providing support services and vessels. Again, many of its staff members have given freely of their own time to work on the project. The U.S. Navy generously lent a considerable quantity of magnetic sensing equipment from its Magnetics Branch on two separate occasions. The personnel to operate it, William J. Andahazy, Bruce R. Hood, and Douglas G. Everstine, donated their time and expertise far above and beyond the call of duty. The Teledyne/Hastings Raydist Corporation lent its Raydist positioning system for one of the surveys and helped with data conversion on the others. Klein Associates provided the side-scanning sonar at a more than reasonable cost and sent their most knowledgeable and congenial technician, Garry Kozak, to operate it. The Institute of Nautical Archaeology, under the leadership of George Bass and J. Richard Steffy, committed considerable time, money, and effort to the excavations undertaken in 1976 and 1980. Gordon Watts, former underwater archaeologist for the state of North Carolina, has provided assistance, advice, and encouragement. So many staff members in all of the above agencies have shared their time and expertise, that it is impossible to thank each of them individually.

This study was ably directed at one time or another by Dr. James Merrill, of the University of Delaware, and by Dr. Philip K. Lundeberg, curator of naval history, National Museum of American History, and thanks are due both gentlemen. The study was submitted as a dissertation to George Washington University.

Early support for the project was made available to me while a Fellow at the Winterthur Museum, with funding from the National Endowment for the Humanities. As a Smithsonian Fellow at George Washington University, again with NEH funding, it was possible to continue the study. The Mariners' Museum, under the direction of William D. Wilkinson, has since been most generous in its support, both in terms of research time and operational assistance. The staff of the museum has been uniformly helpful and understanding; John Tilley generously commented in detail on the manuscript. Finally, funding for the direct support of the Yorktown project has been received for two years from NEH, which has made possible the in-depth survey of the site. It also made possible a research trip to England to complete this project.

The owners of the various manuscript materials and illustrations have been most generous in permitting their publication. Quotations from Crown Copyright Records in the Public Record Office appear by permission of the Controller of Her Majesty's Stationery Office.

Last, I owe thanks to my wife Geales for her patience and understanding; without her help I might have finished sooner.

Yorktown's Captive Fleet

1

The Campaign
in the South

IN A LETTER of March 7, 1781, Lord George Germain, the British secretary of state for American affairs, wrote, "So very contemptible is the Rebel Force now in all Parts, and so vast is Our Superiority every where, that no resistance on their Part is to be apprehended, that can materially obstruct the Progress of the Kings Arms in the Speedy Suppression of the Rebellion."[1] Two months later George Washington recorded in a gloomy tone in his diary, "Instead of having everything in readiness to take the Field, we have nothing and instead of having the prospect of a glorious offensive campaign before us, we have a bewildered and gloomy defensive one."[2] Yet within six months of this dark forecast Washington and his forces were victorious in what was to prove the decisive battle of the American Revolution. The critical factor in that victory was sea power. The developments that led up to the victory at Yorktown had a history not of months but of years, dating back to the early part of the war.

After two years of the struggle in North America, the British had altered their overall strategy. Their initial actions were based on the assumption that the rebellion was centered in Boston and was attributable to a few fiery radicals. If the uprising in Boston could be quelled, the other colonies would fall in line. The lesson of the first years of the war was that this approach was doomed to failure. The rebellion was general, and Boston was only the most immediate manifestation of the problem. In consequence, a new approach was adopted around 1778. The intention was to conquer and hold those colonies that were most loyal and most easily taken. In addition to Canada, Florida, Bermuda, and the Bahamas, all of which were already under control, an attempt was to be made to extend dominion over the southern colonies; the effort would begin with Georgia and South Carolina and eventually extend to include North Carolina, Virginia, and Maryland. As plantation economies dependent on exports, these colonies were peculiarly susceptible to control from the sea, by blockade and riverine warfare. With control of the southern colonies, the northern colonies would find themselves cut off and must eventually wither and succumb.[3]

Lord George Germain was the main promoter of this scheme, though it undoubtedly had its origins among the strategists of the day. Germain, born Lord George Sackville, had had a fairly distinguished military and diplomatic career, having risen by 1759 to the command of all the British forces cooperating with Prince Ferdinand of Brunswick in the Lower Rhine. At the Battle of Minden in August of that year, however, he hesitated and withheld his forces from action until the decisive moment had passed. For this misjudgment he was dismissed from military service, and the court martial, which he requested, only confirmed his condemnation. As a result of the acrimonious public debate, his political life was virtually at an end until the ascent of George III led to different attitudes in court. Germain was then appointed lord commissioner of trade and plantations, as well as secretary of state for the colonies, under the administration of Lord North, in 1775. He held the latter post until the resignation of Lord North's government in 1782. A resolute campaigner in the American war, Germain may have been seeking to redress old grievances through his determination to win. The death of his wife of twenty-four years in June 1778 can only have hardened his resolve.

To implement his plan for the reconquest of the American colonies, Germain selected Sir Henry Clinton. Born in Newfoundland, where his father was governor, Clinton was raised in New York when his father became governor of that colony. His military service began with the New York militia, though he first saw active service with the Grenadier guards. As a lieutenant colonel he served in the forces allied with Prince Ferdinand of Brunswick, to whom he was eventually appointed aide-de-camp. After distinguished service under the man responsible for Germain's disgrace, Clinton returned to England; he was finally detached to America. Serving under Generals Howe and Burgoyne, he again distinguished himself, particularly in the Battle of Bunker Hill. He was sent to North America again in 1776 with a commission to serve as second in command to Sir William Howe. Clinton continued to serve with distinction until the disastrous capture of Burgoyne at Saratoga in October 1777. Howe returned to England, and Clinton found himself in command of the British forces in North America. It was his responsiblity to implement the new strategy, to put into effect the plans developed thousands of miles away from the war itself.

Germain's orders to Clinton, dated March 8, 1778, outlined the intended campaign. Failing an immediate and decisive action against General Washington, he was to undertake to gain control of all the seaports from New York northward, thus cutting off all possible commerce in New England. He was then, when fall made operations in the South more feasible, to attack Georgia and South Carolina, with the intention of conquering them and raising loyalist troops there. Germain continued:

> *While these Operations are carrying on every Diversion should be made in the Provinces of Virginia and Maryland, that the remaining troops, which can be spared for offensive Service, in conjunction with the Fleet, will admit of. The great number of deep Inlets and navigable Rivers in those Provinces expose them in a peculiar manner to naval Attacks, and must require a large Force to be kept on foot for their Protection, and disable them from giving any assistance to the Carolinas. The seizing or destroying their Shipping would also be attended with the important Consequence of preventing the Congress from availing themselves, as they have done, of their Staple Commodity, Tobacco, on which, and the Rice and Indigo of Carolina & Georgia, they entirely depend for making Remittances to Europe. Should the Success we may reasonably hope for attend these Enterprizes, it might not be too much to expect that all America to the South of the Susquehannah would return to their Allegiance, and in the Case of so happy an Event, the Northern Provinces might be left to their own Feelings & Distress to bring them back to their Duty, and the Operations against them confined to the cutting off all their Supplies, & blocking up their Ports.[4]*

This outline, which was to be the foundation for the actions of the next four years, was based on sound reasoning by strategists who recognized the peculiarities of this war, peculiarities without precedent.

A series of position papers written by Richard Oswald summed up the factors that affected the British decision to pursue the war in the South. One of the wealthiest London merchants, with extensive holdings in the Carolinas, and destined to be one of the British negotiators at the 1783 Paris Peace Conference, Oswald argued in February 1778 in favor of the establishment of a series of seacoast posts, supported by the navy. These would serve as fortified harbors, both protecting ships and at the same time being protected by ships. They would resolve the critical problem of supply, which constantly plagued British forces in North America. The American people were either unwilling or unable to produce sufficient food and supplies within the conquered districts to support the king's army. In consequence, the army had to communicate with the ships that brought supplies from England; the sphere of military operations was thus strictly limited. The control of seaports enabled the control of trade as well, a critical element in subduing the rebels. Oswald further explained his ideas in 1779, stressing that primary reliance must be placed on the navy in the pursuit of such a war. He wrote, "There has been a great mistake in people's conceptions of the nature of this American business from the beginning; by which their attention has been improperly, I may say fatally, turned too much to the Land Service." He explained that the wide extent of the continent, the relatively small number of troops that could be sent to America, and their inability to occupy more than a small portion of the country at any one time had made the task set before the army virtually impossible. In contrast, he proposed a blockade of the coast, to be supported from "Ports of Rendevous for Shipping," which would be held by the army; the navy was to bear the primary burden, however. As for the army, "after these Troops were placed in their Seaport Garrisons, we should have thought no more of them farther than to pay & victual them properly." This was precisely the scheme that worked so successfully eighty years later in the American Civil War, resulting in the slow strangulation of the trade of the Confederate states.[5]

Oswald's unusual approach to the American war recognized its peculiar character. This was a war of the people; a defeat in arms did not necessarily imply a defeat in reality:

This American Land War is like no other War that ever was read, or heard of before. It prescribes action & conquest, but carries no coercive powers along with it over the Inhabitants of the Country. It courts Allegiance, but cannot enforce any, either by Contribution of Property, or Penalty of Person. Where the Inhabitants chuse to be quiet, they lose nothing, & we gain nothing. They allow us to pass through their country; & as we halt at night, to take possession. If we chuse to remain there, we have made a Conquest. If not we quit it in the Morning. In this manner we penetrate but conquer nothing. If in our progress we at last meet with Opposition, or an embodied Force in hostile array, We are ordered to encounter it. We do so, & suppose that Army is defeated & disappears. What shall we do next. We call upon the Inhabitants then, to give us assurance of their Amity & Submission, by oath or affirmation. They decline it, & won't tell us their reasons. Whether from Principle, as not inclining to our government, or from prudence, not being certain of a permanent protection—it is to us the same thing. We must leave them as we found them, and so must go in search of new adventures. We have a great deal to do. But must not go too far off, as we must eat. We would gladly Save our English Supplies as they come from a great way, & yet not being certain that the Country will kindly help us, & that it would displease them to be forced, we must not cash ourselves upon uncertainty & so must keep within a proper distance. At last we hear the Enemy which we beat is recruited & not far off, in the high grounds. We march thither, attack & dislodge him, & get possession. But it not being safe to stay, for fear of his getting between us & our Provisions, we quit it, & return by a different route, trying always for conquest or at least for as much as might pay for the Expences of the Expedition. But with the same effect as formerly, the Inhabitants taking our Money, giving us good words, & making the same excuses as they did on the former occasion.[6]

This classic description of what would later be called guerrilla warfare epitomized the plight of the British in America. By sim-

In 1755 H.M.S. Norwich *visited Yorktown. A midshipman on board, John Gauntlett, is thought to have executed this drawing at that time. Though the artist has misplaced several of the houses, the town looked much the same in 1781. The fortification in the center was the sole defense of the town until Cornwallis arrived. Though not shown, there was at least one wharf along the shoreline. (Courtesy of The Mariners' Museum, Newport News, Va.)*

ply prolonging the war, the Americans made victory more likely. They knew that the expense of the war was unpopular politically at home, that they might win by waiting.

The British ministers wished to press the war in the South for two reasons. First, tobacco, the most valuable product of the colonies, continued to be exported. Not only did England lose the benefits of this trade, but it was a primary means of financing the rebellion.[7] Second, since fewer actions had been fought in the South, more loyal citizens might be found there. The sentiments of the planter class seemed always to have leaned toward England. There can be no question that the first objective, that of controlling the trade of this critical area, was a worthy one; but the second, that of rallying a loyal citizenry, proved illusory. Clinton wrote in the spring of 1781, concerning the choice of Portsmouth, Virginia, as a post "with a view of putting our friends of Princess Ann &c. under cover and protection but by your account a small house will I fear be sufficient for them all."[8] For the above reasons, however, the conquest of the Chesapeake region was to become an idée fixe with Lord George Germain.

In the spring of 1779 Clinton dispatched a small force under Maj. Gen. Edward Mathews to raid in Virginia. On April 29 it sailed from New York under the convoy of Commodore Sir George Collier, the senior naval officer in America. After a stay in the Chesapeake area, particularly Portsmouth, for about a month, the expedition sailed back to New York. Clinton had been unable to spare sufficient forces to take up a permanent post, in consequence of which he sent the contingent as a raiding party to destroy supplies. Its orders were to remain only if there was a massive uprising by the citizens in support of the king. Failing that, the entire force had returned to New York. Germain was at first pleased to learn of the expedition, then disappointed to discover what a temporary enterprise it had been. After its conclusion, he wrote to Clinton to urge an attack on Charleston. He continued:

> *The other Enterprize you meditate on the side of the Chesapeak Bay, cannot, I am persuaded, fail of accelerating the great end of all the King's American measures, the suppression of the Rebellion; and I shall hear with particular pleasure that you have found means to establish a post at Portsmouth in Virginia, as that situation appears to be so well circumstanced as a station for the Men of War & privateers to intercept the Trade of that Province & Maryland whilst they persist in Rebellion, which with that of Carolina & Georgia have furnished the Congress with the chief means of purchasing supplies for carrying on the War.[9]*

While Clinton's enthusiasm for these expeditions was at best lukewarm, the same could not be said of his second in command.

Charles, Earl Cornwallis, was the eldest son of a prominent family; educated at Eton, he entered military service in 1756. Like his contemporaries, he served under Prince Ferdinand of Brunswick and was present at the Battle of Minden. Unlike Germain, however, Cornwallis found his reputation enhanced by that action, and he returned to England after a promotion to captain. He was opposed to the political actions that precipitated the American rebellion, but once hostilities commenced, he willingly served the king in his attempts to suppress the uprising. Acting under the command of Sir William Howe, Cornwallis demonstrated ability and skill. He won the Battle of Brandy-wine, successfully occupied Philadelphia, and returned home to be promoted to the rank of lieutenant general. Sent back to America in April 1778, he was to serve as second in command to Clinton, with a reserve commission as commander in chief should Clinton resign. Cornwallis, unlike his superior officer, was an enthusiastic believer in Germain's overall strategy and sought to put it into effect immediately. With an up-and-coming military career, he wanted action and victory, not the apparent sluggishness of Clinton's campaign. In consequence, Cornwallis maintained a regular correspondence directly with Germain, to the constant annoyance of Clinton; the difference in the temper-aments of the two men was to lead to grudging cooperation, if not open hostility, in the months ahead.

Sir Henry Clinton, faced with orders from Germain to open a serious southern campaign, chose to press the attack on Charleston, and the full efforts of the British forces in North America were directed at that objective, starting in December 1779. With the conquest of Charleston on May 12, 1780, Clinton dispatched Lord Cornwallis with a substantial force to subdue the backcountry of South Carolina while he returned to New York. Charleston became a fortified post, and the focus of the war shifted to Lord Cornwallis, whose South Carolina enterprise was fraught with problems. Germain was not about to forget his interest in the Chesapeake, however, and he continued to urge the project from time to time.

Clinton himself seems to have recognized the desirability of beginning serious action in the Chesapeake region, though his motives differed from those of the strategists in England. He envisaged a series of small actions that would divert rebel atten-tion from Lord Cornwallis in South Carolina, thus facilitating his attempts to subdue the Carolinas. It had become his opinion, and apparently that of Cornwallis as well, that the rebels' source of men and supplies for the South was Virginia. By forcing the militia to look to their home territory, they would be prevented from rendering assistance to the forces in North and South Caro-lina. Such an effort required concerted action by the army and the navy, the realization of which proved elusive. Clinton wrote to Adm. Marriot Arbuthnot, commander in chief of the navy in North America, on July 5, 1780, expressing his disappointment at Arbuthnot's lack of cooperation. He had that morning proposed to the admiral that a post be established at Portsmouth, in consequence of a dispatch he had received from Germain. But Arbuthnot believed that the requisite ships could not be spared from his defense of New York. As he was under no apprehension that the Americans might occupy the post in strength before the British, he apparently felt no sense of urgency. Clinton therefore reluctantly agreed to postpone the expedition until naval cooperation could be guaranteed.[10] Clinton and Arbuthnot had little respect for each other, and this was not the first time they had found it difficult to act in a cooperative venture.

The weakness of a joint command such as this was recognized by Sir George Brydges Rodney, who wrote to Lord Germain in December 1780:

> *Permit me to add that if Adm——s would consider, the difficulty of making Different Commander in Chief agree, they would find it answer their own and the Nation's expectations better if there was during this very Important Crisis—but one Commander Chief, by Land, or Sea, Responsible for the War both in America and every part of the West Indies, all difficultys would then be removed and no officer presume to Judge whether, he was or was not, to obey the orders of a Superior Officer, because he was not in sight of a Superior flag and had a Commission as Commander in Chief upon a particular Station.*[11]

There was no resolution of the problem during the American Revolution, and the dilemma of joint command was to return to haunt the British forces the next year, when delay would prove fatal.

Clinton reiterated his request for naval support on August 26, 1780: "From letters I received yesterday from Earl Cornwallis in South Carolina, I am become entirely of opinion that some very early Expedition into Chesapeake Bay is absolutely necessary."[12] There was continuing pressure from Lord George Germain to undertake a diversion in support of Cornwallis in the Chesapeake. He wrote to Clinton on October 4, in consequence of discouraging news received from Lord Cornwallis in South Carolina. He urged that a post be established immediately in Virginia, in the expectation that this would have the effect of diverting the Virginia and Maryland militia, which had been sent south to oppose Cornwallis. He further urged that such a project be "speedily executed, as no accounts have been received of the sailing of any second Armament from France for North America."[13] Germain was obviously concerned that a British incursion into the Chesapeake might be preempted by a French move; he further recognized the vulnerability of any post there in the face of a superior fleet. Since the Franco-American alliance of 1778, the British had good cause for concern over possible naval intervention. In contrast to the practically nonexistent American naval force, the French navy was at least the equal of the British navy at this time. With the arrival of fleets under d'Estaing and Guichen, the war in North America had taken on a more serious air. Both Clinton and Germain had every reason to be concerned at the possibility of a major French fleet gaining control of the East Coast of North America, a possibility that was realized a year later.

By the time Germain had written, however, Clinton had succeeded in getting the proposed expedition into an advanced state of readiness. Arbuthnot had complied with his second requisition for ships, and assigned seven vessels to the project under the overall command of Captain Gayton, H.M.S. *Romulus*.[14] The preparations were further facilitated by the arrival of Admiral Rodney, visiting briefly from the West Indies with the principal British fleet. Exercising his seniority, much to the disgust of Arbuthnot, he took supplies and ships for his own fleet and ordered full cooperation with the expeditionary force preparing for the Chesapeake.

After Arbuthnot's grudging assistance, Clinton must have been pleased indeed with Rodney's understanding aid; he wrote to Cornwallis in South Carolina on September 20:

> *I have always thought Operation in Chesapeak of the greatest importance, and have often represented to Admiral Arbuthnot the necessity of making a Diversion in Your Lordship's favor in that Quarter, but have not been able till now to obtain a Convoy for*

John Gauntlett pictured Gloucester Point across the York River from Yorktown in 1755. Small even as towns went in the 18th century, Gloucester Point did boast a very small fortification on the beach. (Courtesy of The Mariners' Museum)

> *this purpose. I have Communicated to Sir George Rodney my Wishes to send an Expedition thither, and he has most chearfully Consented to grant every necessary Naval Assistance. In the course therefore of a very few days it will be dispatched, every thing having been in great forwardness before Sir George's arrival, in consequence of Admiral Arbuthnot's having sent me all the Ships he could spare for that Service.[15]*

This expeditionary force was placed under the command of Major General Leslie, who was ordered to "pursue such Measures as you shall judge most likely to answer the purpose of this Expedition, the principal object of which is to make a Diversion in favor of Lieut. General Earl Cornwallis."[16] The convoy carrying Leslie and his troops sailed from New York on October 17 and arrived in Virginia on the twenty-second; a post was established at Portsmouth on October 27, 1780. In the meantime, after a brief incursion into North Carolina, Cornwallis had withdrawn his army to South Carolina, himself bedridden with a fever and his prospects much dimmed by the defeat of Major Ferguson at King's Mountain. Without the immediate possibility of a move into North Carolina, let alone Virginia, Cornwallis thought bet-

ter of the benefit which a diversion in the Chesapeake might
provide him. Writing in his stead, due to Cornwallis's illness,
Lord Rawdon informed General Leslie that he could be of most
assistance if he were to abandon the Chesapeake and move to
North Carolina and the Cape Fear River. Though his first letter,
written October 24, left Leslie to make the final decision on the
basis of his understanding of Clinton's orders, a second letter
written October 31 contained positive instructions to be followed unless in direct conflict with those orders.[17] In consequence, Leslie gave up his plan to establish a post in Portsmouth, and reembarked his troops. The short-lived expedition
to Virginia ended when the fleet sailed from Hampton Roads on
November 23. Though headed for the Cape Fear River, the
ships were met by H.M.S. *Galatea* en route, with orders from
Cornwallis to proceed to Charleston. The fleet arrived there on
December 14, and Leslie effected a junction with Cornwallis
soon thereafter.[18] Clinton gave his approval of this move in a letter of November 12, reiterating that support of Cornwallis was
the primary goal of the venture.[19] Leslie must have appreciated
some of the importance attached to the Virginia post by the Min-
istry, however, for he wrote on November 19:

> *I left the works entire, and I still hope you will be enabled to
> take up this ground, for it certainly is the Key to the wealth of
> Virginia, and Maryland, it is to be lamented, we are so weak in
> Ships of War, for there's a fleet of Sixty sail expected hourly from
> the W. Indies, besides the Valuable Ships or Craft ready to Sail
> from the Chesapeake. Had we gone up the River we should have
> benefitted as Individuals, loaded with plunder, and Tobacco, but I
> am confident we should have lossed some of our large Ships, for
> they get aground on every Move, even the King's Ships, who
> never want for pilots.[20]*

Even during the course of his short visit, Leslie had appreciated
some of the opportunities the Chesapeake presented to the British, and some of the problems as well.

When news of the abandonment of Virginia reached Lord
George Germain, he expressed considerable consternation. On
January 3, 1781 he wrote Clinton at some length, voicing his

disappointment in the action, the unfortunate results that might be expected from it, and the hopes he still entertained for such an expedition. His first concern was that this second abandonment of Portsmouth within two years must necessarily make cautious any potential loyalists, who had been twice left to the mercy of the rebels. He also emphasized the importance of cutting the supply lines for the southern army, thus aiding in the reduction of the colonies of North and South Carolina. Perhaps most significantly, however, he urged action in the Chesapeake because of activity which he had reason to expect from the French. The fleet under d'Estaing that had sailed to the West Indies had been brought into play in a cooperative venture with the Americans, an attack on Savannah in September 1779. Although the effort failed, there seemed every reason to expect that similar ventures would be attempted in the future, perhaps with the Chesapeake as target. As it seemed highly probable that troops would be sent from France in the spring, it seemed equally likely that they would be sent to secure the Chesapeake, once word of its abandonment was received. Germain consequently pressed again for action in Virginia.[21] The strong terms in which he urged this move were carefully calculated, with an ulterior motive. He had for some time felt that Clinton was not pursuing the war with the vigor that might reasonably be expected. In the preparation of this letter, he was assisted by William Knox, his undersecretary of state for America, to whom he wrote:

> *I hope you will see Dalrymple as he may possibly throw some fresh light upon Clinton's intentions, tho' I confess I expect little exertion from that Quarter and I feel more disappointed and less sanguine about the success of the war in America than I have ever yet done. . . . I mean in consequence of former orders and to enforce as strongly as possible the Establishing a Port in the Chesapeake but when we are to act with such a man as Clinton we must be cautious not to give him an opportunity of doing a rash action under the sanction of what he may call a positive order. . . . But there is no use in fretting when we can not do more than has been done from hence, and the rest must depend upon those who are trusted with the Execution of the war. I would be happy if our Generals had more Activity.[22]*

Apparently Knox drafted this crucial letter of January 3, 1781, and sent it on to Germain for approval. Germain, at his country estate, wrote back:

> *I return you the Letters Extracts for what you say to Clinton is so well Connected with what he will have already received, that it must Convince those who may read the Correspondence, that we have ever had in view a Settlement in the Chesapeak, and have never alter'd our opinion about it, he has always adopted the Idea, has promis'd to Execute this Plan, but is never Steady when the most favourable circumstances invite him to pursue it. I should think he will feel hurt at seeing his Conduct set in the true light and that if the Jealousy of Lord Cornwallis does not outweigh him, he will take the opportunity of quitting his command. I shall not be sorry to see him here, if he does not resolve to act with more steadiness and Activity.*[23]

Knox, ghostwriting for Germain, had made it clear that time was of the essence in the pursuit of victory. He wrote, "The Circumstances of this Country cannot support a protracted War, nor bear to have any considerable part of the National Strength remain inactive or unemployed. Every Advantage must therefore be seized, every Occasion profited of, and the Public Service be made the great Motive and Object of all Our Actions."[24] Clinton had, in the meantime, already taken action that would satisfy most of the demands in the minister's letter before it was received.

On December 14, 1780, Brig. Gen. Benedict Arnold, recently gone over to the British side, was ordered to the Chesapeake with approximately 2,000 men and a naval convoy. He was to disrupt the supply lines and depots of Virginia as much as possible and then establish a permanent post at Portsmouth, to which loyalists might come. Once that post was established, Clinton made it clear that he did not expect it to be abandoned or risked, lest every hope of the loyalists be dashed.[25] In spite of rough weather and a seriously dispersed convoy, Arnold arrived in Virginia by the end of the year. He immediately undertook an expedition up the James River, attacking the warehouses of Richmond and the shipping in the river. The public stores in Richmond were largely destroyed, while the tobacco and shipping were left intact, since they seemed to be largely the property of loyalists. After Arnold had seen to it that the stores had been "purified by the Flames," he withdrew and occupied Portsmouth, as ordered.[26] As was the case when the expedition under Leslie came into Virginia waters, a number of prize ships had been taken, by both the navy and the army. Certain of these were sent back to New York under convoy, while others were held in the Elizabeth River, along with the naval vessels that remained to help in the defense of the post.

Arnold quickly realized that Portsmouth would be a difficult post to defend since it was spread out and broken up by water. He therefore urged that Clinton send him more men and further offered a novel approach to the subjugation of the colony. While others had proposed to take advantage of the extensive river system of the Chesapeake to provide access to the interior, it seems always to have been the intention that naval vessels would be used. Arnold, recognizing the difficulty of using deep-draft vessels in the shallow waters, proposed to have constructed fifty light boats, which "would enable us to move with double the Celerity that the Militia could do, with every Exertion. The Rivers and Creeks in this, and the neighbouring States, in that respect, gives us every advantage." The boats to be built were designed to carry about eighty men each, while drawing only 12 inches of water.[27] It would appear that Arnold had in mind the construction of boats similar to the gundalows with which he had successfully delayed the British on Lake Champlain in 1776. The construction of these small boats was authorized by Clinton, and a number were built; circumstances did not permit their full development, though the concept was sound.[28] Arnold, however, soon found himself wholly on the defensive.

Since the arrival of the French expeditionary force in Newport, Rhode Island, in July 1780, the British had been apprehensive about actions the French might initiate. In addition to the five-thousand-man force under the comte de Rochambeau, there was a naval squadron under Admiral Ternay present, on which a watchful eye was kept. When Admiral Arbuthnot received orders to dispatch five of his ships to the West Indies, there was considerable concern in New York over the possible result of such a move. Clinton urgently requested that he not send the

An engraving issued in 1793 depicting the then successful and widely respected Lord Cornwallis. (Courtesy of The Mariners' Museum)

ships requested, lest the French achieve superiority at sea. Thus, on December 19, 1780, Admiral Arbuthnot reported to Lord George Germain that he had not dispatched the ships. He stated that the risk that the French would use their temporary superiority to convoy a large part of the American army to the South posed too great a hazard to Lord Cornwallis. In consequence, he continued to guard the vessels at Newport, though he added grumpily, "If the superiority at sea would give the enemy such decided advantage over us, why do we not avail our selfs, who are at present possessed of it?"[29] Notwithstanding Arbuthnot's attitude, there was real reason for concern.

The French apparently received a request from the state of Virginia to "protect the American commerce in the Chesapeake Bay and attempt to destroy the fleet of Mr. Arnold which was laying waste the shores of that State."[30] In consequence, a ship of the line, two frigates, and a cutter were dispatched under the command of Captain Le Gardeur de Tilly and entered Hampton Roads on February 8, 1781. At their approach the British withdrew into the Elizabeth River, which was too shoal for anything larger than a frigate to enter. Finding the fleet well protected by the narrowness of the river and the shore batteries of Portsmouth, the French stayed in Hampton Roads for ten days and then sailed again for Rhode Island. Although the post at Portsmouth had been held, there was by no means universal acclaim for the actions of the British fleet on this occasion. John McNamara Hayes, stationed in Charleston, voiced his criticism of the forces there for not sailing to the Chesapeake to attack the small French squadron that had entered the Bay. Captain Barclay, of H.M.S. *Blonde*, had received timely notice from Captain Symonds, in Portsmouth, of the presence of the French, but he took no action to intercept them. Hayes commented, "But alas! They were not Tobacco Ships, and therefore not *deemed* an object."[31]

While this lack of cooperative action may have had its roots in the jealousy which had developed between the army and the navy over the distribution of prizes, it may also be that Barclay was privy to the greater scheme of things. The forty-four-gun *Romulus*, convoying transports back to New York after landing

Leslie's force in South Carolina, had been captured by the
French squadron on its way to the Chesapeake. In addition to
this blow, there was a more important indication of the significance of the French vessels in the Chesapeake, as suggested in a
letter written to Arnold by Clinton: "Appearances at Rhode Island give some reason to suppose that the Ships seen last
Wednesday were the Avant Garde from that place. Should they
pay you a visit from Rhode Island, you may rest assured every
attention will be paid to your Situation, and that our Movements
will be regulated by theirs."[32] Clinton soon had cause to back up
his promise with action.

It rapidly became clear to Arnold that Clinton's information
from Rhode Island was correct and that a move against Virginia
was underway, with the French navy to support troops under
Lafayette. In the face of such an attack, a concerted defense by
the army and the navy was obviously required. Unfortunately,
the forces in Virginia were suffering from the same lack of harmony that afflicted the services in general. They had been quib-
bling over the distribution of prize moneys, and neither service
had formal command over the other. As the Virginia militia
gathered, Arnold wrote to Clinton on March 8:

> *I have every reason to believe that [the enemy] have collected their
> Force to co-operate with the French ships and Troop which they
> hourly expect from Rhode Island. I have had several
> Conversations with Commodore Symonds upon the subject of the
> defence of this place, and His Majesty's Ships. He seems
> undetermined how to act. At one time he proposes opposing the
> Enemy at Crany Island Bar—at another of bringing his Ships up
> to Town. At present he is between both, and has lain there near
> four weeks, permitting the Enemy's Ships to go out & come in as
> they please. He informs me, that his orders from the Admiral are
> to get all the Ships in Shoal Water, out of the reach of the
> Enemy, and I believe he is sincerely inclined to follow his
> Instructions. . . . I am clearly of opinion that if the Commodore
> gives up Craney Island Bar, that every King's Ship and
> Transport here will fall a Sacrifice in Forty Eight hours after the
> Arrival of a superior fleet and Army to ours.*[33]

Arnold seems eventually to have prevailed on Captain Symonds,
of H.M.S. *Charon* and senior naval officer in Virginia at the

time, to cooperate with his plan for defense. He wrote Clinton again on March 12: "Commodore Symonds at my earnest request has at last consented to attempt to stop the Enemy's Ships at the Bar, below Craney Island, should they attempt to come up here. He is preparing Ships to sink for that purpose, and was to have moved his Frigates down to the place two days ago. They are (for what reason I know not) still remaining in their old station."[34] Arnold was thus preparing to weather a siege in the classic fashion. He had canceled all expeditionary excursions, withdrawn within his lines, and sought to use the shipping in the harbor to block access to his post by water. In the full knowledge that his force was inferior to the enemy expected, he sought to hold the post until relief could be sent from New York. Neither Arnold nor Symonds seems to have been inclined to force an action against the partially assembled rebel force. They were content to take a defensive position and await developments.

They did not have long to wait. On March 5 the French began embarking troops in Rhode Island, and their fleet sailed with two thousand men on March 8. Since the death of Ternay, Commodore Destouches was in command. They were apparently trying to take advantage of the fact that Arbuthnot was remasting H.M.S. *Bedford*, using spars removed from H.M.S. *Culloden*, lost off Long Island earlier. Arbuthnot swiftly completed that task, however, and on March 10 he sailed from Gardiner's Bay, at the tip of Long Island, where he had been watching the French. In the meantime Lafayette had been marching south with a body of continental troops to join the Virginia militia. Arbuthnot caught up with the French squadron on the morning of March 16, having been favored by a following wind and sped along by his copper-bottomed ships. Lines of battle were formed, the ships in the vans engaged, but the action never became general. After damage had been inflicted on both sides, the French withdrew into the haze, and Arbuthnot, instead of pursuing, saw to his crippled ships. The next morning he sailed between the Capes of Virginia. With the Chesapeake secured, Arnold had little to apprehend from the forces gathered on land; they were powerless to act without superiority at sea. Arbuthnot notified the Board of Admiralty of the successful outcome of the engagement and of the effect it would have on the land forces. He had blockaded Lafayette's small force in Annapolis, and he

A miniature of Sir Henry Clinton painted in 1793, when the general was in retirement, his career shattered by events in North America. (Courtesy Victoria and Albert Museum. Crown Copyright)

expected the militia to become disaffected and disperse. In short, "the plan of the Rebel campaign is intirely disconcerted." The French fleet returned in frustration to Rhode Island, and arrived safely, though Arbuthnot had set out in hopes of forcing a second engagement. Having forestalled Washington's effort to retake Virginia, the admiral retired to New York.[35]

Clinton recognized the critical nature of this attempt, the importance it had whether won or lost. He had written on March 14: "It is a bold move to evacuate Rhode-island, and proceed to the Chesapeak so encumbered, liable to be followed by an unencumbered superior copper fleet. God send our old Admiral success!"[36] The significance of the engagement was also perfectly clear to Lord George Germain, and he was jubilant when news of the British victory reached him:

> *The Plan of the Enemy was certainly judiciously laid, and if Admiral Arbuthnot had not had the good Fortune to overtake the french Fleet before they entered the Chesapeake, the Destruction of General Arnold & his small Corps would probably have been effected, which must have put a Stop to Lord Cornwallis's Progress, & blasted all Our hopes of recovering the Southern Provinces this Campaign. . . . Indeed had we any doubt of the Wisdom of the present Plan of pushing the War in that Quarter, and of the vast Importance of the Possession of Virginia, the Conduct of the Rebels would confirm Us in Our Judgment, for they could not give stronger Proofs of the high Opinion they entertain of its Importance, than by the great Efforts they made, and the hazards they ran, in their Attempts to perserve it.[37]*

Thus, after years of planning and inaction, a post in the Chesapeake had finally been established and held against an enemy action. That the control of the Chesapeake was of importance was taken for granted; that naval superiority was critical to the maintenance of that control was now abundantly evident.

2

~~~~~~~~~~~~

Focus on the Chesapeake

RECOGNIZING THE PERILOUS POSITION in which Arnold would have found himself had the expeditionary force from Rhode Island succeeded in reaching Virginia, Clinton moved to reinforce the post on the Chesapeake. He assembled about 2,000 men under the command of Maj. Gen. William Phillips; as soon as he learned of the naval success of Admiral Arbuthnot, he dispatched them to Virginia in a fleet of transports, escorted by several frigates. When these arrived in the Chesapeake on March 26, 1781, Phillips joined Arnold and took command of the forces in Virginia. With the arrival of the reinforcement and the ships attached to it, Arbuthnot returned with the main British fleet to New York. He had failed to force the French into a second engagement, but he had maintained the security of the Chesapeake until relief from New York could arrive.[1]

Phillips was ordered to make the relief of the army at Portsmouth his first concern, but Clinton then outlined further objectives in his instructions. He was to act under the orders that Lord Cornwallis, then in North Carolina, might issue, in an effort to cooperate with and support his actions. Should direct orders be lacking, the army was to endeavor to disrupt the supply lines through Virginia and destroy any American magazines and warehouses. In cooperation with the navy Phillips was to select a permanent post that was both easily defended and suitable as an anchorage for large ships, should it appear that Portsmouth was not satisfactory for such a task.[2] In informal conversation with Phillips before he left New York, Clinton made it clear that he was not to limit his activities to the support of Cornwallis in the south. If enough men could be gathered for the task, Clinton hoped to hold the entrance of the Chesapeake with a permanent post supported by the navy, and then move northward by water to retake Maryland and possibly lower Pennsylvania. It was said that there were many loyalists in that region, particularly on the Eastern Shore; he was depending on them to flock to the flag once given the opportunity. The area was sufficiently remote from Washington in New England to be safe for such actions, yet the move would divide the colonies in half if successful. The cooperation of the navy was a critical aspect of the plan, however. It was necessary that it control either Chesapeake or Delaware bays, and preferably both, in order that communications with New York could be maintained and the rear of the army protected. It was thus with some hope of rallying the countryside to the king's cause that Phillips left for Virginia.[3]

With the threat of the French fleet past, Arnold and Phillips concentrated on the disruption of rebel commerce and supply lines in western Virginia. Although Phillips was incapacitated by the fever that eventually killed him, Arnold led an expeditionary force up the James River, departing on April 18. He captured and burned the Virginia state navy's shipyard on the Chickahominy River, captured and destroyed some shipping at Petersburg as well as a large quantity of supplies, and captured eleven ships at Osborne's Landing on the James, where he burned an indeterminate number of others.[4] At the same time a force was left in Portsmouth to hold the mouth of the Chesapeake. In an effort to further annoy and disrupt the rebels, Phillips made use of the naval force that had been left to him: "I have imagined it right to give the Enemy a general jealousy and, therefore, in addition to two Sloops of War Stationed off Annapolis I sent the Armed Brig Defiance—The Sloops Savage and Swift with a small Armed Vessel to cruize in Potowmack—the Sloop Bonetta at the Mouth of York River—The Formidable and Spit fire Armed Vessels off Newport News, to check the Enemy in James River—The Vulcan Fire ship stationed at Portsmouth as a Guard Ship, and the Commanding Naval Officer in the Guadaloupe, with the Thames Frigate, in Hampton Roads."[5] Phillips was beginning to follow the ideas laid out by Clinton, controlling

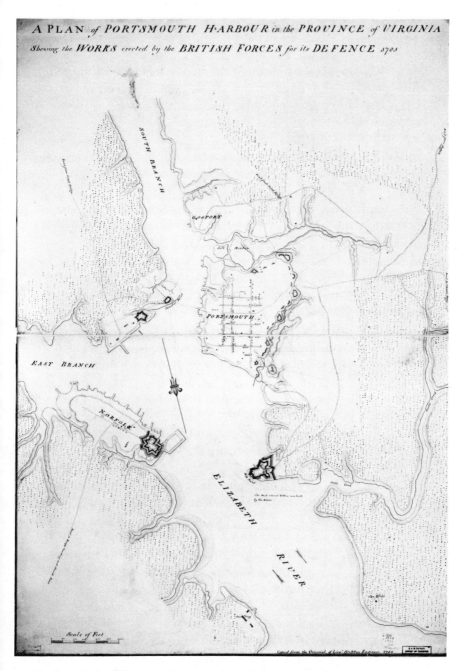

A plan of the Elizabeth River and the defenses erected around
Portsmouth, Virginia, in 1781. The widely separated
fortifications, as well as the possibility of being blockaded in the
narrow river, caused the British to abandon the post in favor of
Yorktown. (Courtesy of the Library of Congress, Geography and
Map Division)

all of Chesapeake Bay through the deployment of his shipping. He was thus able to offer mobile and swift opposition to any land-based force and generally to disrupt the routine of the countryside.

While Phillips was employing the naval force at his disposal in an intelligent fashion, it cannot be said that the two services were acting entirely in harmony. Since one of his objectives in going to Virginia was to establish a safe harbor for ships of the line, Phillips was somewhat dismayed by the lack of interest expressed in the project by the senior naval officer present upon his arrival, Admiral Arbuthnot. The admiral seemed indifferent to the choice of harbor, or even to the presence of such a harbor. Phillips complained of this to Clinton, who responded: "With regard to your Establishing another Station in Chesapeak for large ships, I need only refer you to my Instructions—which stated that Idea only on the Supposition that the Admiral or Naval Commanding Officer, should require it for a Security to the King's Ships; but if they do not seem to wish it, there is no necessity at present of entering further upon that Subject, as such a proposal will of course come first from them."[6] This lack of concord in Virginia was, in all likelihood, the result of a larger disagreement between Arbuthnot and Clinton. Clinton had requested the admiral's recall or transfer, which had been promised in 1780. In the spring of 1781, however, Arbuthnot was still in command. Clinton apparently made it a point not to communicate with him, to the certain detriment of the war as a whole. He described himself as "unwilling to trouble the Vice Admiral with a Consultation upon Operations, which his Removal from the Naval Command here would of course prevent his being concerned in."[7] This overall situation was further aggravated by a local situation that developed as a result of Arnold's raid up the James. The ships captured at Osborne's Landing had been taken by the army in a cannonade from the shore and sent downriver with army prizemasters on board. They were seized by the navy, however, and naval prizemasters put aboard. Because they were valuable, and the cargo of tobacco with which they had been loaded was eminently salable, a fairly major dispute developed over the rights to these prizes. The result was a case that dragged on through the High Court of Admiralty for years to come while the parties bickered over the equitable distribution of the proceeds.[8] In the short term it resulted in discord among the supposedly cooperating forces. When Cornwallis's subordinate General Leslie reached Portsmouth in late May, he commented: "I am sorry to observe there's no harmony between the Sea & Land, nothing shall be wanting on my part to unite both parties. I wish to God all Prises were immediately destroyed."[9] It was into this situation that Lord Cornwallis marched.

Lord George Germain had repeatedly made it clear that he viewed Chesapeake Bay as an object of great importance. Lord Cornwallis had on numerous occasions expressed his agreement. Even Sir Henry Clinton viewed a move into the Bay as the natural result of a successful campaign in the Carolinas. When he left Charleston in June 1780 and put the southern campaign in the hands of Lord Cornwallis, he wrote in his orders:

> *Should your Lordship so far Succeed in both provinces, as to be satisfied they are safe from any Attack during the Approaching Season . . . I should wish you to assist in Operations which will certainly be carried on in Chesapeak, as soon as we are relieved from our Apprehensions of a superior Fleet and the Season will admit of them in that Climate. This may happen perhaps about Septr. or if not, early in October. I am clear this should not be attempted without a great naval Force, I am not so clear there should be a great land force . . . the only thing in which we all agree is that our next Operation must be in Chesapeak.*[10]

Clinton had reiterated his desire that Cornwallis consider a move to the Chesapeake region when he dispatched the first expedition under General Leslie to take Portsmouth. On November 6, 1780, he had written Cornwallis concerning the advantages he expected to derive from a post at Portsmouth. At the least he expected the forces there to be able to stop the trade of the Chesapeake and thus limit the foreign exchange that had its source there. With a larger, offensive force, he hoped to be able to mount an aggressive campaign in Virginia that he supposed would cause the loyalists to come forward. This, along with the control of the James River, would prevent the Americans from accumulating and transporting supplies to the South through this critical area. He urged Cornwallis to consider establishing

his winter quarters in Virginia, which he would no doubt willingly have done, had he been able.[11] Faced with the opposition of
the wily and tenacious General Nathanal Greene, however,
Cornwallis was unable to leave the Carolinas to take up a post in
Virginia. Following an exhausting and unrewarding campaign in
North Carolina during the first months of 1781 and his Pyrrhic
victory at Guilford Court House, Cornwallis had withdrawn to
Wilmington, North Carolina, arriving in early April. He was
depressed about the likelihood of making any further progress in
the conquest of North Carolina and wrote to Clinton on April
10, 1781. He asked for any specific orders Clinton might have
concerning his future operations and urged his own project: "I
cannot help expressing my wishes that the Chesapeak may become the Seat of War, even (if necessary) at the expence of abandoning New York." He felt that until Virginia was subdued, he
would not be able to hold North Carolina. He no doubt viewed
this project as a cooperative venture with the navy, since, he
added, "the Rivers in Virginia are advantageous to an invading
Army." He was evidently considering operations on a far wider
scale than those which had been proposed by Clinton.[12] Without
waiting to receive a response from New York, Cornwallis
marched from Wilmington on April 24, moving his entire force
to Virginia. An embittered Clinton, sometime after the eventual
defeat at Yorktown, annotated the aforementioned letter in the
margins as follows: "For unfortunately the very reasons his
Lordship assigns for recommending operations in Virginia mili-
tate against them unless he had been sure of a covering Fleet.
That he had friends in N. Carolina cannot be doubted, that he
had any in Virginia may be. If the Chesapeak had become the
seat of war, & N. York evacuated to enable us to carry it there, it
certainly would have been the speediest way of finishing the
war—for the whole army could probably have been anihilated in
one campaign commencing in July."[13]

Notwithstanding this recriminating attitude of a later date,
Clinton had himself suggested a move by Cornwallis to Virginia.
Writing on April 13, 1781, he had suggested that Cornwallis
come immediately to the Chesapeake by sea with such troops as
he could spare to follow by land. He made it quite clear, how-

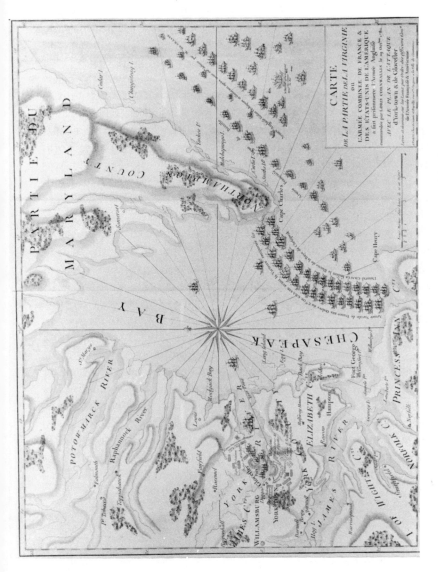

A map printed in Paris soon after the Battle of Yorktown depicting the French fleet under Admiral de Grasse in two positions. They are shown, somewhat fancifully, blocking the entrance to Chesapeake Bay as well as engaging the British fleet under Admiral Graves in the battle of September 5, 1781. (Courtesy of The Mariners' Museum)

ever, that this move was to be contingent upon having first secured the Carolinas, and only those troops that were not needed
there were to come to Virginia.[14] Sir Henry was apparently concerned that the reinforcements he had sent to the Chesapeake
might not prove adequate to the size of the campaign that seemed
to be taking shape there. In consequence, he was readying a second reinforcement to leave for Virginia under Colonel Voit, a
force that sailed around the first of May. Further, having heard
of the severe illness of General Phillips, he was preparing to dispatch General Robertson, the military governor of New York,
whom he despised, to take command in Virginia. This plan was
abandoned, however, when he heard that Cornwallis had decided to move his force into Virginia. During the first week of May
the detachment from Arnold's force which had raided Petersburg was returning down the James River when word reached
them that Cornwallis sought to effect a juncture with them at
Petersburg. In consequence, they returned upstream and met
Cornwallis's army when it finally marched into Virginia. The
feverish General Phillips wrote to Cornwallis, "It will give me
infinite satisfaction if this Corps of Troops proves of Service to
your Lordship's operations."[15]   wrong! see p 26

Upon the arrival of his force in Virginia on April 17, 1781,
Cornwallis began immediate action against the small army under
Lafayette. This force, which had been dispatched to cooperate
with the French fleet defeated on March 16, had served as the
sole opposition to the British in Virginia. Lafayette had played a
cat-and-mouse game with the British, keeping them constantly
on the march around the state in fruitless chase. Lafayette was
fully aware of the precarious state of his affairs, as indicated in a
letter he wrote to Washington on July 4, 1781:

> *Your desire was that I should hold my ground in this state. We*
> *were Happy Enough as to Recover every part of ground But*
> *what is under an immediate protection of shipping—our numbers*
> *are very small, But our Movements are Offensive, and we appear*
> *larger for action. We never encamp in a body, and our numbers*
> *are much exaggerated. . . . Had we Beat Him, We might have*
> *acquired More Honour—But Had we been compleatly Beat this*
> *State was lost, and Your Expeditions interrupted. . . . But my*

prospects are distant, my lotte instant, and danger very near at hand—I do however put on a good face—there is no detachment from the Ennemy but what a detachment marches against them and they generally retire—Children Sing when they are afraid.[16]

In fencing with the British, Lafayette was taking advantage of the weakness in the British effort which the strategist Oswald had recognized several years before. The young Frenchman had written on May 31 to Governor Thomas Jefferson of Virginia: "The vast Superiority the Enemy have acquired in Virginia, is not without some loss in other Quarters—Overrunning a Country is not to conquer it, and if it was construed into a right of Possession, the French could claim the whole German Empire."[17] There were, in any event, greater developments afoot that would supersede Lafayette's holding action.

During the spring of 1781 rumors flew around New York about the possibility that the French fleet in North America might be reinforced. After the close call of the battle of March 16, Clinton intended to take no chances with French sea power, and he had so indicated in a letter to Lord George Germain. Writing on April 5, he expressed his concern that if the French presence were reinforced, his position would be in extreme danger. He was particularly concerned about the very real possibility of the arrival of a French naval force. He stated that the success, even the safety, of the forces in the Chesapeake would "depend upon our having a decided Naval Superiority in these Seas." He therefore pressed for immediate notification in the event that intelligence should be received from France suggesting that the status quo was changing.[18] On the day that Clinton was writing his request, the notice he sought was being sent. The secretary of the Board of Admiralty wrote to Admiral Arbuthnot that the squadron which had been preparing at Brest under the command of Admiral de Grasse was expected to sail momentarily. It was said that there were twenty-six ships involved, though it was thought that six of them were to be detached to the East Indies.[19] With this information, there was legitimate cause for concern about the American station. Though the target of the force was unknown, the fact that it was headed toward North America was certain.

The sailing of this fleet was the culmination of several years of American negotiation, negotiation aimed at redressing the naval imbalance on the North American coast. When Washington learned that de Grasse had sailed, he called a high-level planning conference with the comte de Rochambeau in Wethersfield, Connecticut. It was their purpose to plan the effective utilization of their forces, to take advantage of the naval superiority that would be theirs should de Grasse reach America. Reports of the outcome of the conference vary, since Washington intentionally put out false information concerning the upcoming campaign. He even went to the extreme of writing letters intended for capture by the British; this planted information led Clinton to believe that New York was the certain target of the French and American effort.

The truth of the allied intentions is perhaps best revealed in a letter Washington wrote in response to an inquiry from Noah Webster in 1788. Webster had been asked to write the history of the revolution for a geography book soon to be published, and he wrote to inquire what had been the original goal of the 1781 campaign and what was the thinking behind the actions. He said, "In writing history, it is of infinite consequence to know the *springs* of action as well as the *events*."[20] Washington answered that in 1780 he had planned a joint operation with the land and naval forces of France, with the expectation that it would take place in 1781. There was no formal decision as to the point of attack, since it was impossible to know that far in advance where the enemy might be weakest. The actual objective was of secondary importance if the fleet arrived, as it would be possible to move the allied forces to the chosen area by water "with the greatest celerity." Though the final target had not been chosen, Washington let it be known that it was New York in order to divert support from the actual objective. He continued, "New York was thought to be beyond our effort & consequently the only hesitation that remained was between an attack upon the British army in Virginia or that in Charleston." He took considerable pains to deceive the British into believing that New York was the objective, and no less pains with his own army. Obviously, secrecy was of the utmost importance in this critical time. It was indeed a critical time, as "our affairs were then in the most

A model of H.M.S. Charon *built by Maj. Raban Williams during the 1930s. It is owned by Welholme Galleries, Great Grimsby, England. (Photo courtesy of the Science Museum, London)*

ruinous train imaginable." Washington appears to have viewed this joint action with the French as the last hope of a waning cause, for he continued to Webster: "Some splendid advantage . . . was so essentially necessary to revive the expiring hopes & languid exertions of the Country, at the crisis in question, that I never would have consented to embark in any enterprize; where-in, from the most rational plan & accurate calculations, the fa-vourable issue should not have appeared as clear to my view, as a ray of light. The failure of an attempt agst. the Posts of the ene-my, could, in no other possible situation during the war, have been so fatal to our cause."[21] That splendid advantage on which Washington was depending, the French fleet, was en route.

Clinton, having received advice of the sailing of the fleet under de Grasse, was seriously concerned, not only for the safety of New York but the entire British establishment in North America. Having only received an unofficial report of the fleet, he wrote to Lord George Germain for confirmation on May 18. He stressed that even a brief naval superiority could be critical in "our Insular and detached Situation." He was particularly concerned for the safety of his expeditionary force in Virginia. He wrote that should the fleet be intended for the North American continent, he would consider it advisable "to give up all operation in Chesapeak while there is a possibility of the Enemy being Superior at Sea."[22] Clinton was fully cognizant of the exposed position of the post in Virginia in case of a real naval superiority. He was therefore more than willing to sacrifice a campaign to which he had grown less attached by the day, should it have become necessary.

While Clinton reflected on the possibility that activity in Virginia might have to cease, Cornwallis still hoped to accomplish something there. He wrote to Clinton on May 26:

> *From the experience I have had, and the dangers I have undergone, one Maxim appears to me to be absolutely necessary for the Safe and honorable conduct of this War, which is, that we should have as few posts as possible, and that wherever the King's Troops are, they should be in respectable force; By the vigorous Exertions of the present Governors of America, large bodies of Men are soon collected, and I have too often observed that when a Storm threatens our friends disappear. . . . I shall take the liberty of repeating, that if Offensive War is intended, Virginia appears to me to be the only Province in which it can be carried on, and in which there is a Stake; But to reduce the Province, & keep possession of the Country, a considerable Army would be necessary, for with a small force, the business would probably terminate unfavorably, though the beginning might be successful.*[23]

While Cornwallis still hoped to undertake a solid offensive, Clinton was increasingly concerned about the likelihood of de Grasse's arrival and the threat to New York. He wrote to Cornwallis on June 8, 1781, and sent copies of intercepted American dispatches which suggested that New York was the intended target of the combined French and American force which he now knew was forming. Little suspecting that these captured papers were plants, Clinton was alarmed about the safety of New York. As it appeared that he was to be the intended victim, and more forces would be drawn away from those few which now opposed Cornwallis, he requested reinforcements from the southern army. He had little desire to concentrate large quantities of troops in Virginia and suggested that at least 2,000 men could be spared for the defense of New York. He was prepared to leave a larger force there if Cornwallis intended to attack Maryland and attempt to rally the loyalists who were presumed to be numerous there. Even so, however, he expected to receive a considerable force from Virginia.[24] In later letters he detailed the corps and equipment he wanted shipped to New York for its defense.

While Clinton was primarily concerned for the safety of New York, others continued to think of the safety of the Chesapeake. In his minutes of a meeting held June 17 with Admiral Arbuthnot and Commodore Affleck, Clinton recorded: "The Admiral & Commodore expressed their Fears that Le Grasse might get Possession of the Chesapeak before us, particularly York River. But I told them, I had, I hoped, provided against that by advising Lord Cornwallis to take Post at York Town. That I had left his Lordship at Liberty with respect to operations; I had however recommended one in particular. But if his Lordship should not find that of mine expedient & had none of his own to propose I had ordered great Part of his Troops to return to me during the sickly Season."[25] Clinton had no intention of entirely withdrawing British forces from the Chesapeake; in view of the importance attached to the area in ministerial circles, it would hardly have been prudent. His goal seems to have been the reduction of the force to a point where it would become less of a target for the French and would at the same time improve his own position. He wrote Cornwallis on June 19, "But if, in the approaching inclement season, your Lordship should not think it prudent to undertake operations with the troops you have . . . I cannot but wish . . . that you would send me as soon as possible what you can spare from a respectable defensive."[26]

Having been instructed to establish a defensive post before sending troops to New York, Cornwallis set about the examination of those recommended. Based on the intelligence he had received, his preference was for Yorktown. But when he exam-

An Admiralty model of H.M.S. Guadaloupe, *the 28-gun ship launched in 1763 which was a significant member of the captive fleet. Note that the carvings on the model have been left incomplete, as they were on the draughts of the ship. (Courtesy of the National Maritime Museum, London)*

ined the town on June 29, he concluded that to defend it and still send troops to New York was beyond his capability. He believed that both Gloucester Point and Yorktown would have to be held in order to properly defend the post and shipping, an approach that would require a large commitment of men. In consequence he wrote to Clinton on June 30 that he was abandoning the Peninsula and moving his entire force to the vicinity of Portsmouth. At the same time, he had requested that transports be prepared to carry troops to New York, it being his intention to retain only those men necessary to defend Portsmouth. He had little enthusiasm for the idea of a greatly reduced force holding only Portsmouth. He called it "a sickly defensive post in this Bay, which will always be exposed to a sudden French attack, and which Experience has now shewn makes no diversion in favour of the Southern Army." Unspoken is the fact that Cornwallis had no desire to be stranded in the "sickly defensive post," without any chance at action or glory.[27] In consequence, he seems to have decided to embark virtually his entire force for New York, with the intention of leaving few, if any, men in Virginia, while he returned to Charleston. Marching toward Portsmouth with part of his army, he was able to report to Clinton that the first reinforcements for New York were nearly ready to sail by July 17. Once he had abandoned any hope of future activity in the area of the Chesapeake, Cornwallis was acting with considerable alacrity in leaving the area.

Although Lord Germain had no way of knowing of the move that was underway, he did have a copy of Clinton's instructions to General Phillips issued after the attempt by the French to invade the Bay was foiled on March 16. Clinton had implied to Phillips that his role in the Chesapeake was a temporary one, that he could shortly return to New York, leaving a small garrison behind. In consequence of this, Germain wrote on May 2, 1781, to Clinton:

> *Your ideas therefore of the Importance of recovering that Province appearing to be so different from mine, I thought it proper to ask the Advice of His Majesty's other Servants upon the Subject, and their Opinion concurring entirely with mine, it has been submitted to the King, and I am commanded by His Majesty to acquaint you, that the Recovery of the Southern Provinces, and the Prosecution of the War by pushing our Conquests from South to North, is to be considered as the chief and principal Object for the Employment of all the Forces under your Command which can be spared from the defence of the Places in His Majesty's Possession untill it is accomplished.[28]*

The only deviation which Clinton was permitted was the temporary withdrawal of forces from the South during the summer, when they might be used in more temperate climes. Even then, however, Germain made it clear that conquered territory was not to be given up, but held; the long-term goal was stability: military, economic, and political. In the face of this positive order from England, Clinton was forced to alter his plans radically. He received Germain's letter on June 27, 1781, but he waited over a week to take action on it. By letter of July 8, with a confirmation and amplification on July 11, Clinton reversed his position with Cornwallis. He explained that his request for troops did not take precedence over the requirement that a defensive post be maintained in Chesapeake Bay. This post had to serve for not only the protection of the loyal citizenry but the British fleet as well. Cornwallis was instructed to give highest priority to the establishment of a permanent post and to delay all sailings until that had been done. As a result, Cornwallis wrote on July 20 to General Leslie, in command of the troops about to sail from Portsmouth: "By a Letter I have received this Instant from the Commander in Chief it is necessary to stop the sailing of the Expedition, which you will be pleased to do & remain with the Transports in Hampton Road untill you hear further from me. You will be pleased to communicate this to the Commodore & make an Apology to him for my not writing to him."[29] In consequence of the minister's action, local jealousies and disagreements were set aside to enable the pursuit of the overall strategy. The decision to remain in Virginia was thus not the result of the opinions or efforts of Clinton, Cornwallis, or Washington, but of a strategic plan that had been developed years before. The repercussions were to be staggering.

3

*The Move
to York*

WITH THE RECEIPT of Clinton's letter of July 11 announcing his about-face under pressure from Lord Germain, Cornwallis found himself the surprised victor in his war of nerves with the commander in chief. He wrote from Portsmouth on July 27, informing Clinton that he had detained the sailing of his expedition. Clinton had been sharply critical of Cornwallis's decision to send all or none of his troops, and Cornwallis defended his actions.[1] It was a perfunctory effort, however, as he now had the choice of a post facing him. Clinton's statements concerning the need for a naval facility had been immediately seconded by Admiral Graves, in a letter of July 12: "I need only say to your Lordship that there is no place for the great ships during the freezing months on this side the Chesapeak, where the great ships will be in security, and at the same time capable of acting— And in my opinion they had better go to the West Indies than be laid up in Hallifax during the winter. If the squadron is necessary to the operations of the Army, Hampton road appears to be the place where they can be anchored with the greatest security and at the same time be capable of acting with the most effect against any attempt of the Enemy."[2] The goal, then, was to establish a fortified harbor that would serve to protect the British fleet in North America and allow the necessary symbiosis between the army and the navy to continue through the winter months.

Cornwallis had expressed his dislike for Portsmouth previously, as had the navy. It was observed that while a fleet might remain secure in the Elizabeth River, it could easily be bottled up by a very few ships in Hampton Roads. The choice was thus narrowed to two alternatives: Old Point Comfort or Yorktown. As Admiral Graves had expressed his approval of a Hampton Roads base, Old Point Comfort was examined first. Lieutenant Sutherland, the engineer in charge of the survey, reported that the site of the old colonial fortification, Fort George, was the most suitable spot to erect works on the point. He was by no means happy with the spot, however. Fort George had been a simple earthwork, with a few guns, and was in complete disrepair. The ground stood only two feet above the high water mark and thus did not command the channel. Further, the channel passed in close proximity to it, making it possible for attacking ships to bring their full broadsides to bear at close range. The width of the channel at that point, nearly 1,500 yards, made it almost impossible to prevent ships from bypassing the fort on the other side of the river, if they chose to do so. Finally, it seemed unlikely that a fort could provide significant protection to a fleet anchored there. The site possessed no protected harbor behind the fort in which a weaker fleet could take shelter from a stronger force. The ships would have to anchor within the range of the fort's guns, thus losing much of the advantage to be derived from such a post. Lieutenant Sutherland and the naval captains who made the examination therefore agreed that Old Point Comfort was unsuitable for the requirements of the army.[3] Cornwallis was determined to take immediate action, and began to move within two days after receipt of that report. As he wrote to Sir Henry Clinton in New York, on July 27:

> *Your Excellency will see that a work on Point Comfort would neither command the entrance, nor secure his Majesty's ships at anchor in Hampton Road. This being the case, I shall, in obedience to the spirit of your Excellency's orders, take measures with as much dispatch as possible, to seize and fortify York and Gloucester, being the only harbour in which we can hope to be able to give effectual protection to line of battle ships. I shall likewise use all the expedition in my power to evacuate Portsmouth and the posts belonging to it, but until that is accomplished it will be impossible for me to spare troops.[4]*

On the same day, Cornwallis notified the senior naval officer in Portsmouth, Captain Hudson of H.M.S. *Richmond*, of his newly

An Admiralty model of a sloop of the period 1745–46. This represents the class of 24-gun vessels to which H.M.S. Fowey belonged. (Courtesy of the National Maritime Museum, London)

chosen destination for the fleet, which stood ready in Hampton Roads. He wrote that he expected to come aboard the *Richmond* on the morning of July 29 and anticipated that the fleet would make sail for Yorktown on that day, "if wind & tide should suit."[5] Hudson had apparently been under orders from Admiral Graves in New York to return the *Charon* and the *Loyalist* to New York. They were to serve as convoys while the transports were carrying troops and then to join the main fleet at New York. In consequence of the move to Yorktown, however, and the requirement that Hudson cooperate to the fullest extent of his abilities, he was forced to write to Graves that the ships would not be sent at the present time. With the acquiescence of the naval commander, the move to Yorktown was underway, only two days after Old Point Comfort had been pronounced unsuitable.[6]

In undertaking this move Cornwallis utilized virtually everything afloat in the Portsmouth area. In addition to the naval vessels in the harbor, he employed the transport vessels that had come from New York in several convoy movements, two victuallers that he was holding out of a supply fleet from England, and prizes and private vessels that were under his protection.

The sailing of the fleet was somewhat delayed. Lafayette sent the following description to General Greene on July 31: "The enemy's fleet have not yet sailed from Hampton road. It consists of 30 ships 18 sloops loaded with horse, a 50 gun ship, and several frigates. The ships are full of troops, and nine other vessels are getting ready at Portsmouth. Lord Cornwallis, Tarleton and Simcoe are still at this place; but I expect they will soon go on board. They give out that they are going to Baltimore; but I think a part are destined to New York, and another part to

Charlestown. Nothing but a garrison will be left at Portsmouth, though this may also be evacuated."[7] Lafayette's sense of the destination of the fleet was uncannily accurate, if somewhat outdated.

Cornwallis reported briefly on the move to Yorktown in a letter to Sir Henry Clinton. Though he was on board the *Richmond* on July 29, the fleet was hampered by contrary and strong winds, and four days were required for the voyage to Yorktown.[8] The 80th Edinburgh Regiment and a number of Hessians were embarked in small craft, described as "long boats" but possibly including some of those Arnold had built during the preceding winter. One of the Hessians, Captain Johann Ewald, of the Field Jäger Corps, reported on the difficulties of the move. Encountering strong headwinds, the fleet was forced to anchor near Old Point Comfort, but the anchors on the small boats were not large enough to hold in the wind, and dragged. Efforts to moor the boats to the ships in the fleet were unsuccessful, and they were cast off on their own. Fortunately, toward midnight the wind finally abated. Ewald continued:

> One must not think that these boats were properly manned by sailors. There was only a single sailor and a midshipman in each boat, who sat at the helm. All the others, especially the soldiers, had to do the rowing, which our men learned so well that they were completely safe on the water. The most unpleasant thing during this shipment was that the men were so closely packed in the boats, one against the other, that no one could move. In addition to this, the terrible heat of the sun and the lack of water worked a double hardship on us, because from dire necessity we had to drink water that was mixed with salt water.

They succeeded in taking possession of the town on August 1, 1781.[9]

Ewald reported that the troops in the boats were landed on either side of the river and were the first to enter the towns of Yorktown and Gloucester Point. Although the British had heard alarm shots from the militia the night before, the Americans had evidently left the post. The Hessians "took possession of the place and a battery of two 18-pounders abandoned by the enemy."[10] This sea battery, the sole defense of the town, had been the subject of some debate earlier in the summer, and agreement to let it remain in place must have been reached. The reasons for attempting to hold the post had been outlined in a letter from an unknown American, dated June 27, 1781:

> *I had the Pleasure of receiving your Letter by Capt. Dixon last Night. We are pleased with the Marquis's attention to our Country, & I approve highly of his Plan of rendering it as little an Object of the Enemy as possible—but if the Cannon are moved from Y-town the Enemy will immediately send up their Ships, Privateers & Boats & plunder not only Gloster, but the whole Coast of York River on both sides, & this before we can possibly remove our Negros, Stocks or even Furniture out of their way. I humbly conceive that the 2 or 3 Guns at Y-town are no Object sufficient to induce the Alexander like Cornwallis to make a serious Attack upon that Place—but as they are of importance to us, they may lead him to send a small Detachment to dispossess us of them & such an Attempt I am in hopes we should be able to frustrate. The Work is insignificant open behind and we have only now Militia to defend it.[11]*

It was immediately evident to the militia that this tiny force would prove to be no hindrance to the British massed in the river, and they wisely withdrew and left the town open to Cornwallis.

Lafayette wasted no time in bringing the change in British plans to the attention of Washington, recognizing the effect it must have on future operations. He wrote on August 6 that the fleet which he had believed destined to New York had sailed, apparently for Baltimore. Taken completely by surprise, Lafayette quickly marched his force northward toward Fredericksburg. On the way he received word that the ships had entered the York River, however, and in consequence he turned his march to take up a position on the peninsula. He must have been somewhat humbled by this swift turn of events, for he wrote, "His lordship plays so well, that no blunder can be hoped from him to recover a bad step of ours." He also recognized the opportunity which was presented, for he continued, "Should a fleet come in at this moment, our affairs would take a very happy turn."[12] In a later letter he accurately analyzed the fortifications which were under construction at Yorktown. "I should infer that

*A French engraving by Baugean shows a British transport of
the early 19th century embarking artillery. Transport ships like
these formed the backbone of the captive fleet at Yorktown. Note
that the vessel is clearly numbered on its side in this view,
presumably to avoid some of the confusion which prevailed at
Yorktown concerning these vessels. (Courtesy of The Mariners'
Museum)*

they are working for the protection of one fleet, and for a defence
against another."[13] While Cornwallis dug in, Lafayette abandoned any thought of a move to the northward and settled in to
watch over the British force.

With the safe arrival of the first embarkation, the bulk of the
British shipping was directed to return to Portsmouth to collect
the garrison remaining there. Captain Hudson of the *Richmond*
reported to Admiral Graves on August 12: "We arrived here on
the 2nd instant and the troops were immediately landed at York

and Gloucester; and the Guadaloupe, Swift and Loyalist with the transports, returned to Portsmouth for the total evacuation thereof. The Army having brought very little artillery with them by the first embarkation, the Earl requested that I would order guns on shore to Gloucester from this ship and the Charon (the only two now here) which I complied with, and that side is now tolerably well fortified."[14] The evacuation of Portsmouth proved a tedious task. It was the responsibility of Brigadier General O'Hara, who wrote on August 5, "I am affraid that we shall have so much to do in loading the enormous quantities of Stores, & the means of doing it so feeble, that I am persuaded I shall spend my Christmas here."[15] A week later his report was equally pessimistic, though the end was in sight: "I wish I could tell you that we make great dispatch in embarking the stores—but we have very few Negroes that are able to work. In a fortnight, I am affraid not sooner, we shall be able to leave this Place & bury the last atom of confidence the people of America will ever place in English *Proclamations* & *Declarations*."[16] On August 18 O'Hara boarded the fleet, and for the third time in three years the loyalist population of Portsmouth was abandoned to the fury of the rebel forces. The next day, the American militia colonel Josiah Parker, of Smithfield, reported: "General O'Hara . . . accompanyed by a vast Concourse of runaway Negroes and are now on board their shiping in Elizabeth River, prevented from proceeding on their Voyage a Yorcktown by a contrary wind protected by the Guadaloup & Foy Ships of War. At five o'clock this morning I entered the town. The enemy's works which consist of a number of well constructed & well finished redoubts & batteries with a bomb proof & block house surrounded with well pointed abbatis are left compleat."[17] With the evacuation of Portsmouth the move to Yorktown was complete, and the British forces were concentrated in one major defensive post.

While the post at Yorktown was being established, Cornwallis kept up a regular correspondence with Sir Henry Clinton in New York. Clinton continued to inquire after the availability of troops to strengthen his position, and Cornwallis continued to maintain that he needed every man to build the required fortifications at Yorktown. This correspondence was largely carried on by water, with a regular traffic in ships going back and forth with dispatches. It was not always a simple matter to make the trip, as is indicated by this report of Admiral Graves to the Admiralty on August 20:

> *The Swift Brigantine 14 guns and 60 men on board, Richard Graves Commander, with dispatches from the Chesapeake, proved so leaky, that in order to bail at the Hatchways, they had taken their lumber and stores upon Deck; in so distressful a situation they found themselves attacked by the Holker Privateer carrying 18 guns and full of Men; it was impossible to show a cannonade, they therefore with great spirit boarded the Enemy twice, but the Privateer having greatly the advantage in sailing, disentangled and made away, leaving their Enemy to pump and bail or drown; fortunately she arrived, and hauled on shore; she had two men killed and two wounded.[18]*

The problems the *Swift* was suffering seem to have been endemic to the fleet as a whole. Many of the vessels on the American station were in less than optimal condition. Graves continued: "Wooden bottoms in the Cheasepeke, and at Carolina are eat up presently; there is nothing resists the worm, but Copper. The Small Men of War upon the out posts here are so perforated by the Worm, we find a necessity of hauling them frequently on shore to prevent their sinking; this will oblige me to keep every thing upon Copper in the Country, and to send home as Convoys all the Wooden Bottoms."[19] This was certainly a problem for Cornwallis since of his entire fleet only the *Charon* and the *Guadaloupe* were coppered. In fact, the *Fowey* was so riddled with rot and worm that in at least one report she was listed as "irreparable."[20]

A second group of dispatches was carried by the *Richmond;* though there were certainly other dispatch boats available, Captain Hudson seems to have been anxious to get back to the fleet at New York. He had brought the last of the Portsmouth garrison to Yorktown by August 22, and on the twenty-fifth he sailed for New York. Though he may have taken a few transports with him, he did not lead the convoy filled with surplus troops which Clinton was hoping to see. This is confirmed by the deposition of John Buchanan, the master of the privateer *Goodrich.* He had captured two Dutch vessels in May, the *Leendert & Matthy's* and the *Margaretta Catharina*, both of which were carried into Portsmouth. Unable to get them convoyed to New York, Buchanan moved them with the British forces to Yorktown. When the opportunity to carry them to New York under the protection of the *Richmond* arose, Buchanan sought permission to send the vessels:

> *Captain Hudson replyed that he would take under his convoy and give Sailing Instructions to the Ship Margaretta Catherina, provided the Ship Goodrich would attend her and take her in Tow, that he might not be detained by her, as he was proceeding*

A watercolor by British artist Samuel Atkins depicting a brig similar to many of the commercial vessels in use at Yorktown as transports. (Courtesy of The Mariners' Museum)

round to New York with Dispatches, but that he would not take under His Convoy, nor give Sailing Instructions to, nor wait for the Ship Leendert & Matthy's, as she appeared to be a dull or heavy sailor . . . [she was left with] orders to embrace the first Convoy for New York, which at that time was expected to sail in Two or three Weeks, as Captain Hudson the Senior Officer had appointed the Charon for that purpose.[21]

Cornwallis had to maintain communications not only with New York but with Charleston, which was still a part of his command. In consequence, he dispatched H.M.S. *Guadaloupe* to Lieutenant Colonel Balfour, who commanded there. He admonished him in a letter of August 27, "You must not keep the Guadaloupe on any account, except for a Convoy for our Clothing, Stores, Convalescents, etc., as it is a great favour that I obtained from my friend Symonds to let her go."[22] She did not get far, however, as is made clear in the letter which Capt. Thomas Symonds of the *Charon*, then senior officer in the York River, sent to Admiral Graves:

Lieut. Genl. Earl Cornwallis having made a requisition for the Guadaloupe to carry his Dispatches to So. Carolina, I gave Capt. Robinson orders to proceed thither and he left this River at 8 am on the 28th. On the next day in the evening, he discovered a Fleet off Cape Henry & their not answering the Signals made to them & perceiving some ships in chace of him, he bore away for this Port. The Loyalist which was Ordered down by Capt. Hudson lay between the Horse shoe & the Cape to relieve the Bonetta, endeavoured to make her escape, but one of the Enemys Frigates came up with her about noon, when an Action commenced just below Towes marsh which continued for 3/4 of an hour & on the Loyalist being also attacked by a ship of the line & having her Maintopmt. shot away she struck.[23]

The long-heralded French fleet thus arrived on the American coast, disrupting lines of communication and capturing one of the smaller British ships.

There was confusion and consternation in the camp at Yorktown, with various reports as to the size and composition of the fleet. In order that he might provide an accurate report to Admiral Graves, Symonds sent the lieutenant of the *Charon* and a pilot to reconnoiter from the land. Symonds then reported that: "Between thirty & forty sail lay between the Horse shoe & middle, sixteen or seventeen if not more he took to be ships of the Line, besides these, one Line of Battle ship & two Frigates with the Loyalist are laying off Toes marsh in full sight of us, so that this River is effectually blocked except a chance of a small schooner or row boat escaping the Enemys vigilance. I am landing cannon from the Charon & shall cooperate with Ld. Cornwallis in everything he wishes for His Majestys service."[24] The fact that Symonds was landing guns from the *Charon* makes it evident that both he and Cornwallis recognized immediately that the arrival of the French fleet could only mean the beginning of the siege for which they had been preparing. The Hessian Ewald reported: "Now head banged against head in York and Gloucester. Now they hastily began to unload all the magazines and guns which had been brought from Portsmouth, but which—through negligence and laziness—were still on board the ships lying at anchor in the York River between the two towns. Now, if the French had been in better readiness, or perhaps had had better intelligence, the ships could be shot to pieces."[25]

The French fleet, having successfully blockaded Chesapeake Bay, anchored in the vicinity of Lynnhaven Inlet. Several ships were dispatched to guard the mouth of the York River, to ensure that Cornwallis was unable to escape up the Bay with his force. De Grasse had brought with him roughly 3,000 men from the French forces in the West Indies, under the command of the marquis de Saint-Simon. These were landed at once, both to unburden the warships and to reinforce Lafayette: "September 1st, our troops got in boats and were landed without the slightest molestation from the forces composing the army of Lord Cornwallis, although he had a ship of the line, three frigates, and several smaller vessels. The English general might have prevented us from doing anything, and even repulsed us, had he not despised our small army."[26] These forces were landed on the shores of the James River, near Jamestown Island, and certainly something might have been done from the beach to hinder their landing. It may be said in Cornwallis's defense, however, that any naval action would have been difficult in the face of the massive force that separated him from the James. On September 5, while the French ships were watering, the British fleet under

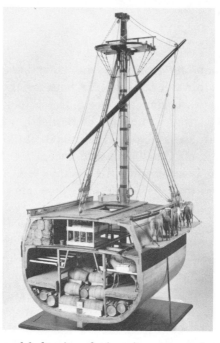

A cutaway model showing the interior construction of an 18th-century horse transport, one of the several types of support vessels involved at Yorktown. (Courtesy of the National Maritime Museum, London)

Admiral Graves appeared off the Capes of Virginia. Though the French sailed out to meet them and did not return to the Bay until September 11, the ships blockading the York River were left behind. This was the result not only of the haste with which the fleet sailed to meet the British but also of the recognition that containing Cornwallis was of paramount importance. When the victorious de Grasse returned to the Chesapeake, he found that the Rhode Island squadron under the comte de Barras had arrived, strengthening his position substantially. Most importantly, Barras brought with him the heavy artillery belonging to Rochambeau, so necessary to the upcoming siege. The forces under Washington and Rochambeau had been marching southward, and with the certain arrival of the French sped up their march. While some marched all the way to Williamsburg, others were embarked in small transports from both Head of Elk and Annapolis. They too were landed along the James, at Archer's Hope, and the forces assembled at Williamsburg.

Washington had come overland from New England, and upon his arrival in Williamsburg, made arrangements to visit Admiral de Grasse to coordinate their movements. On September 18, 1781, he set out with his principal aides and Jonathan Trumbull, his secretary, to visit the fleet. They were rowed in small boats out to the *Queen Charlotte*, lying off Archer's Hope. The *Queen Charlotte* was a small, speedy cutter that had been captured by the French while on a voyage from Charleston to England. Washington was not long in reaching the fleet, where his welcome was reported by Trumbull:

> *Come early in the Morng. in View of the Fleet—a grand Sight! 32 Ships of the Line in Lynn Haven Bay just under the point of Cape Henry, about 60 miles from where we had first embarked— get alongside the Admiral about 12 o'clock—go on board— received with great Ceremony & Military Naval Parade—& most cordially welcomed. The Admiral a remarkable Man for Size, Appearance & plainness of Address—with Compliments over, Business is proposed & soon dispached to great Satisfaction; after which Dinner is served & then we view the ship & see her Batteries & accomodations—a noble prospect—the World in miniature. After receiving the Compliments of the Officers of the fleet, who are almost all come on Board the Admiral's ship, we take our Leave about Sunset to go on Board our own little Ship—saluted by the Admirals Guns, & the Manning of all the Ships of the fleet, who from the Yards Tops & etc. give us their several Feu de Joyes—or Vivè Le Roy.*[27]

Following this festive reception on board the *Ville de Paris*, Washington returned to Williamsburg up the James River by what proved to be a long, difficult voyage. The prime purpose of the trip had been achieved, however. De Grasse had agreed to continue in the Bay, thus guaranteeing naval superiority while the land forces undertook the siege of Yorktown. Further, he had agreed to extend his stay from his planned departure date of October 15 to the end of that month. Control of the seas, the one factor that had always eluded the American revolutionary forces, was at last a reality. If only for a limited time, Washington had the weapon he had lacked; with the cooperation of the French navy, the reduction of Yorktown was virtually assured.

4

~~~~~~~~

The Trap
Closes

CLINTON AND THE OTHER OFFICERS of the British army were by
no means blind to the cause of Cornwallis's entrapment or to the
best solution to it. They had long recognized the critical role sea
power must play in support of any significant action by the army
in North America. Clinton had made this clear to Germain on
several occasions, though it was a factor the minister was well
aware of. Clinton had written to him again on September 12: "In
this Situation of Affairs Your Lordship must be sensible that so
far from being in a condition to undertake Offensive Operations,
I may perhaps be unable to preserve our present Possessions. For
(as I have often had the honor of Suggesting to your Lordship) if
the Enemy retain only a few weeks Superiority at Sea, we shall
certainly be beat in detail."[1] De Grasse with his fleet had assured
the Americans of that superiority at sea, and it was only by over-
coming it that the British stood any chance of redeeming Cornwallis and his army.

When de Grasse and his fleet arrived on the American
coast, he was expected by the British, but his destination and
date of arrival were unknown. Adm. Thomas Graves was in
command of the squadron in New York and served as the commander in chief for the British fleet in North America. It was his
firm expectation that if de Grasse came to America, he would be
notified of the arrival and reinforcements would be sent from the
West Indies. In late August he had received intelligence that the
French squadron blockaded at Newport for nearly a year was
preparing to depart. These ships, as a part of a fleet under Admiral Ternay, had helped to bring the army under Rochambeau to

America in 1780 and served to support that general's actions. Following Ternay's death, command had passed to Commodore Destouches and then to Commodore Barras in May 1781. Since this was far and away the largest naval force the Americans could muster at the time, it was a matter of constant surveillance by the British New York fleet. Graves was preparing for an action with it when more important news was received:

> *The 28th [of August] Sr. Samuel Hood arrived off the Hook with fourteen sail of the line, four frigates one Sloop and a fireship from the West Indies. I was at that moment settling a plan with Sr Henry Clinton for attempting the French squadron in Rhode Island, as the French troops were mostly with General Washington in the Jerseys, we had only waited for the repair of three of the Squadron and the troops were ordered to embark, but the same evening intelligence was brought that Mons du Barras had sailed the Saturday before, with his whole squadron. As Sir Samuel Hood had brought intelligence from the West Indies that all the French fleet from the Cape were sailed, I immediately determined to proceed with both squadrons to the Southward, in hopes to intercept the one or both if possible.[2]*

The danger to Cornwallis was at once evident to Clinton, although it was not clear at that time whether the fleet was intended for Virginia or New York. Clinton was always nervous at the prospect of losing New York, a fear Washington had played upon by leaking erroneous information. In consequence, when Graves set out to meet the French fleets, he did not know their final destination, though it was soon clear. When it became evident that the object of the campaign was Lord Cornwallis, Clinton wrote to Graves of his plans for defense, in a letter of September 2. He had gathered between three and four thousand troops and embarked them on troop transports, ready to sail. He intended to hold them in readiness until he received word from Graves that his action against the French had proved successful, at which time they would sail for Virginia.[3] Thus Clinton was prepared to follow up a naval victory with a decisive military reinforcement.

Having sailed from New York, Admiral Graves looked into Delaware Bay, but found no French fleet. He then continued to

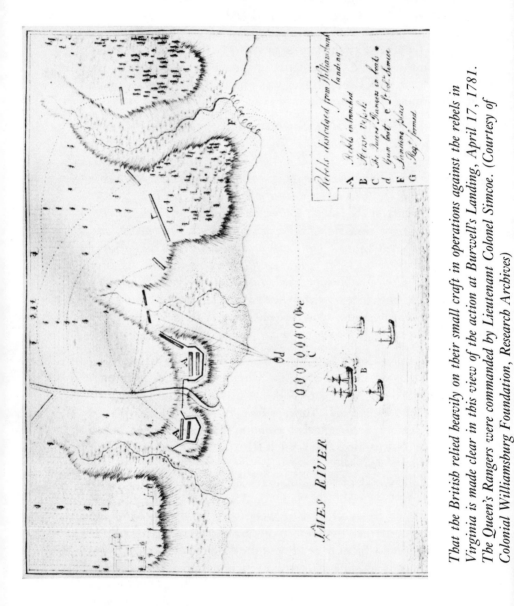

That the British relied heavily on their small craft in operations against the rebels in Virginia is made clear in this view of the action at Burwell's Landing, April 17, 1781. The Queen's Rangers were commanded by Lieutenant Colonel Simcoe. (Courtesy of Colonial Williamsburg Foundation, Research Archives)

the Chesapeake, where on the afternoon of September 5 de Grasse's fleet was discovered at anchor. Upon sighting the British, the French made hasty attempts to stand out of the Bay, cutting their anchor cables and abandoning shore parties. The British fleet, in the advantageous windward position, waited. Graves chose to form the line of battle and not engage the French until they had done the same. He thus sacrificed his advantage of surprise and confusion, as well as position. The French fleet outnumbered the British twenty-four to nineteen. Fighting in parallel lines, the two fleets never engaged in the rear, either through lack of courage or confusion of signals. The result of this partial engagement was considerable damage to the van of the British line, less to the French, and no damage at all to either rear. For the next five days, the fleets remained in sight of one another, sailing parallel courses; neither side sought to reopen the battle. The British were busy making what repairs they could at sea, given the poor condition of their ships and their lack of replacement timber. De Grasse had a firm awareness of the importance of his cooperation with the allied army, which he dared not jeopardize in another action. The French finally broke away and sailed back to the Chesapeake, reestablishing their earlier blockade of the Bay. While de Grasse was out, the squadron under Barras had arrived, with the consequence that the combined fleet substantially outnumbered the British.

Knowing Clinton's intention to attempt to relieve Lord Cornwallis once control of the sea lanes was assured, Graves wrote him on September 9:

I am sorry to inform you the enemy have so great a naval force in the Chesapeake that they are absolute masters of its navigation. . . . The French fleet at sea consists of twenty four sail of the line, large ships and two frigates. We met them the 5th, coming out of the Chesapeake, and had a pretty sharp brush. . . . In this ticklish state of things your excellency will see the little probability of anything getting into York River but by night, and of the infinite risque to any supplies sent by water. How far a diversion made in the neighborhood of York may effect any good purposes your excellency is by far the best judge. All that I can say is that every resistance the fleet can make shall not be wanting for we must either stand or fall together.[4]

This discouraging news was sent to Clinton only a day after he had written to Graves to inform him that the troops were embarked and ready to sail for Virginia. He only awaited word from Graves that it was safe for the convoy to depart, word that would apparently not be forthcoming.[5]

Recognizing the perilous situation in which Lord Cornwallis found himself, Graves had attempted to communicate with him on September 8, the day before he wrote to Clinton. He probably intended to convey dispatches from Sir Henry Clinton concerning the possibility of relief from New York, though it seems likely that he would have reported on the action of September 5 as well. He sent these dispatches on board the frigate *Richmond*, Captain Hudson, in company with the *Iris*. When he left Yorktown two weeks before, Hudson had joined the fleet under Graves, and he was now sent back into the Bay, presumably because of his knowledge of conditions there. The *Medea* had entered the Chesapeake on September 6 and reported a "considerable force" there, though this consisted only of the ships blockading the York River. Between the departure of the *Medea* and the arrival of the *Richmond* and the *Iris*, the squadron under Barras entered and seized control of the Chesapeake. In consequence, Hudson was unable to enter the Bay, both the *Richmond* and the *Iris* were captured by the French, and the dispatches were never delivered to Lord Cornwallis.[6]

Any hope that Clinton might have maintained of a turnabout was dashed by the letter Graves sent him on September 15, written on board his flagship, the *London*, off Cape Charles: "The whole Fleet are now at anchor above and about the Horse shoe shoal—so that a frigate has no chance of getting even a boat forward and the French cruisers are out—We think it impracticable to force so strong a fleet advantageously posted, in a strong situation, and that a shattered fleet as ours should not be exposed to a Storm at the Equinox. We therefore determined to shelter at N. York. And I fear that nothing by Sea can be got up to Lord Cornwallis."[7] With that, Graves set sail for New York to refit.

Clinton, on the strength of the earlier letter from Graves, had called a council of war in New York, gathering together his principal officers on September 14 for a recapitulation of the status of Cornwallis and the chances of relieving him. The primary question hinged on the abilities of the navy:

> *Whether is it most adviseable to commit a Reinforcement of five*
> *or six thousand men to the Hazards of the Sea during our present*
> *Naval Inferiority, and endeavor to relieve Lord Cornwallis*
> *immediately at all Risks; or to wait until we either receive more*
> *favorable Accounts from our Fleet, or the Junction of Rear Adml.*
> *Digby's Squadron affords a more certain Prospect of Success in the*
> *Attempt. It was the unanimous opinion of all the General*
> *Officers present that it would be most prudent to wait for more*
> *favorable Accounts from Rear Admiral Graves, or the Arrival of*
> *Rear Admiral Digby.*[8]

Rear Adm. Robert Digby, coming to replace Arbuthnot as head of the North American fleet, represented a vague and distant hope. In consequence, an order was issued on September 19: "The Troops Embarked for the Expedition are to land tomorrow Morning at 6 o'clock at Coles Ferry on Staten Island, and encamp on such ground as the Deputy Quarter Masr. General (who will attend for that purpose) shall point out."[9]

Clinton had considered for a time an alternate possibility for the relief of Cornwallis. On September 3 he ordered wagons to be prepared for the transportation of twenty days' provision for eight thousand men, as well as a group of flatboats and pontoons on wagons to be used in crossing rivers.[10] It was evidently his intention to mount a diversionary raid, possibly against Philadelphia, in the hope of slowing or diverting entirely Washington's march south. However, as he wrote to Lord Germain on September 12, he soon had reason to abandon this plan. He had realized that, with the French fleet in command of the Chesapeake, Washington must recognize his strategic advantage. He would therefore be unlikely to sacrifice an almost certain victory to counteract any diversion that might be mounted by Clinton. In addition to the slim chance of success, a diversion might be prolonged, and the opportunity to directly aid Cornwallis might be lost through delay. Clinton had come to the conclusion, in agreement with Cornwallis, that the best hope lay in a direct move to Yorktown, however it might be achieved.[11]

Clinton now considered a land march to Virginia as a possibility. It was discussed at a council of war on September 17 but fell victim to precisely those considerations that had made the role of the navy so critical throughout the war. Expert testimony was taken from Messrs. Goodrich and Burnby, who were apparently well acquainted with Virginia. It was their opinion that it would not be possible for an army of any consequence to draw subsistence from the countryside, especially if that countryside were hostile. They doubted that Washington could have subsisted without outside support, but were certain that a British army could not. Since it would be impossible to maintain a reasonable train of supplies by land, and water transport was not available, additional troops in Virginia would only have compounded the problem. The board unanimously concluded that "an Army could not act there alone without the Communication & Cooperation of the Fleet." They therefore decided that any attempt at relief should be "deferred until the Admiral thinks it may be undertaken with less Danger than at present." With this decision, any further consideration of actions by land was abandoned; all hopes were on the fleet.[12]

Cornwallis was not slow to recognize his precarious position. In earlier correspondence he had referred to the importance of sea power in controlling Virginia and realized the risk which would be entailed if the control of the seas should be lost for even a brief time. Consequently, he must have given serious consideration to the possibility of abandoning Yorktown, suddenly rendered so vulnerable, and trying to salvage some remnant of his army. Though expedient, this alternative was hardly an honorable one, and not a route he would willingly have chosen. Whether he went north or south, the march would have been difficult, the losses great, and the outcome doubtful. Lafayette sensed the possibility that retreat might be attempted, through North Carolina, and wrote to Gen. Allen Jones on August 27, 1781, "It is of the highest importance every obstruction should be thrown in their way." He ordered every boat on the Roanoke River collected and destroyed, lest they facilitate a move to the southward by the British.[13] Following the unsuccessful Battle of the Capes, the question must have seemed even more pressing. Maj. James McHenry of Maryland wrote to General Greene, September 11,

A model of a British landing barge of the 18th century.
Whether most of the small craft involved at Yorktown were of
this type or the flat-bottomed boats more typical on the
Chesapeake is unclear. The number of men shown in the boat is
perhaps conservative, in light of contemporary reports. (Courtesy
of the Science Museum, London. Crown Copyright)

1781: "Cornwallis seems to hesitate between a brilliant defence, and the chance of being relieved, and, abandoning everything, to risque a retreat. His boats upon carriages give him the opportunity of crossing the James river. When this is accomplished, he may head the rivers. But this is an undertaking full of extremest hazard and difficulty; and in the end may not improve his situation."[14] Cornwallis must have turned the matter over in his mind for several days; he finally put his faith in sea power, the weapon he lacked.

In a letter to Clinton dated September 16, he informed him of his decision to try to hold the post. Clinton had suggested that relief would be forthcoming as soon as the naval forces were augmented, and Cornwallis chose to pin his hopes on that development. He was cognizant of the gamble he was taking, for he wrote, "If I had no hopes of Relief, I would rather risk an Action than defend my half-finished Works." To stay, in expectation of help from New York, seemed less of a risk, however, than to attempt to break out. He computed that he had provisions for six weeks, if he turned out all nonessentials from the post. He concluded, "I am of opinion, that you can do me no effectual Service, but by coming directly to this place."[15] Having made the decision to stay, Cornwallis pressed forward with his preparations for the oncoming siege.

While the bulk of the French fleet was out on September 5 and the days following, the ships blockading the York River fell down to Lynnhaven. With the return of the fleet, the tight blockade was reestablished, to the consternation of the British. Lt. Bartholomew James of the *Charon* had been sent down in a small captured schooner to keep an eye on the movements of the French, and he recorded in his journal for September 11:

> *At four o'clock in the morning the enemy began to advance from the Shoe, at which time the schooner lay becalmed about three miles from them, and by bringing with them a sea breeze they came very near me before I could get any wind; at six o'clock one of the headmost ships fired a shot at me, at which time, having received the wind, I cut away my boat and hopped off, with all I could drag on her, and fortunately escaped "Monsieur." At noon I made the signal for a further advancement of the enemy, and at four o'clock ran up the harbour like a scalded cock, the French fleet having anchored in the mouth of the harbor at Too's Marsh. On this evening, the tender becoming useless, I hauled her on shore.[16]*

That was the last opening the British were given as far as contact with the Atlantic went. From that point on the French maintained a tight blockade of both the Bay and the York River.

As Washington saw the trap closing, a minor development nearly became a major crisis. The reinforcement that Admiral Graves had been promised for New York, should de Grasse come to America, finally arrived. Admiral Digby reached New York on September 24 with three ships, the number being variously reported in Virginia. Washington sent a courier to inform de Grasse of the new additions to the fleet, with unexpected results. De Grasse replied that, in view of the enhanced position of the British fleet, he intended to leave the Bay and cruise off the Capes of the Chesapeake. He had no desire to be caught again in a disadvantageous position, as was the case on September 5. Washington was much alarmed at this possibility, and wrote in the strongest terms on September 26: "Give me leave in the first place to repeat to Yr Excellency that the enterprise against York under the protection of your Ships, is as certain as any military operation can be rendered by a decisive superiority of strength and means; that it is in fact reducible to calculation, and that the surrender of the british Garrison will be so important in itself and in its consequences, that it must necessarily go a great way towards terminating the war, and securing the invaluable objects of it to the Allies."[17] After a second conference with his captains, de Grasse agreed to maintain his blockade. In order that his fleet might be in a less exposed position should the British attempt to take the Bay a second time, de Grasse eventually moved from the anchorage at Lynnhaven to the mouth of the York River, where they anchored "en Ligne en Ligne."[18]

With the blockade of the river, the fleet made captive therein ceased to serve in its primary, or naval, capacity. While command continued to be vested in Capt. Thomas Symonds of the *Charon*, the senior naval officer, the ships were essentially serving as a support element for the land forces. This fleet contained not only naval vessels but a large collection of transports, victuallers, armed merchant ships of private ownership, and smaller boats. In consequence, although there was by no means sufficient firepower to force the blockade, there was an ample supply of shipping to be used in the defense of the town. A description of the armed vessels was offered by Col. Richard Butler, of the 9th Pennsylvania Regiment, on September 7:

Several sailors having deserted from the ships, I obtained an account of their naval force which I sent to the Marquis de la Fayette, viz:

Name of Ship	No. of Guns	Pounders
Charon	44	18 and 12
Guadeloupe	32	12 and 9
Old Foway	24	9 and 6
Bonetta, sloop of war	16	6
Brig Defiance, with	16 Carronades	18
" Spitfire	12 "	12
Sloop Formidable	10 "	12
" Rambler	10 "	4
" Susannah	14 "	4
" Tarleton	10 "	4

Four of the above named small vessels were ordered two miles up the river to cover a working party who were building a redoubt . . . had two or three fifty gun ships been passed up, on the arrival of the French fleet, it would have so far accelerated our approaches and secured the river carriage of provisions, etc., that matters would have been rendered very easy and all their shipping would have fallen, also, these very heavy guns with which they have covered the river, and will thereby impede the passage.[19]

The heavy guns Butler described as having been put in place on the fortifications seem to have been drawn largely from the ships in the harbor. Though some were undoubtedly carried to Yorktown by the ordnance transports, others must have been the armament of the ships themselves. This is confirmed by the journal of a Hessian soldier, J. C. Doehla, who wrote on August 31: "I was on unloading duty. All the munitions and provisions were unloaded from the ships riding in the harbour, the lower tiers of guns from the warships and frigates brought into the earthworks and all the ships completely emptied. Also, some fire ships were prepared in order, when the French fleet should sail into the harbor, to send the same among them."[20] It seems certain that a great deal of the artillery for the defense of the town was drawn from the ships in this fashion.

This removal of guns and stores from the principal ships must have gone quickly for Captain Symonds wrote to Admiral Graves on September 8:

Most of the Cannon and Ammunition of the Charon are landed, and great part of the Crew in Tents and employed in enlarging the Sea Battery, and assisting the Army; the Guadaloupe is moor'd head and stern, opposite a Creek above York Town to enfilade a Gulley should the Enemy attempt to cross. The Fowey's ammunition and provisions are ashore, and she is hauled close in, and her men assisting at the Batteries. The Bonetta at Gloucester side, Captain Dundas ashore with his officers and men to man the Batteries, assisted by thirty of the Foweys men. Captain Palmer of the Vulcan, lays prepared to Act should the Enemys ships return, and come up, and has three Horse vessels, fitted, to act on the same service.[21]

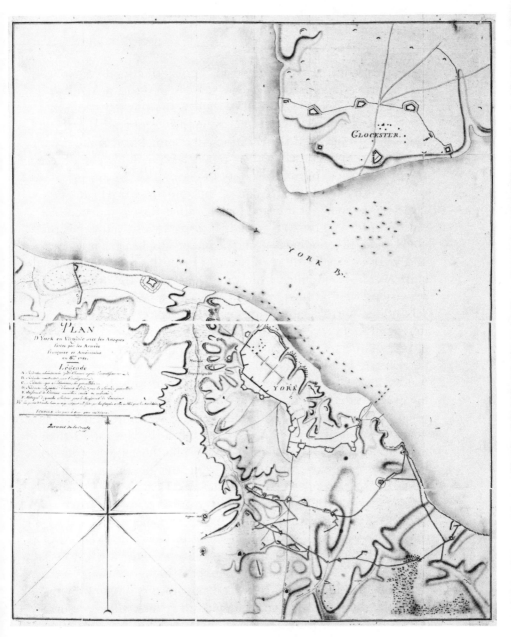

This French map from the Rochambeau Collection shows the line of ships scuttled along the shoreline at Yorktown. It also depicts a line of ships projecting into the river, placed to force vessels sailing up the river into the center, within cannon range. The secondary anchorage on the Gloucester Point side is shown as well. (Courtesy of the Library of Congress, Geography and Map Division)

It is remarkable that the ships had been so thoroughly stripped and incorporated into the defenses so early in the campaign. The French had not even returned to the Bay by this date, and in a postscript to the above letter, Symonds reported that "the French ships have left their station after some Fleet, some say it is a Fleet from the Sowd. Others report it is possible to be a Fleet from New York, but no certainty of either."[22]

Even by the end of August, the ships had began to serve largely as support for the land forces, rather than as independent entities. On August 29 Symonds informed Cornwallis that the ships under his command would be out of supplies in a few days, and were especially short of bread. Cornwallis replied that the ships would be supplied from the magazines of the army when provisions were needed, an unusual arrangement for naval vessels under normal circumstances. He further urged that Symonds make every effort to buy what he needed from the merchants of the town, since his own supplies were limited. He particularly recommended that rum be bought in town, since it was said to be plentiful there. This particular transaction probably explains the large number of rum bottles found in the excavations of the wrecks at Yorktown in 1934. It was quite unusual on board ship to carry any quantity of rum in bottles rather than casks, but not at all unusual on land.[23] The shortage of supplies was a severe problem for Cornwallis, one that became more critical as the siege approached. With the allied armies encamped in the vicinity of Yorktown, his ability to forage in the area was increasingly restricted. This may explain his magnanimous gesture on September 26, when he wrote to Governor Nelson, of Virginia, offering to let all noncombatants leave the town. Wives and families of former residents were permitted to leave, as were those of male inhabitants who had remained until now in the town. In addition, they were allowed to remove their personal effects by wagon, if the governor saw fit to send transportation for them.[24] Two days later the investment of the town was completed by the allied French and American forces.

The York River and the harbor it provided were both the reason for the choice of Yorktown and one of the principal weak spots in its defenses. With the broad beach along the York shore and the massive French naval presence, the British feared that an effort might be made to stage an attack on the soft underbelly of the post. That Cornwallis moved to block this possibility is made evident by the journal of St. George Tucker, a Williamsburg resident, who reported on October 2:

> *This Afternoon from Mr. Moores I cou'd discover two of the French ships which were concealed by a point of Land from Wormley's Creek—I discovered by the Assistance of a Glass from seventy to an hundred horses dead on the shore of York or floating about in the River—This seems to indicate a Want of Forage & no Intention of pushing a March. I could also discover that the British had sunk several square rigged Vessels near the Shore and at the distance of one hundred and fifty, or two hundred yards from it—Whether this was meant as a precaution against the French landing from their Ships in Case of a general Assault I can not determine.*[25]

This effort to block the channel had been undertaken soon after the French fleet returned to the Chesapeake. The Hessian Captain Ewald recorded that "on the 16th [of September] we began to sink ten transport ships between York and Gloucester to obstruct the entrance."[26] Further detail on the disposition of the shipping before the town was offered in an intelligence report received by Washington after the interrogation of a man who left the town by boat on October 4: "Ten or twelve large merchant ships have been sunk before York, and piles have been driven in front of these vessels, to prevent our ships from approaching the Town sufficiently to debark Troops; which they are infinitely afraid of—The Charon and Guadeloupe are moored before York, in such a manner as to defend the town rather than the passage of the River. Twelve large barks in form of half galleys containing 110 men each, have been collected some days since. . . . his disposition announces that he is exceedingly afraid of our ships passing before York."[27]

Cornwallis had used a defensive tactic that by this time was becoming standard for the British army in America. Ships had been sunk during the defense of Savannah, to good effect. The presence of at least a dozen ships drawn up along the shore and hauled in until they grounded must have presented a formidable sight. It certainly offered a good platform from which to defend the beach, and a superb obstacle to an amphibious assault. From contemporary maps and surviving wreckage, it appears that this line of defense was constructed with the colonial wharf as its center point. The wharf extended out to deep water and would have provided a firm mooring as well as access to at least some of the vessels. Drawn into shallow water as they were, these scuttled vessels were by no means totally submerged. Rather, they probably only sank down a few feet below their normal waterlines in most instances, and their upper decks certainly continued to be manned.

As preparations by Cornwallis continued, the attackers gradually tightened their grip on Yorktown. The blockade of the York River by the French, which seems to have been rather haphazard early in September, was drawn closer after Washington's visit to the fleet. The British decided to take an aggressive stance and initiate some action to keep the French in their place. Captain Symonds wrote to Admiral Graves on September 29:

> *On the 21st the enemys Ships advanced, consisting of three sail of the line and a frigate from a report of our guard boats their not keeping that look out which might be expected from advanced ships, I ordered four vessels belonging to the Quarter Master Generals department, to be fitted as fire vessels with the utmost expedition, and directed Captain Palmer of the Vulcan to proceed in the night whenever the wind offer'd, to endeavour to destroy the enemy or drive them from the post they had taken, as it prevented a communication from New York or the Eastern Shore. He took a favorable opportunity of the night of the 22nd about twelve o'clock to slip with the other vessels and run down to the French squadron, and though he did not meet with the success which was to be wished, he obliged all the enemy's ships to cut, and two sail of the line were run ashore and on board each other.* [28]

Further light is shed on this venture by Lt. Bartholomew James, who commanded one of the vessels in the attack. He described the vessels as "patched up and very ill-fitted out, being all of them schooner and sloops." Additionally, they were commanded by lieutenants from the naval ships in three cases, but by a lieutenant from a privateer in one instance. The four commanders

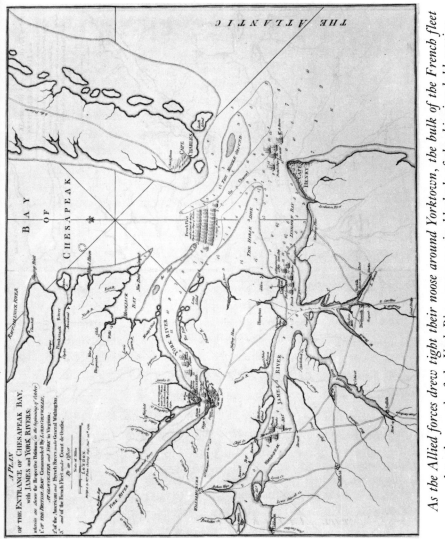

As the Allied forces drew tight their noose around Yorktown, the bulk of the French fleet moved to the mouth of the York River to secure its blockade of the shipping held captive there. A few ships were left at the mouth of the Chesapeake, and others supported the landing of men and supplies on the James River. (Courtesy of The Mariners' Museum)

apparently asked to be placed under the orders of Captain Palmer of the *Vulcan*, the experienced captain of the only formal fire ship in the harbor. Captain Symonds thought it expedient to allow each man to act as he saw fit, however, rather than attempt a concerted effort, much to the chagrin of James. James reported of the action of the twenty-second:

> At two o'clock we came within sight of the enemy, and were advancing, with every probability of success, when from some cause, unaccountable as strange, Mr. Campbell, of the privateer, set fire to his vessel. This proved as unfortunate as dangerous, for the enemy, who was before keeping no look-out, cut their cables, beat to quarters, and having fired twenty or thirty shot at us, retreated in a precipitate and confused manner. Mr. Conway at this time set fire to his vessel, and soon after Mr. Symonds to his; when, seeing the French launches rowing towards us and no probability of grappling the enemy, and running a risk of my retreat being cut off, in which case no quarter is gave, I set fire to my vessel, with no other view than to prevent her falling into the hands of the enemy. The Vulcan was within her own length of a seventy-four's bow, and must have burnt her had not the light from the first vessel discovered her before she reached that length. However, bad as this sad business ended, we ran two ships of the line on shore, and, if pursued with any enterprising people, in that situation [they] might, in my opinion, have been destroyed at last.[29]

That the failure of the fire ship raid may be directly blamed on the small vessels accompanying the *Vulcan* was made clear in the testimony offered at the court martial of Captain Palmer. The lieutenant of the *Vulcan* described the attack:

> When we hove too, we were in sight of the French ships, & not seeing the other vessels come up, we waited for them. The first Thing that we saw, was the four vessels coming up, 3 miles astern of us, all in Flames;—As the alarm was given by this, Captain Palmer thought it most prudent to push on, and accordingly made all the sail he could instantly for the French ships; as soon as we came nigh they hailed us 3 Times; we could not understand what they said, after that they fired a shot which

went right thro' us; Captain Palmer desired me to tell the People
to go into the Boat and stay there myself, to prevent their taking
her away, & he took the Helm himself.[30]

With only the captain and the gunner on board, the *Vulcan* bore
down on the anchored French ships. The gunner described the
final moments of the attack: "Capt. Palmer took the wheel himself, & he ordered me to go down & get the Prime Matches
ready; the Distance we were then from the French Commodore
was about the Length of our own Ship—I got the Matches
ready—Captain Palmer came down from the Quarter Deck, I
went into the Boat, and Captain Palmer sat Fire to the Ship.
There were numbers of the French People jumped overboard &
their Boats were chock full of Men—we then put off, and pulled
up for little York, & as we went, we perceived the French Ships
going on Shore."[31] Though the attack caused the French some
little discomfiture, and they withdrew their ships downstream a
bit, it was largely unsuccessful. Following the abortive fire ship
raid, Symonds fitted out two more transports as fire ships, and
later a third was added. He viewed them as reserves to be held in
case of an assault by the French fleet, however, not as weapons
to be used in a repeat of the September 22 fiasco.[32] This was tacit
acknowledgment that Cornwallis and his forces were now, in
fact, trapped and on the defensive. The combined French and
American forces were beyond their capability to oppose, and for
help they had to look outside, to New York.

5

~~~~~~~~~~~~

The Battle Won

FOLLOWING ITS UNSUCCESSFUL ENGAGEMENT with the French, the main British fleet, under Admiral Graves, had at last returned to New York on September 21, where he was informed of the decision to rely on the navy for the relief of Yorktown. Graves agreed to cooperate with the army in any way he was able and to the fullest extent of his abilities. He observed, however, that his fleet had been much damaged in the recent engagement with the French. Asked how soon he could be ready to put to sea again, he replied, "The Injuries received by the Fleet in the Action, added to the complaints of several very crazy ships, makes it quite uncertain how soon the Fleet can be got to Sea."[1]

Graves was not simply hedging to avoid a repeat of the Battle of the Capes; New York was chronically short of supplies and all the requisite materials for repairing ships. As soon as he had word of the battle of September 5, Commodore Affleck, still in New York, had begun making preparations to refit the fleet. As he wrote to the Board of Admiralty on September 14, however: "I am making every preparation possible for the supply of the Fleet in Masts, Yards & Rigging as well as provisions on their return, but the deficiency of all these Articles are not to be described and without the arrival of supplies from England and a mast ship from Halifax which the Warwick is gone for, the demands of the Fleet cannot be complied with."[2] Unfortunately, there seemed little hope of getting additional supplies in time. The principal source of supplies for the British navy in America was the station at Halifax, Nova Scotia. The command at this station had been transferred in August 1781 to Capt. Andrew

Snape Hamond, and he was still trying to establish a regular flow of material. He had been trying to get a convoy for a store-ship destined for New York since mid-September, with no success. There were thus no supplies en route to New York when they were needed. By the time word could be gotten to Halifax, it was too late. It was not until October 14 that Hamond wrote the captain of H.M.S. *Chatham:*

> *Having received Intelligence that His Majesty's Fleet has returned to New York, after having been engaged with the Enemy off Chesapeak Bay, it is of the utmost Importance to His Majesty's Service that every possible supply of Stores should be sent from hence to the Fleet as soon as possible. I am therefore to require that you will take the Young William Mast Ship under your Convoy and join Admiral Graves's Fleet with all possible expedition, acquainting the Admiral that the Storeship will be forwarded by the Assurance, or the first ship of war that calls off this port.[3]*

In the face of such a shortage of materials, it is little wonder that Graves found it difficult to patch together his battered fleet. With inadequate supplies of food and water and jury-rigged repairs to masts and yards he must have felt himself a scant match for the thirty-six French ships of the line now blocking the Chesapeake.

While waiting for the fleet to refit, Sir Henry Clinton was less than sanguine about the prospects for success. As commander in chief he had to consider not only the consequences of the loss of Lord Cornwallis's army but the possible repercussions of the various attempts which might be made to relieve his position. He was ever fearful of endangering the post at New York, and he thought out some of the ramifications of the project in a series of notes written on September 23. He had until that day been of the opinion that the French fleet blockading the Chesapeake consisted of twenty-six ships. Having just learned that the number was, in fact, thirty-six, he was reconsidering his position. It had been his theory that any fleet blockading the Chesapeake must necessarily be divided by the large shoal lying between the two capes. To cover the area adequately, one would have to blockade both channels, with the consequence that an invading fleet need not take on the blockader's full force. He had thought that with luck in the choice of wind and tide, it might have proved possible to run past the French and get into the Bay; thus troops could have been landed for the succor of Cornwallis. He was less sanguine about getting the ships back out than he was about getting them in. With his new knowledge of the true strength of the enemy, he now doubted whether such an attempt could succeed at all. He wrote, however, that "the Object is so important, the Consequences of Success so apparent, that some Risk should be run to attain it." He was at the mercy of the navy, and if they chose not to make the attempt, he could see no alternative. He fully recognized the probable result of a failure, since with the loss of the army under Lord Cornwallis, "there will be little Hope of British Dominion in America— except by an Exertion, of which I fear our Country is not capable." Because of the critical importance of the effort, he was inclined to make it, no matter how risky, for "if we try we may succeed, and that Success may be most decisive; if we do not try, we cannot succeed." With no other avenue of support open, it was evident that the plight of Lord Cornwallis was directly attributable to the British naval weakness. Given a siege, whether the post "is well fortified or supplied with Provisions is out of the Question; complete in all these, it must finally fall, if not relieved by a Superior Fleet." He summarized his thoughts on the entire campaign: "If the Corps in Virginia is lost, there is but one cause to impute it to,— *the Want of an adequate Fleet.*"[4] So Clinton waited, expecting the navy to complete its repairs so that the fleet might sail by October 5; that was the date he had been given and the date he had forwarded to Lord Cornwallis.

There were those who thought that whatever action was being taken was insufficient to the task at hand, as was made evident in a letter Lord Germain received from one of his correspondents:

> So considerable a part of our force cutt off & besieged, and so considerable a one remaining hitherto inactive not to say careless of the fate of the other, are objects of too great moment & too striking to remain silent under . . . I do not believe the most sanguine admirer of my Lord Cornwallis or of his army could expect him to hold out longer than from two months to ten weeks.

Any relief to be given him by land is utterly impracticable from the numbers & size of the Rivers on the western side of the Chesapeak as well as from want of numbers in Sir Henry Clinton's Army: It is then to be attempted by Sea & the passage up the Bay is at all risks to be forced; for one, I own I am glad of it, let the attempt be ever so desperate, because the failure can not have worse consequences than remaining idle at New York.[5]

If there was reason for concern among the officers of the army and the navy, there seems to have been a very real effort made to keep morale among the troops up. On October 5, the day the fleet should have sailed from New York, Capt. John Peebles, encamped at Staten Island, wrote in his journal: "Accounts rec'd from Lord Cornwallis that he has four months provision is well fortified, his Army in good spirits, & in no apprehension, so we were told."[6] Almost two weeks later, with the fleet still in New York, he wrote, "An express from Lord Cornwallis who finds himself hardly press'd & wants assistance. . . . The Navy people does not seem to be in a hurry on this occasion."[7] This apparent lack of coordination between the forces was one of the most prominent features of the entire campaign. Neither Clinton nor Graves had authority over the other; they were to operate in tandem but not necessarily in unison. Neither seems to have trusted or respected the other, and even within the services jealousy and distrust were rampant. In consequence, it was difficult to get agreement on any plan of action, let alone coordinate all the disparate elements involved.

There was considerable jealousy between Admiral Graves and Sir Samuel Hood, who commanded the squadron that had come from the West Indies. Each thought the other incompetent, and it is thus with caution that one must consider Hood's report of a meeting of naval officers called by Graves on October 8:

Soon after we were assembled, Mr. Graves proposed, and wished to reduce to writing, the following question, "Whether it was practicable to relieve Lord Cornwallis in the Chesapeake?" This astonished me exceedingly, as it seemed plainly to indicate a design of having difficulties started against attempting what the generals and admirals had most unanimously agreed to, and given under their hands on the 24th of last month, and occasioned my

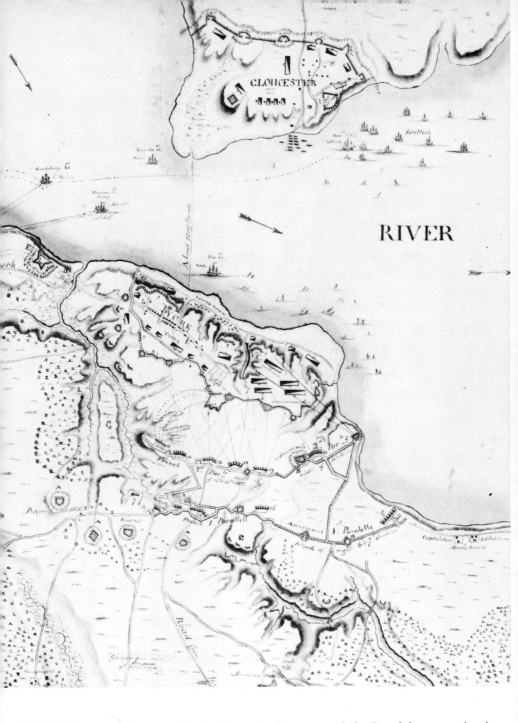

This British manuscript map clearly shows the Charon *and the* Guadaloupe *acting in support of the Fusilier's Redoubt, as well as the fire directed at these ships by the French. The locations of the various ships seem fairly accurate; it is thought the ship* Fox *shown on the Yorktown shore is, in fact, the* Fowey. *(By permission of the British Library)*

replying immediately that it appeared to me a very unnecessary and improper question, as it had already maturely discussed and determined upon to be attempted with all the expedition possible.[8]

Certainly, one must assume that had there been a supreme commander, there would have been no question of possible dallying by the navy. Given the supply problems he faced, Graves may have moved as expeditiously as possible to refit the fleet. He would not have been much of a commander, however, had he not carefully reflected on the ramifications of the project to be attempted, win or lose.

In October, with each day dragging by, it finally became evident that the fleet must soon sail. On October 10 Clinton issued orders for the troops on Staten Island to reembark. All of their baggage and artillery were put on board a single transport.[9] On the morning of the eighteenth, Graves reported that "we embarked all the Troops on board the Men of War from the Transports, where they had been in readiness for us some days, to the amount of Seven Thousand, one hundred and forty-nine (Officers included)."[10] On the nineteenth, all the major vessels having crossed the bar, the fleet finally sailed from New York to attempt the relief of Cornwallis. The troops were apparently housed on board the men-of-war so that the fleet would not be delayed by the slower transports; further, there would be no need to defend the helpless transports in the event of a general engagement. Captain Peebles described the accommodations of the army on board: "The troops went on board by seniority of Companys, & were dispos'd of on the middle and lower decks, 6 to a mess between the Guns. Appartments made for the Officers on the middle deck before the Wardroom, of canvass curtains, & Cotts slung betwixt the Guns. The Comr. in Chief & his Suite & Col. Marsh in the Admirals appartments on the upper deck, & mess there. The rest of the officers eat in the Wardroom, where all the Gentlemen seem to be very civil about 20 at table a very good dinner, and plenty of Wine, with freedom & ease."[11] Clinton was himself a considerably less than enthusiastic sailor, if we may judge from a note he had sent Admiral Arbuthnot concerning a meeting in June 1781. He stated that he was willing to visit the admiral on board his ship, "but if there should be the least motion, I fear I shall not be able to do any Business."[12] In all likelihood, he did not savor the delicacies of the admiral's mess. Nonetheless, with troops jammed into the gundecks, and the officers making the best of it in the wardroom, the fleet sailed to meet the French.

Clinton, by a letter of October 14, had advised Cornwallis that the fleet was soon to sail, and had outlined his various plans of possible action. He explained that his first intention was to attempt to sail directly into York River, should that prove practicable. Failing that, he would attempt to land his forces so that they could march to Gloucester, presumably sailing around the French at the mouth of the York. His third preference was for a landing on the James River, at Newport News or Jamestown, in the hope of effecting a junction with Cornwallis somewhere on the Peninsula. Failing that, he hoped that Cornwallis might escape upriver to Queen's Creek and cross with the bulk of his troops to Jamestown Island, where they might be evacuated. This whole plan of action was spelled out in considerable detail, in a letter Cornwallis was destined never to receive.[13] Once having formulated his plan, Clinton assumed the role of passenger while the fleet was at sea. He wrote on October 19 of his expectations, however:

> *I understand nothing of the [naval] matters, you know, but my oracle S. S. Hood, seems to think that if they meet us at sea, we have everything to hope from our better sailing, & I could add from the superior abilities of all our naval chiefs; the stake is great, if we don't play for it we can not win it, if we do we may. While afloat I am only a passenger. If the Navy succeed and we are put ashore we will try for a junction with his Lordship if I succeed in succourring L. Cornwallis I shall resign the command to him, I should have done so last June but in the then & since threatened state of this post it was impractible; I had then or I have now but too much reason to wish to quit this command.*[14]

Thus, after nearly a month of delays, Clinton sailed on a campaign which he was well aware might be his last, a campaign critical to the preservation of British dominion in North America.

• • •

The French blockade of the York River was still firmly in place when Washington surrounded Yorktown and began to open his first siege line on September 28. With the town encircled, the focus centered on the construction of trenches from which to undertake the siege. This work was, of course, hampered by gunfire from the British lines, as well as from the ships anchored in the harbor. The *Charon* and the *Guadaloupe* were anchored to enfilade the swampy creek just above Yorktown, an area defended only by the ships and its impassability. They also served to support the Fusilier's Redoubt, located on the Williamsburg Road. This small star redoubt, manned by the 23d Regiment (Welsh Fusiliers) was critical to the defenses of the town, since it covered the only road across the swamp. It was the subject of concentrated attack from the French, who established a trench opposite it, about 1,000 feet distant. While this trench was being dug, the two ships kept up an annoying fire, which the French determined to avenge. When the bombardment opened on October 9, the firepower hurled at the town was staggering. Not only did Washington's army far outnumber that of Cornwallis, but he had roughly twice his artillery capability, thanks to the French.

Some of the earlier shots to be fired from the trench erected by the French were not at the town, but at the shipping in the harbor. In retribution for the annoying fire which they had suffered during the preceding week, they turned their guns toward the river. Captain Symonds of the *Charon*, ashore with the great bulk of his crew, described the action during his later court martial:

> *On the 10th October about 6 in the Evening during the Siege of Yorktown, Virginia, observing the Charon to be struck by two shot from the Enemy's Battery, and soon after seeing a Smoak, I directed the Ship to be hailed, to inform the Gunner and Carpenter of it, who were on board, and I sent off the Master and Boatswain, with as many men as could be collected, with Bucketts to extinguish the Fire, But they were all obliged in about an Hour, to return on shore as fast as they could to avoid being destroyed by the Flames of the Ship. She continued burning the whole night and till she was burnt to the Waters Edge.[15]*

The lieutenant of the *Charon* testified that when he got on board, the ship was already in flames, and the carpenter was attempting to scuttle the ship by boring her under the starboard counter. The gunner, who was on board during the entire incident, gave further details on the disaster:

> *Between 3 and 4 o'clock in the afternoon, on the 10th of October, I sent the Men up to unreeve the Main and Fore topsail Halliards, when the Enemy fired from their Batery on shore, at the Men, there came a shot in upon the Main Deck and lodged there. So soon as it lodged there came smoak from the Deck, the men took it by Rolling it into a Tin Kettle, and put it into a Match Tub below, we threw two Bucketts of Water upon the Shot, it made the Water so hot we were not able to put our fingers into it. Soon after this another red hot shot struck the ship and set her on fire.*[16]

It was the opinion of Symonds that this second shot landed in the sail room, on a spare suit of sails. In any event, the fire was soon out of control. Asked whether everything possible was done to save the ship, the carpenter replied, "Everything that was in the Power of men; Nothing more could be done."[17]

The use of heated shot, cooked in a portable sheet-iron oven until red hot, was a standard technique to be used against ships. As demonstrated by the burning of the *Charon*, it could be devastatingly effective. The loss of the *Charon* and the several transports that took fire from her was described in vivid terms by an American surgeon, Dr. Thacher, who watched the spectacle from shore:

> *A red-hot shell from the French battery set fire to the Charon, a British 44-gun ship, and two or three smaller vessels at anchor in the river, which were consumed in the night. From the bank of the river, I had a fine view of this splendid conflagration. The ships were enwrapped in a torrent of fire, which spreading with vivid brightness among the combustible rigging, and running with amazing rapidity to the tops of the several masts, while all around was thunder and lightning from our numerous cannons and mortars, and in the darkness of night, presented one of the most sublime and magnificent spectacles which can be imagined.*[18]

It is apparent that the destruction of the largest and newest naval vessel in the harbor made a profound impression on the British. Their morale could not have benefited. In the morning following the burning of the *Charon*, all shipping that was not directly incorporated into the line of scuttled ships along the Yorktown beach was withdrawn to the Gloucester side. The *Guadaloupe* had succeeded in escaping to that side before the *Charon* burned, and no vessel of any value ventured across the river again.

Even on the opposite shore of the river, where there were no allied gun emplacements, the ships were not entirely safe. Though they were not fired upon from the Gloucester side, the reach of the allied cannonade, as described on October 11 by the Hessian Doehla, was impressive:

> *I went on ship watch on the water. Today there was stupendous cannonading on both sides; during these 24 hours 3,600 shot were counted from the enemy, which they fired at the town, our line, and at the ships in the harbour. These ships were miserably ruined and shot to pieces. . . . I saw with astonishment today on my watch how the enemy cannon balls of 24 and more pounds flew over our whole line and the city into the river, where they often struck through 1 and 2 ships, and indeed even struck 10–12 times in the water; yes, some even went clear across the river to Gloucester, where they even injured some soldiers on the beach.*[19]

In the face of this blazing torrent of cannonballs and shells, the defenses of the town were fast crumbling. Not only were the ships much damaged, but most of the buildings in the town were riddled with holes or knocked down entirely. Virtually the only refuge to be found in the town was in small bunkers and dugouts, which offered some measure of safety. The picture for the defending forces was not bright.

While Washington had written that the "enterprise against York . . . is as certain as any military operation can be rendered," early in the siege he recognized a critical weak link. Although the French had the fleet under Cornwallis contained in the river, the British retained control of the upper part of the York River, at least as far as West Point. This not only allowed them to forage through an extensive territory, but left open the possibility of escape upriver. Washington had raised this point with de Grasse when he visited the fleet, and requested that he attempt to send several of his ships past Yorktown, to form an upriver blockade. De Grasse at first demurred, then agreed to consider the matter. He had not taken any action, however, by September 28, when the town was surrounded and Jonathan Trumbull, Washington's secretary, recorded in his journal: "By this Approach of the Main Army, & the Lying of the french Shipps in the Mouth of the River, the Enemy are now compleatly invested except by Water above the Town, where they are yet open & their Boats are troublesome up the River for some Distance—To Close them on this side, the Genl. has proposed to the Admiral to run some ships above the Town, & take their station there."[20] The British ability to resupply from the countryside weakened the effectiveness of the siege, and the possibility of escape existed, but one of the immediate difficulties was the length of the communications lines the allied forces had to maintain. Gloucester had been invested by Genl. George Weedon, who, in order to communicate with Washington, had to send runners around West Point, nearly a 100-mile trip.

That the river was not a safe avenue of communication is made clear by an order which Virginia Governor Nelson sent out on September 25: "You will please to stop all Vessels coming down either of the Branches of York river with provisions of any kind whatever, at Frazier's and Ruffin's Ferry, and if possible have them stored at those places: the danger attending Vessels coming down the River at this time being infinitely too great to hazard the Loss of any others—three having been captured by the Enemy this day."[21] In addition to stopping the traffic on the river, other stopgap measures were proposed, pending the anticipated action of the French. General Weedon, who was most directly concerned with the problem, wrote to Washington on October 3: "The Enemy make a practice of going up York River and plunder in our rear. I have detached a Battalion to cover and protect the Inhabitants if possible, but would suggest the propriety of Arming some Boats at Cumberland & Fraziers Ferry with orders to Cruise as low down as within sight of the shipping at York which would effectually stop their Depredations. . . . If some Armed Vessells are sent down to prevent their Boats plundering above, we shall shortly be able to cut off their foraging in

any part."[22] The control of foraging was Weedon's primary role on the Gloucester side, since that area was the weakest in the allied perimeter, and little else could be undertaken.

While Weedon proposed alternatives to the forcing of the river by the French, an ongoing correspondence between de Grasse and Rochambeau indicated that the project was not dead. Rochambeau wrote on October 3:

> *The left bank of the upper part of the river is steep, which would indicate to us that it has ample depth; but all the pilots here, about whom I have not replied to you, claim that the river is good everywhere, going up, to the confluence of the two branches. That which gives them pause, is that the enemy having first sunken only four vessels on the bank below, to force your vessels to place themselves in range of their batteries which are elevated, from thence they have sunk eight others, which block less than half the river, of which development I am informed by General Washington.*[23]

That Rochambeau had failed to provide the pilots to whom he referred seems to have been one of the major stumbling blocks to an ascent of the river. De Grasse wrote him on October 5, "In spite of my desire to have our ships do all they can, they can accomplish nothing because of the lack of pilots. I do not have

An inset on a French manuscript map depicting the destruction of H.M.S. Charon *on the night of October 10, 1781. The ship is shown third from the right, with the several transports which also took fire during the night, and Yorktown in the background. Even at this early stage in the battle the scuttled ships, with their rigging stripped, gave a vivid impression of destruction. (Courtesy of the Edward E. Ayer Collection, The Newberry Library, Chicago)*

one on my ships who wants to enter the river, and I would have to have several, one for each vessel."[24] De Grasse can hardly be blamed for not risking his ships in strange waters, partially blocked by sunken hulks, without any guidance from those who knew the river's channels. Cornwallis had been obliged to sink the additional ships to force the French into the middle of the river because of the placement of his guns. While the elevation of the guns on the bluff at Yorktown provided them with ample range, it meant that they did not command the beach or the river near the beach. It is not possible to depress a smooth bore gun sufficiently below the horizontal to command such a low area, lest the ball roll out the muzzle. To avoid allowing the French to ascend the river along the Yorktown shore and below the fire of the guns, obstructions had to be placed in their path.

Washington seems to have despaired of de Grasse ever sending ships up the river. He apparently concurred in the plan proposed by Weedon to arm local vessels, and ordered him to undertake that project. Weedon responded on October 13, "I am honored with your Excellencies dispatch of yesterday, and shall use my utmost endeavors to effect what you recommend. I saw the utility of manning and bringing down the River the privateer Cornwallis and all the vessels from Cumberland & Franzens Ferry some time since, and eight days ago wrote Governor Nelson on the subject, supposing he might by his authority had it instantly adopted."[25] The lack of faith which the Americans placed in de Grasse was ill-founded. On October 15, orders were given to the *Experiment* (50 guns), the *Vaillant* (64 guns), and the *Triton* (54 guns) to ascend the river with the first favorable wind.[26] The necessary wind did not come in time, however, and it was not until after the conclusion of hostilities that the ships were finally on their way into the harbor.

The pounding which the town was taking from the besieger's artillery was fast reducing Cornwallis's ability to defend the post, regardless of any naval action. Recognizing their precarious position, the British began to destroy materiel that might prove of value to the Americans should they win. The Master's log of H.M.S. *Fowey* reported on October 13: "P.M. bored holes under the Starboard fore chains to sink the Ship pr. order from Captain Symonds. A.M. at 7 two shells fell into the Provision Tent, which destroy'd one Puncheon of [Rum] 4 Barrels of Flour 27 Pieces of Beef and 6 firkings of Butter allso the Ships and Warrant Officers Books they being put there for safety."[27] Two days later Captain Robinson of the *Guadaloupe* received orders from Captain Symonds to scuttle his ship. Other shipping was also destroyed at this time. Certain of the private vessels in the harbor also seem to have fallen victim to the hectic final efforts of the British. One of these was the schooner *Sally*, a private vessel that had carried dispatches from New York; her owners reported in a later claim:

Being at York Town . . . the sixteenth day of October last, Richard Pindar Commander of the Brigantine Spitfire employed in the Quarter Master General's Department in an arbitrary and forcible manner without any authority took from the said Schooner Sally her Mainsail, Foresail, Jibb and Square Sail, notwithstanding he was forewarned by the Deponent not to unbend said Sails and was challenged to produce his Orders for so doing which he could not do. . . . The Deponent further says that by means aforesaid the said schooner was rendered unfit for Sea and he was thereby prevented putting to sea, and said Schooner of course fell into the hands of the Enemy and was captured, as was also the Deponent.

In defense of the actions of Captain Pindar, Captain Vallancey of the Quartermaster General's Department testified that

during the Siege of York the Sails of all vessels private as well as Publick were ordered to be taken to make tents of for the sick and wounded Soldiers of Lord Cornwallis's Army at Gloster Point there not being houses sufficient for them—Captain Pindar as well as other people had orders to take all such Sails from the Vessels then in harbor for that purpose. As to the vessels sailing it was actually impossible as the River was at that time closely blocked up by the French fleet and this Gentleman's vessel fell with the Capitulation of the town and I Submit to you if he is not in the same situation as other merchants and owners of vessels whose Craft and Sails were all taken at that time for the Publick Service.[28]

Certainly by the end of the battle, any distinction between public and private vessels must have seemed academic.

The devastation already evident in the harbor can only have been increased by the necessity of destroying material from the town itself. The Hessian Captain Ewald reported: "All the artillery and baggage horses, for which there was no forage, were killed and dragged into the York River. Several days after their death these poor animals came back in heaps with the tide, nearly up to the sunken ships. It seemed as if they wanted to cry out against their murder after their death. The sight of these horses was saddening to a person of feeling. But what should we have done if we did not want the enemy to have them? Voltaire says, 'La raison de guerre, c'est la raison de guère.' "[29]

This gruesome spectacle of destruction was surely demoralizing to an already weakened British army.

Met with overwhelming firepower, and with diminishing likelihood of aid reaching him from New York, Cornwallis began to seriously consider the possibility of breaking out of Yorktown. That this might happen had long been realized by the allied commanders, and orders were issued to render it more difficult. The

American effort at Gloucester was primarily directed at contain-
ment, rather than reduction, as indicated in a letter from
Weedon to Washington, September 29, 1781. He reported that it
was not within his capability to undertake a normal siege on the
Gloucester side, as he had not a single entrenching tool. He was
not particularly concerned about this lack, however, since he regarded the British post at Gloucester as secondary, and liable to
one of two possible developments. He suggested that the post
would either be evacuated entirely or held so that the cavalry
could break through the lines there and push into North Carolina. He observed that, while the latter was a desperate move,
they were dealing with desperate men.[30] Weedon must have realized that his scant force was unlikely to be able to stop a concerted escape effort by Cornwallis, and he therefore took preventive
measures in case of such a move. He wrote on October 12 to all
the lieutenants of the militia in the surrounding counties in a
circular letter:

> *The present Situation of the Enemy subjects them to Certain
> Captivity unless they force a passage thro' Gloster County and
> penetrate by rapid marches either to the North or South. I am
> desired by his Excellency Genl. Washington to take every previous
> precaution, and tho' an attempt of that sort is little to be expected
> yet Policy Dictates to us to be guarded at all points. I have
> therefore to request of you to hold a body of Ax men constantly in
> readiness, as also a body of Armed men, that in case Lord
> Cornwallis should throw his Army on this side York River, and
> force a passage thro' the Defences of this Camp, he may meet with
> Opposition at every defile in your County by your throwing
> down Trees, braking up Roads & Bridges, and opposing him
> wherever you can taking care to drive off all your Stock of every
> kind upon the first knowledge you have of his advance.[31]*

Having killed most of his horses, Cornwallis would have found
such a march difficult at best.

Driven to the final extremity, however, he determined to
try just such an escape, on the evening of October 16; Cornwallis described the effort in a later letter to Clinton:

> *I had therefore only to chuse between preparing to surrender next
> day, or endeavouring to get off with the greatest part of the*

Troops, and determined to attempt the latter. . . . Sixteen large Boats were prepared, & upon other pretexts were ordered to be in readiness to receive Troops precisely at ten o'clock; with these, I hoped to pass the Infantry during the night, abandoning our baggage, & leaving a detachment to capitulate for the Town's people & for the sick & Wounded, on which subject a Letter was ready to be delivered to General Washington. After making my arrangements with the utmost secrecy, the Light Infantry, greatest part of the Guards, & part of the 23d Regiment embarked at the hour appointed & most of them landed at Gloucester. But at this critical moment the Weather from being moderate & calm, changed to a most violent Storm of Wind & rain & drove all the Boats, some of which had Troops on board, down the River. It was soon evident that the intended passage was impracticable, & the absence of the Boats rendered it equally impossible to bring back the Troops that had passed, which I had ordered about two o'clock in the morning. In this situation, with my little force divided, the Enemy's batteries opened at day break. The passage between this Place & Gloucester was much exposed, but the boats having now returned, they were ordered to bring back the Troops, that had passed during the night, & they joined us in the forenoon without much loss.[32]

Commenting on this attempt at escape, which was foiled not by military action but by weather, Banastre Tarleton stated succinctly, "Thus expired the last hope of the British army."[33]

Having failed in his attempt, Cornwallis determined that he had done all that he could hope to do in defending his post. He later wrote to Sir Henry Clinton: "I thought it would have been wanton & inhuman to the last degree to sacrifice the lives of this small body of gallant Soldiers who had ever behaved with so much fidelity & Courage, by exposing them to an Assault, which from the numbers & precautions of the enemy could not fail to succeed. I therefore proposed to capitulate."[34] An emissary was sent out onto the parapets with a white flag, his presence announced by the beating of a drum. An American reported the scene: "Had we not seen the drummer in his red coat when he first mounted, he might have beat away till doomsday. The constant firing was too much for the sound of a single drum; but when the firing ceased, I thought I never heard a drum equal to

A view of Yorktown and the York River taken from Gloucester Point, drawn during the battle by Lt. Col. Simcoe. The Dutch flag on the vessel in the center of the picture suggests that it might be the Leendert & Matthy's, *a prize vessel trapped in the river by the action. (Courtesy of Colonial Williamsburg Foundation, Research Archives)*

it—the most delightful music to us all.'"" Debate over the specifics of the Articles of Capitulation went on for over a day, until the final details were settled. They were signed on October 19, 1781, by both Cornwallis and Symonds, as commanding officers of the two services in the town. One of the subjects dealt with specifically was that of the shipping in the harbor: "Article XIII—The shipping and boats in the two harbours, with all their stores, guns, tackling and apparel, shall be delivered up in their present state to an officer of the navy appointed to take possession of them, previously unloading the private property, part of which had been put on board for security during the siege."[36] Washington had determined to hand over the shipping to the French, in recognition of the critical role they had played in the battle. This was both a gesture of good will and of pragmatism, since only a well-equipped naval force could possibly have dealt with the shattered mass of ships lying in the harbor.

In writing his official report to Admiral Graves, Thomas Symonds had to report that of the five naval vessels in the harbor only one, the *Bonetta*, was afloat after the battle. Of the thirty-two transports and victuallers which he listed, only two were

reported afloat. The scene was described by St. George Tucker in his journal:

> *Thursday 18th . . . On the Beach of York directly under the Eye hundreds of busy people might be seen moving to and fro—At a small distance from the Shore were seen ships sunk down to the Waters Edge—further out in the Channel the Masts, Yards & even the top gallant Masts of some might be seen, without any vestige of the hulls. On the opposite of the river the remainder of the shipping drawn off as to a place of security. Even here the Guadeloupe sunk to the Waters Edge shew'd how vain the hope of such a place. . . . A painter need not to have wish'd for a more compleat subject to imploy his pencil without any experience of Genius.[37]*

What de Grasse had failed to accomplish with his ships, Washington had done with his artillery.

The tactical significance of the fleet under Cornwallis was less actual than potential. The shipping he maintained in the river was the one loophole in an otherwise foolproof siege. It was a factor over which Washington had no control. In spite of his efforts, the ships continued to play a vital role in the battle until the day of the surrender. Had Cornwallis made more effective use of the naval forces at his command, rather than waiting for relief from New York, and had he not encountered bad weather on the night of October 16, the outcome of the battle might have been different. As it happened, the battle was to have massive political repercussions on a global scale. It was to have its effect locally as well, though it was a very different, and human, impact. A Hessian soldier wrote: "October 20. We remained in the line again. The French naval officers and sailors began to go over our ships and set up their white flags. The Americans also put up white flags on the great sea fort. Things were quite different for us now. First of all, we received no bread, only flour; secondly, we got no more rum, but had to be satisfied with water; thirdly, we have many more masters than before."[38]

The relief fleet carrying Sir Henry Clinton and his army from New York had left October 19, the day that Cornwallis formally surrendered. They could not have known this, of course, but were quickly enlightened when they arrived at the mouth of the Chesapeake. On October 24 they were greeted by several small craft carrying refugees from Yorktown, including the black pilot of the *Charon*, who had left the day before the capitulation. All bore the same depressing news; silent guns and rumors of surrender. The appearances were confirmed when the fleet was joined by *La Nymphe* from New York, bearing dispatches from Cornwallis dated October 15. They concluded: "The Safety of the Place is therefore so precarious that I cannot recommend that the Fleet and Army should run great Risque, in endeavouring to save us."[39] Recognizing the implications of this news, Graves immediately dispatched a ship for England to notify the government. He cruised off the Capes for several days, but saw no profit in attempting to force the Chesapeake at this late date. The French showing no inclination to come out for a second fleet engagement, Graves finally turned toward New York where he debarked Clinton's troops. The relief effort had been too late; whether too little was academic.

The allied forces were not unaware that Clinton intended to make an attempt to relieve Cornwallis, and they had therefore hastened the siege to the extent that they were able. In addition, however, Washington saw an opportunity to capitalize on Clinton's expedition. He had been informed of the size of the detachment by Thomas McKean in Philadelphia, as had General

Heath commanding the American forces in Boston. It was suggested by McKean, and seconded by Washington, that some attempt might be made on New York, under the circumstances:

> *It would seem that the Enemy are making, not a detachment only from their Army, but that almost their whole Force from N. York is to be employed on their meditated diversion—should this prove to be the Case, their remaining Force will be so small, that it will become a Matter worthy of your most serious attentions, to make some Attempt upon them in their Defenceless State.— The particular object to which you will direct your Attention is not for me, at this distance, to determine—your own judgement must dictate, according as you shall be made acquainted with particular circumstances.*[40]

Notwithstanding the appeal of striking at the very heart of the British army in North America, there was simply not enough time to gather an army and march on New York. Fortunately, Heath seems to have realized this before committing himself to what might have been a disastrous effort. Like the idea of following up the victory at Yorktown with an attack on Charleston, this project died aborning.

Given the length of the Atlantic voyage, there was a considerable time lag before the ministers in England learned of the fate of the campaign in Virginia. Germain had been informed by Clinton of the defeat at the Battle of the Capes and of the plans to relieve Cornwallis. He wrote to William Knox, his undersecretary of state for North America: "I never saw a more critical situation than that in which we stand, but we must wait the knowledge of an Event which is decided by this time, it is an anxious interval, and no orders can be sent from hence. . . . If I thought anything could be done here to spirit our fleet and army immediately in America, I should have return'd with your messenger, as we must now depend upon Providence and the valour of our sea and land forces, I shall not alter my first intention of returning to Town on Thursday about 12 o'clock."[41] The experience of watching a war across the ocean must have been akin to watching the stars, knowing that what you are seeing has taken place ages before. Any developments that might arise hardly seemed to warrant cutting short a vacation in the country.

When it became evident that the effort at relief from New York had failed, Clinton wrote Germain with the news: "This is a Blow, my Lord, which gives me the most serious concern, as it will in its consequences be exceedingly detrimental to the King's Interest in this Country; and might, I flatter myself, have possibly been prevented, could the Fleet have been able to Sail at or within a few days of the Time we first expected. At least I am persuaded we should have saved to His Majesty's Service great part of that gallant Army together with its respectable Chief, whose Loss it will now be impossible I fear to repair."[42]

The confirmation of the disaster occasioned considerable turmoil in the political circles of England. Added to the loss of General Burgoyne's army at Saratoga four years before, this defeat was viewed by many as decisive. There were those who argued that the reduction of the rebellious colonies was impossible, and others who argued that it was not worth the cost. When the defense was made that the fault lay with the misconduct of the generals and admirals, there were none waiting in the wings who were any more likely to succeed. In consequence, the king called upon Germain to propose a policy for the subjugation of the colonies that would succeed under the extraordinary circumstances which prevailed. Germain answered "that we ought to maintain what we possessed and act offensively by Sea only."[43] Clinton was informed by Germain of the new, defensive policy in a letter dated January 2, 1782. Greater emphasis than ever before was placed on the importance of the navy:

> *The Posts and Districts which are now in His Majesty's possession may be maintained, and such Detachments may occasionally be spared for such joint Operations with the Navy against the Ports and Towns upon the Sea Coasts of the Revolted Provinces, for destroying their shippings and stores and obstructing their Trade, as may be necessary to prevent them from acting offensively against us. The Prosecution of such a Plan necessarily supposes that Our Naval Force in America will be superior to that of the Enemy which I trust it will be at all times hereafter during the Continuance of the War, such Measures being taken for the purpose as promise to be effectual.[44]*

This was, in large measure, a reiteration of the policy Germain had been pursuing for the past four years, though viewed from a

Washington and His Generals at Yorktown *was painted by Charles Willson Peale soon after the battle. In the background may be seen Yorktown and its windmill; in the river are the masts of the scuttled ships, the French ships that finally entered after the battle, and the carcasses of the horses killed by the British garrison to prevent capture. (Courtesy of the Maryland Historical Society, Baltimore)*

defensive rather than an offensive position. In any event, it was not long before both Clinton and Germain were removed, and the implementation of the policy fell to Clinton's successor, Sir Guy Carleton. It was essentially his role to oversee the dismantling of the British military structure in North America over the next two years.

Early in 1782 the House of Lords opened an inquiry into the causes of the loss of the army under Lord Cornwallis. Copies of much of the pertinent correspondence were gathered, and on March 6, 1782, the House formed itself into a committee of the whole to pursue the inquiry. Though no minutes were kept and no formal resolution was adopted, a proposed resolution has survived that succinctly summarizes the apparent sentiments of the group:

> *Resolved, That it is the opinion of this Comm. that the immediate Cause of the Capture of the Army under Earl Cornwallys in Virginia, appears to have been the Want of a Sufficient Naval Force to cover and protect the same.*

> *Resolved, That the Undertaking the Expedition to Virginia, and neglecting to support the same with an adequate Fleet, was highly blameable in the Minister, or Ministers who plan'd the same.*[45]

Thus, while Clinton and Cornwallis were to engage in an acrimonious and bitter dispute for some time to come, attempting to lay the blame for this defeat, the Lords recognized that the fault lay not with the actors but with the playwright.

6

*After
the Battle*

IMMEDIATELY AFTER THE SURRENDER CEREMONY, Washington dispatched his aide-de-camp, Col. Tench Tilghman, to report the news of the fall of Yorktown to the Continental Congress. Though the news had already been received through the governor of Maryland, Congress was pleased to have a first-hand account of the action and, more particularly, of the captured materiel, including the shipping. Unfortunately, Tilghman had left in great haste, and his report was rather sketchy; the members of the committee appointed to interrogate him decided that the information he gave was not sufficiently reliable to warrant publication. They did, however, make a record of his statements relative to the shipping that had been captured: "The number of seamen was not ascertained at the time of his departure, but is probably small—that the vessels amount to about 100 Sail, fifty of which may be called transports: that among the shipping, are the *Guadaloupe*, a frigate of 28 guns, and *Bonetta* Sloop of War, with two or three other armed vessels: that most of them are sunk, but can easily be raised."[1] Though his report was substantially correct, it reflected the confusion and lack of accurate information in the American camp regarding the shipping.

This confusion resulted in large measure from the fact that although the Americans had possession of Yorktown, it was the French, on their ships in the Chesapeake Bay, who were responsible for the shipping in the harbor. The man in whose lap fell the task of taking account of the captured British ships was Capt. Guillaume-Jacques-Constant de Liberge de Granchain, chief administrative officer under Admiral de Barras. Granchain had been sent ashore by Admiral de Grasse to reconnoiter the possibility of an ascent of the York River by the French ships. He and another captain reported to Washington on October 8, 1781, and by the eleventh had concluded that there was no major obstacle to a French assault of the river. While the other captain was sent back to de Grasse with this report, Granchain remained attached to Washington's headquarters as a liaison officer.[2] He represented the French interests in the bargaining sessions at which the Articles of Capitulation were drawn up and was then apparently seized upon by the Americans as the only readily available member of the French navy. As such, he was delegated the responsibility for taking command of the shipping that had suddenly become the property of His Most Christian Majesty, the king of France.

On October 20 Granchain went on board the *Experiment*, one of the French ships that had finally been sent to force the river. He addressed a communique to her captain, Martelli Chautard, which stated in part:

> *I have been on board your ship, monsieur, in order to have the honor of seeing you and of taking your orders relative to the manning of the several ships anchored before York. I am only responsible for this taking of possession as the supposition was that there were no ships of the king in the harbor to carry it out; and I will have the honor to account to you tomorrow in person or by writing of the steps which I have taken for this object, and to ask you to continue this operation, as you are more capable than myself, and as moreover holding me here much longer than originally thought is the reembarkation of the garrisons of the vessels, which should take place tomorrow morning.[3]*

The garrisons referred to were the troops from the West Indies, under the marquis de Saint-Simon, who were to reembark on board the French fleet. The letter continued to outline the steps that would be necessary for getting these troops loaded on transports and to discuss the shipping available, a part of which consisted of the recently seized prizes. "There are further on the Gloucester shore towards the south of the town a rather large number of small boats and schooners which have all their sails furled on their yards, which could serve for the same operation."[4]

It would appear that the principal concern of Captain Granchain was not with the inventory of the shipping in the harbor,
for which he felt little responsibility, but with the embarkation
of the West Indian troops. He therefore wrote to Captain Martelli Chautard again on October 21, explained his inability to
continue in the position of prize agent for the captured shipping,
and requested that the job be assumed by another. He had not
been entirely idle, however, as he had managed to gather considerable information about the ships:

> *The notes which I have made on the state of the different ships*
> *which I have thought might be of some use to you, I have the*
> *honor of addressing to you, along with a copy of the reports which*
> *have been sent in by Captain Symonds of the Charon and by the*
> *agent of the transports. The latter has promised to give me a*
> *report of those transports, which have been sunk by boring and*
> *which not, and consequently could be raised easily. You would do*
> *well not to sell anything of these. The frigate Guadeloupe is in*
> *this case and it is vital, I believe, to watch attentively to see that*
> *nothing is removed from the rigging and I think it would be*
> *proper to further establish the same policy for all the other ships.*
> *Without that all the prizes will become of no value as one will*
> *find that there is no sale in this country for ships stripped of their*
> *rigging, of their boats, etc.*[5]

While the main consideration of the French with respect to
the newly acquired prizes was the maintenance of their salabili-
ty, there was also concern that all possible use be made of them
to expedite the operations in progress. In addition to using the
shipping, particularly the small craft, to carry the troops of
Saint-Simon, they intended to use several of the ships to house
the British sailors, whom the French had inherited as prisoners
of war:

> *It is indispensable, I believe, to make a collection without delay of*
> *the English naval prisoners and to deposit them on board of*
> *several ships; the Tartar, Andrews and the Bellona appear most*
> *appropriate to me. I have foreseen that you could be caught short*
> *for their feeding and I have spoken to the intendant of the land*
> *forces whom I have ordered to send you every other day at the*
> *beach of York, in fresh three pound loaves, the quantity of bread*

A rather fanciful view of the booming metropolis of Yorktown is given in this French engraving of the period. Notwithstanding the obvious inaccuracies, the French clearly appreciated the important role played by their naval forces in the reduction of the town. (Courtesy of the National Maritime Museum, London)

which you may need. For this object, he reasonably asks that you inform him one day in advance, and that your clerk or another person appointed for the task give receipts. As for the meat, you could address yourself to Messrs. Wadsworth and Carter, suppliers for the land forces at Williamsburg who will deliver to you the number of barrels of rations for which you ask. I do not believe that it is the intention of the General to provide them with drink.[6]

The ships mentioned were transports in the British service and may have served as prison ships during the battle. In any event, they had to accommodate 840 naval prisoners, exclusive of the

crews of the privately owned vessels in the harbor.' This is an indication of the relatively crowded conditions which prevailed throughout the Revolution in prison ships on both sides, though the French tended to be more humane than either the British or the Americans.[8]

In view of the large group of ships that had just been acquired, it is surprising that there was a shortage of vessels immediately following the battle. This apparently resulted from the fact that many of them, while in condition to be easily salvaged, were not readily usable as they were. This was particularly true of the transports, the large majority of which had been scuttled and required raising. The principal shortage seems to have been in the areas of large transports and small craft. In giving instructions for the reembarkation of the troops under Saint-Simon, which had still not taken place on October 22 when he again wrote to Captain Martelli Chautard, Granchain stated: "He desires that all this be done with the greatest haste and without any assistance from the shallops of the army, which are obliged to be employed at other things for supplying it. I am going to ask General Washington for a quantity of flat boats loaded on wagons actually before his quarter. I will conduct these same to York and you would do well to give your orders that they are to be moored and held in reserve for the time when they may be useful."[9] On the same date, the quartermaster general of the American forces, Timothy Pickering, wrote a letter to the American adjutant general, Edward Hand, and requested crews to man small craft: "To give proper dispatch in transporting persons and stores from Gloucester to York and have proper care taken of the boats, I find that about fifty watermen will be very necessary. If Officers experienced in that way were selected to Command them it would be best."[10] Obviously, the French were not the only ones who stood in need of water transport; the business of breaking down the encampment on both sides of the river led to considerable traffic. So much so, in fact, that by October 28 Washington was forced to request the return of the flat boats which Granchain had asked for, "as there were no more than a half dozen in the Port."[11] It may be that Granchain had, in fact, simply held these boats in reserve, and Washington felt that they could be put to better use; more likely, however, the loading of the troops under the marquis de Saint-Simon had been completed, and the French had no further need for the boats. With the withdrawal of the French troops, the problem seems to have gotten worse instead of better. On November 3, 1781, Edward Carrington, deputy quartermaster general for the Virginia militia, wrote from Yorktown: "Capt. Singleton is coming to Richmond to see about the receiving and Storeing the military Stores to be transported by Water from this place. You will be pleased to give him every aid in your power, but in the mean time give attention to forwarding Vessells to York for the purpose of Transporting is pressingly necessary. We cannot get a single Boat here, the Stores to a great amount lye exposed & will perhaps in a short time meet with much danger in going up by water."[12] The shortage of water transportation was a problem for both French and Americans.

The French forces which were to remain in Virginia found that they continued to lack water transport, especially large transport vessels. In addition to the army of Rochambeau, which was to winter at Williamsburg and Yorktown, Admiral de Grasse was leaving four ships. These were to be responsible for the salvage and sale of the prizes, and further for the support and protection of the army. As Rochambeau intended to dispatch some of the newly acquired English cannon to places of safety, he had immediate need of transport vessels and requested these of de Grasse. He replied, on October 24, 1781: "The vessels which I plan to leave you are the Romulus, the Hermione, the Diligente, and the Resolue. As to the transports which you requested of me, if they are not to be found in the York River, I do not see any means for you to procure them; but you could conceivably disarm for a while one of your frigates, and you yourself will find . . . that the frigate Diligente will be, I believe, the most suitable for this operation; you will find by this means, at least, the accomplishment of your object."[13] This naval force, which remained after the main fleet had left, was under the command of La Villebrune, captain of the *Romulus;* it was to him that responsibility for the salvage of the sunken vessels was delegated.

While the French and the Americans had been dividing the spoils and breaking camp, Lord Cornwallis had not been altogether idle. His first concern was to send dispatches reporting the unfortunate outcome of the battle to his superior, Sir Henry Clinton, in New York. He had written a long letter to Clinton, dated October 20, detailing the events of the battle and attempting to exonerate himself of any guilt. Having labored on the composition of this letter, he found that it was even more difficult to get it dispatched. According to the terms of the capitulation, the British sloop *Bonetta* was to be at his disposal for this service:

> *Article VIII—The Bonetta sloop of war to be equipped and navigated by its present Captain and crew, and left entirely at the disposal of Lord Cornwallis from the hour that the capitulation is signed, to receive an Aid de Camp to carry dispatches to Sir Henry Clinton; and such soldiers as he may*

*think proper to send to New York, to be permitted to sail without
examination. When his dispatches are ready, his Lordship engages
on his part that the ship shall be delivered to the order of the
Count de Grasse, if she escapes the dangers of the sea. That she
shall not carry off any public stores. Any part of the crew that
may be deficient on her return and the soldiers passengers to be
accounted for on her delivery.[14]*

This was a real point of irritation to the Americans, in particular,
since it was certain that most of the tories then in Yorktown
would be able to escape the vengeance of the conquering forces.
In any event, the article stood as written, and the *Bonetta*, the
only British naval vessel still afloat, was designated to carry the
dispatches. However, she was not to get off without some difficulty, most of it the result of intentional delay, as is indicated by
Granchain's letter of October 21:

*Lord Cornwallis when I saw him yesterday, monsieur, asked me
urgently that someone should provide water for the small ship
designated to carry his dispatches to New York. Since they could
not succeed in making their sailors work at present as they are
prisoners, he offers to pay French sailors for this service and I
believe that he should not be refused. I forgot to speak of it
yesterday with M. Duprés and have just received a note on the
subject which I forward to you. I beg you to be willing to answer
favorably from feelings of respect for milord Cornwallis. I know
that one would reasonably like to delay the departure of his
communications; this could not be done, however, without
dishonestly making the hindrance of the water last too long. M.
Count de Grasse will find sufficient pretexts for holding it, if he
decides when it is ready to leave that there are disadvantages to
its leaving the bay.[15]*

There were obvious advantages in delaying the communication
between the defeated forces and the British commander in chief,
and these were not overlooked by the allies. On the other hand,
as gentlemen they were bound not to hinder the ship's departure, though they did not extend themselves to hasten it. Apparently, the wonders of the bureaucracy did their work, for it was
not until October 23, 1781, that Colonel Butler, a Pennsylva-
nian, reported that "the sloop of war Bonetta fell down the river,

with her iniquitous cargo of deserters, stolen negroes, and public stores that the British officers had secreted."[16]

The *Bonetta* was a sore point with the American forces, but they apparently had good reason for their concern. After his return to England, Captain Dundas of the *Bonetta* was court martialed on the charge that he had not made every effort to evacuate the loyal citizens in the town. The court martial, held March 12, 1782, found him innocent. The court determined that Captain Dundas had acted strictly in accordance with the orders he had received from Lord Cornwallis and Captain Symonds. It concluded that he had "particularly distinguished himself in his humane Treatment and reception of upwards of 340 of the Loyalists, (besides his Ships complemt.) whom he used with every Attention & Humanity."[17] The acquittal seems to have been based largely on the strength of a report which Lord Cornwallis gave of the events in a letter to the Admiralty dated March 9, 1782:

> *Capt. Dundas was so far from refusing Admittance to the Loyalists into the Bonetta, that he received so great a number, that I was obliged to direct Lieut. Col. Abercromby to go on board, & to turn out several of those who would be least endangered by remaining on shore in order to enable the Vessel to go to Sea. In a Sloop of War, so crowded, & so ill calculated for the accommodation of upwards of 400 persons, there can be no doubt but the Passengers suffered great inconvenience. I was however assured by Mr. Hubbard of Virginia, the Inspector of Refugees, that Capt. Dundas did every thing in his power to contribute to their comfort and convenience, and that he sent them half of the fresh Stock that was killed on board; and that the only reason that some of the Gentlemen who complain of ill usage did not partake of it, was that they kept themselves concealed.[18]*

One can well imagine the sorry plight of the tories who found themselves stranded in the defeated post.

A prisoner of war in New York, Christopher Vail, reported the arrival of the *Bonetta* some days later:

> *I was there when Cornwallis surrendered at Little York. We heard the firing of cannon from the Jerseys for rejoicing, and whenever our people fired the British would fire from their*

This "Sketch of York town, from the beach, looking to the West" was drawn by Benjamin Henry Latrobe on the occasion of his visit in 1796. Though the entire beach area is shown, with emphasis on the remains of the fortifications, there is no indication of any wreckage surviving. (Courtesy of the Maryland Historical Society, Baltimore)

batteries so as to confuse that people should not be informed of Cornwallis capture but it soon came out and in a few days after this a cartel arrived from N. London and I was exchanged. I was on board this Cartel when the Bonetta Sloop of war arrived in New York from Little York. The ship was suffered to depart from Lord Cornwallis without searching and was full of Tories and treasure that was plundered by their army.[19]

Having unloaded her cargo, the *Bonetta* did return to Yorktown, and became the property of the French Navy. As the fleet of Admiral de Grasse had since left, she was temporarily attached to the four ships remaining there. Her real duty was that of dispatch craft, however, and she was sent to the Antilles with messages for the admiral. She was not destined to remain French for long, as she was captured by the British frigate *Amphion* on this voyage. Her capture was effected on January 4, 1782, and she apparently was carrying convalescents at the time.[20]

Though he had finally managed to send off his dispatches, Lord Cornwallis's work was by no means done. He was loath to sit in Virginia while the lengthening shadow of defeat darkened his image at headquarters; it was certainly in his interest to get to New York as quickly as possible. He had foreseen this problem, and Article VI of the Articles of Capitulation granted parole to Cornwallis and his officers, and contracted to provide them with transportation to New York. Thus, on October 23, 1781, Washington wrote to de Grasse, stating: "Lord Cornwallis claims with great earnestness the accomplishment of the Article of the Capitulation which engages to provide Transports for conveying the General and Staff Officers to New York. Mr. de Grandchain was of opinion that your Excellency would probably destine to this service two of the Vessels surrendered to the Marine but that there would be a difficulty in manning them."[21] He then continued to propose that the manning problem be resolved by allowing British prisoners to act as crews, with the proviso that they be exchanged for an equal number of French or American prisoners when they arrived in New York. A further problem arose regarding provisions for the flag vessels which were to carry the officers; apparently the British were unable to supply their own, since all the supplies of the garrison had been taken over as spoils of war by the Americans. Therefore, Washington agreed to supply the ships with salt provisions and biscuit, provided that Lord Cornwallis would return a like amount, of the same quality, to the American forces at Kings Ferry or West Point, upon his arrival.[22]

The ships were finally permitted to depart on November 5, 1781, as the Americans were leaving Yorktown and the fleet of de Grasse was making sail for the West Indies. The passport issued to the ships by General Washington gives the details of their voyage:

> *His Excellency General Washington, Commander in Chief of the Allied Army*
>   *To all Commanders of Ships of War and private armed Vessels belonging to the United States and their Allies cruizing on the High Seas—*

*These are to Certify that the Ship Cochran of 247 Tons
Burthen, Captain Bolton, Commander—Navigated by forty six
British Seamen, Prisoners to his Most Christian Majesty,
transporting the Right Honble Earl Cornwallis, with Twenty Six
other officers, & forty two British Soldiers, Prisoners of War to
the United States of America, under a Flag of Truce—Hath
Permission to pass from Yorktown in Virginia to New York and
Return with an equal Number of healthy French or American
Seamen in Exchange for the present crew—That the wages of
War relative to Flaggs being observed on the part of the said
Vessel she will pass & repass without interruption as afore
mentioned.*

> *Given at Head Quarters near*
> *Yorktown this 4th Day of*
> *November, 1781*

*N. B. Passports granted to two other Vessels as follows Viz.
Lord Mulgrave—320 Tons, Andrew Easterly, Master
        50 Seamen, Carrying 103 Officers, 125 Soldiers, Servants
Ship Andrew—250 Tons, Francis Todnage, Master
        44 Seamen, Carrying 101 Officers, 118 Soldiers, Servants
Sloop Delight—40 Tonns, John Kerr, Master, 3 American
Seamen,
        Carrying 5 British Commissioneds, one Prisoner, 13
Merchants
        To New York & Rhode Island
        Sloop Molly—40 Tonns, Samuel Hicks, Master, 5 Seamen,
carrying 3 officers, 13 merchants, To New York & Rhode
Island.*[23]

Notwithstanding the allowances which were made for the prisoners by the Americans, the voyage was a difficult and unpleas-
ant one. The Hessian Ewald sailed on board the *Andrew*, in the
company of some 99 officers, 143 camp followers and servants, 8
ships' captains, and 100 sailors, probably from the transports. In
addition, "there were some fifty various white and black two-
footed creatures of both sexes. I could not see their faces because
they hid them; they probably were contraband." He offered a
description of the accommodations, which had been jury-rigged:
"Toward midday this whole mixed and motley company was on

board the ship. The cabin had been combined with the sailors' quarters and on both sides three bunks had been built, one over the other, as large as could be made. These bunks, each of a width of two feet, were occupied according to seniority by the two brigadiers on down. The remaining gentlemen, as well as the entire ship's crew and the servants, had permission to look for a place wherever one could be found." There was little discipline, and in short order virtual chaos prevailed. They set sail only to discover bad rations and a shortage of water. Water was rationed to one cup per day per man, the ship drifted aimlessly much of the time, and it was not until November 23 that the *Andrew* reached Sandy Hook.[24] Further details on the voyage were offered by Lord Cornwallis in a letter to Rochambeau: "After a very disagreeable voyage, I arrived here the 19th of this month. . . . The Flag of Truce named the *Cochran* will make sail in a few days, that named the *Andrew* only arrived yesterday, but having made water dangerously in two places will not be able to set out before having been repaired, and we have still not received any news of that named the *Lord Mulgrave*."[25] In fact, the *Lord Mulgrave* never did reach New York. She was blown off course, and put into Charleston, from which the prisoners were sent to New York, finally arriving on December 17.[26]

On November 5, 1781, the last of Washington's troops and the French fleet under de Grasse left Yorktown, the one going to winter quarters, the other to the West Indies. The role de Grasse had played in winning the battle was not overlooked by the participants, and some effort was made to pay him back. A number of the wealthier men of Virginia assembled a token of their esteem which was presented to the admiral. An indication of simpler times, it consisted in part of "12 Lambs, 36 Turkeys, 24 Ducks, 24 Geese, 8 Shoats, 60 bushels Irish potatoes, 10 bushels Turnips, 200 Cabbages," in addition to onions, apples, peas and poultry.[27] The present was no doubt appreciated, given the nature of the preserved food which was commonly available on shipboard. Washington had hoped that de Grasse might stay on the East Coast for a few more months, to follow up the advantage which the victory at Yorktown had created. Both Charleston and Savannah were proposed as potential targets for future concerted campaigns, but de Grasse felt constrained to return to the West Indies. In preparing to leave, he wrote Rochambeau on

October 29, 1781, concerning the shipping which was to be left for his use over the winter: "The arrival of the Romulus in the River should prove to you, my dear General, that I am occupied entirely with you and your operations. I am going to send back the Diligente, if she is not there already, as well as all those vessels which are useless to us, among which number you should find several well suited for the transport of your artillery, which safe after their mission, should be sold to the profit of the equipage of the army."[28] In the five days since his dispatch of October 24, the admiral had revised his position and agreed to provide transports for Rochambeau. Apparently, a sufficiently complete inspection of the shipping that remained in the York River had been made to indicate that few, if any, of the ships were in condition to be commissioned immediately. In the face of this obvious need for transports, de Grasse must have relented and agreed to provide the vessels, particularly since he had several surplus vessels. The French had captured eleven vessels in the process of entering the Chesapeake, and some of these were not required for the fleet's activities. It would appear that it was these ships which were sent to La Villebrune to be used in the transportation of the army's artillery.

This is confirmed by the fact that at least three of the vessels that had been captured before the battle were soon sold to the State of Virginia, by La Villebrune. A letter dated November 17, 1781, from the Virginia agent, refers to this transaction:

> *Captain Villebrun of the Romulus who was left here by the Count De Grasse to transact the business of the Navy has given me all the trouble that was in his power. The ships I purchased for the State were kept down at the Fleet, until they plundered them of a vast quantity of valuable stores, in short I have had more trouble with this transaction than I ever had in my life. I have got the ships in possession, in order to carry up the remains of the Continental Army, at General Washington's earnest request. The ships were kept from me so long that there was neither sailors, officers, nor materials to be procured—expecting that we should be able to pick up some British Tars, with whom there wd. be no danger whilst the Soldiers were on board, I wrote to Col. Dabney to furnish two officers & 40 men for the safety of the ships on their return.[29]*

This view of Yorktown was painted on the spot in 1834 by John Gadsby Chapman. One of a series of historical paintings of scenes associated with the life of Washington, it gives a vivid picture of the decay of the formerly prosperous town. The figures on the small point on the beach presumably are standing on the remains of the colonial wharf. (Courtesy of a private collection)

No doubt La Villebrune made life difficult for the Virginia agent, but there were two sides to the coin. In an earlier letter to the Governor, the agent had stated, "I am like to be much distressed to pay for the two ships I purchased."[30]

The other vessels that remained afloat after the battle were used to return the British naval officers and their crews directly to England. These sailed November 20 under the command of Capt. Thomas Symonds, formerly of the *Charon*:

> *I am to request you will be pleased to acquaint my Lords Commissioners of the Admiralty, that after the surrender of York & Gloucester by capitulation, on the 19th of Octbr. last, His Excellency the Count de Grasse was pleased to grant me three ships for the purpose of bringing to England the officers & seamen made prisoners of war at that time, in consequence of which, the*

*Two Brothers & Bellona late Transports, were fitted out &
sailed from York river the 20th of last month, & the Aurora a
French merchant ship, was appointed to convey the remainder
home.*[31]

Once the paroled prisoners had landed, the ships were to be sent
on to France. A final contingent of naval prisoners was sent to
England on May 4, 1782, on board the chartered vessel *St. Marc
de Riste,* consisting of invalids too weak to have made the earlier
voyage.[32]

If Symonds and the other naval officers had a relatively un-
eventful voyage, the same cannot be said of Lord Cornwallis.
After encountering the unmasked hostility of Sir Henry Clinton
in New York, Cornwallis determined to make his way to England as quickly as possible, to defend himself. He left New
York on December 15, 1781, with a convoy bound for England.
Twelve days out the convoy began to disperse. Cornwallis and
his party transferred to the transport *Greyhound,* which was commanded by Thomas Tonken, who had formerly been agent for
all the transports on the North America coast. On January 14,
1782, separated from the main convoy, their luck ran out:

*We were taken off Scilly by a french privateer of St. Malo who
took all our Seamen out & put french in their room but not one
of them coud steer or was in fact the least of a Seamen, we had
most terrible gales to the NW so that the prize master was
fearfull to go near the french coast & we found ourselves
yesterday near the Start. Lord Cornwallis proposed to him as our
lives were in danger of going to france in our present situation
that in case he consented to go into an English port that the ship
should be his, his Lordship having given his word to the Capt. of
the privateer that neither the officers or servants should in the
least interrupt the prize master from navigating his ship. All my
papers about Transports are destroy'd as well as the letters, but I
will give you every information in my power when I have the
honour of waiting on you.*[33]

Thus Cornwallis fell prey to the French not once, but twice; this
incident also explains in part the paucity of surviving documentation concerning the transports involved in the Yorktown campaign.

When the cartel ship *Two Brothers*, which had brought him to England, was sent on to France, French prisoners were sent on board and Captain Symonds was considered officially exchanged. Thus at liberty to enter the service once again, he immediately petitioned the Board of Admiralty for a formal inquiry into the loss of the *Charon*. Though he wrote on January 17, 1782, the court martial was not convened until March 12, 1782. Symonds was tried jointly with Hugh Robinson of the *Guadaloupe*, Peter Aplin of the *Fowey*, and Ralph Dundas of the *Bonetta*. Testimony was taken from each, and from several of their subordinates, and on March 13 the court stated that it was "of opinion that the said Captains Symonds, Robinson, Aplin & Dundas be acquitted of all Blame on Account of the Loss of his Majesty's said late Ships & Sloop, and they are hereby acquitted accordingly."[34] A similar proceeding was held for Captain George Palmer, of the *Vulcan*, on June 15, 1782, and he was likewise exonerated of all blame.[35] With the termination of this inquiry, official interest in the naval aspects of the battle drew to a close.

Once the main bodies of troops had left Yorktown, the remaining French contingent established itself in winter quarters there and in Williamsburg. Apart from maintaining an armed force in the Chesapeake area, their main reason for being was the salvage and disposition of the sunken ships left at Yorktown. The responsibility for this project rested squarely on the shoulders of Captain La Villebrune, of the *Romulus*. On January 30, 1782, La Villebrune filed an official statement with his superiors in France and gave a detailed report of the progress of his activities. Though he could report that the navigation of the Bay and the rivers was secure, that supplies for the army were assured, and that the military stores had been removed to their various destinations, with respect to the sale of the captured vessels the picture was not so bright: "I have sold as many of the vessels as had solid purchasers, the boats and sloops which are of use in the navigation of the rivers have been preferred and sold. The large vessels, on the other hand, have had little demand and it is feared that they will not be sold before the departure of our forces, which in protecting their navigation gives them a value which they would not otherwise have, as the enemy vessels are superi-

or."[36] That there was a surfeit of shipping available in Yorktown
is confirmed by a letter written by a merchant there to his agent
in the West Indies, December 30, 1781. William Reynolds
wrote, "There are many Vessells here captur'd by the French
fleet, that might be bought on good terms."[37] In addition to the
difficulty of selling large vessels in a war-stricken area, Villebrune also encountered problems in raising those ships that had
been sunk in the York River:

> *I have raised very few of the vessels; the apparatus necessary for
> these operations, which are always difficult in ports, has not been
> given to me, and if I had it at my disposal, the harshness of the
> season and the crew of the Romulus being reduced to two hundred
> thirty men dispersed since my arrival at York on the vessels
> destined for the different expeditions for war supplies and
> provisions for the army, have been insufficient; my first attentions
> will be given to the Guadeloupe, as soon as good weather permits.
> If, Monseigneur, you could send to York the necessary apparatus
> for this operation, I do not doubt that it will be possible to raise
> her.[38]*

Though the picture La Villebrune presented to his superiors in
France was not an optimistic one, there may have been an ulteri-
or motive behind his actions. A letter written to him by Rochambeau on January 24, 1782, six days before his report was filed,
stated in part:

> *I approve infinitely the letter of the 20th which you have done me
> the honor of writing, and I believe that it is reasonable to wait to
> sell all the transports, until we determine whether our operations
> in the spring will not require them in order to have enough for
> our movements, the more so you have strongly pointed out, as one
> third of these prizes belongs to the King, who could at the end of
> the Campaign, make good use of the vessels for his service, and it
> is necessary to count on the Americans for no help, after the
> devastation that the English have done to all their shipping.[39]*

Once having raised the vessels at Yorktown, Rochambeau and La
Villebrune were understandably reluctant to sell them and send
one-third of the prize money to the king while they might still
make use of them for their operations. To reduce their transport
force by one-third would have been reckless and unnecessary.

At the time of the capitulation, the transition from British to American to French control does not seem to have taken place without some dissension, subterfuge, and plundering by all parties concerned, owing in large measure to the unregulated situation which prevailed. Goods belonging to private owners were to be returned to them, naval supplies stored on the ships were to become the property of the French, and war supplies in Yorktown proper were to go to the Americans. There was considerable shuffling after the surrender, as private goods, and presumably others as well, were removed from the ships and taken ashore. Certain of the cases resulted in disputes that were referred to higher authority, as in the instance of a cargo including coffee and cocoa, claimed by both the French and the Americans. Rochambeau finally ordered that the material on shore be turned over to the Americans, and the French were the losers.[40] It would appear that this was the rule rather than the exception, and the condition of the vessels in the harbor suffered as a result.

Another source of conflict and confusion arose during the winter, as the terms of the capitulation agreement were carried out. The ninth article of that agreement had allowed the merchants of Yorktown to preserve their property intact. They were further allowed to dispose of that property and to remove the proceeds for their own benefit. On February 11, 1782, the Continental Congress resolved to allow the traders, having sold their effects, to export their value in tobacco. There was obviously scant enthusiasm among the Virginians for this project, and they did everything possible to hinder it. Ships to carry the tobacco were to be sent from New York and were to be confined to the James River. There was fear, and not without reason, that this venture would serve to mask information gathering, if not any actual military action. There were several incidents with a few individual ships which were sent, and the problem was not finally resolved until December 1782. At that time a fleet of fourteen ships sailed from New York to Virginia and collected over 2,000 hogsheads of tobacco, thus settling the accounts of the loyalist merchants.[41]

La Villebrune found meanwhile that the devastation of the captured vessels proved to be a considerable hindrance to his operations; rather than providing the supplies which he desper-

ately needed, each salvaged vessel proved to be a further drain on
his resources. In another letter of January 30, 1782, he complained of the shortage of uniforms, equipment, and officers,
and continued:

> *The prizes taken in York having been plundered before my
> arrival, they do not offer the means to repair our vessels, in
> particular those which are to be put up for sale, and could not
> now withstand a strong breeze. Though one might find the
> necessary objects to fit them out, I believe that it will be
> infinitely more advantageous to send the rigging and apparatus to
> York, which will be less costly and will give the means after
> having furnished our naval forces for their return to absorb into
> our columns those vessels of which the hulls and spars are
> excellent, but which one could not haul to another area because
> they are disabled.*[42]

He received no relief during the remainder of the winter, and in
a letter of April 5, 1782, La Villebrune again complained: "The
vessels have no less needs than the men; we are lacking especially
sail cloth, cordage, blocks, Brittany cloth for tents, parchment,
oil, and the major part of all the objects necessary for the armament of ships of war and transports."[43] A month later the fleet
was still unrelieved, and the situation was becoming critical. His
crews nearly naked, and his own vessels no longer in condition to
put to sea, La Villebrune attempted to carry on the salvage project: "I have been actually occupied with the raising of the frigate
Guadeloupe. I do not despair of success, but I have few means.
The crew of the Romulus is reduced to 230 men, and it is dispersed among the many transport vessels. As the victuallers of
the army and the Romulus are making considerable water, a part
of the crew is continually occupied at the pumps; if I did not
have a post to guard I would not hesitate to careen her."[44] Ap-
pended to this report, which was dispatched with the British
prisoners on board the *St. Marc de Riste* on May 4, 1782, was a list
of the vessels then afloat in the harbor at Yorktown. Apparently,
La Villebrune was trying to generate some interest in his project
on the home front, in an effort to get supplies.[45] He reported
further in a letter written May 28, 1782: "I have not yet been
able to raise the frigate Guadeloupe; I have only saved all the
cannons, the apparatus which I need to raise her being totally

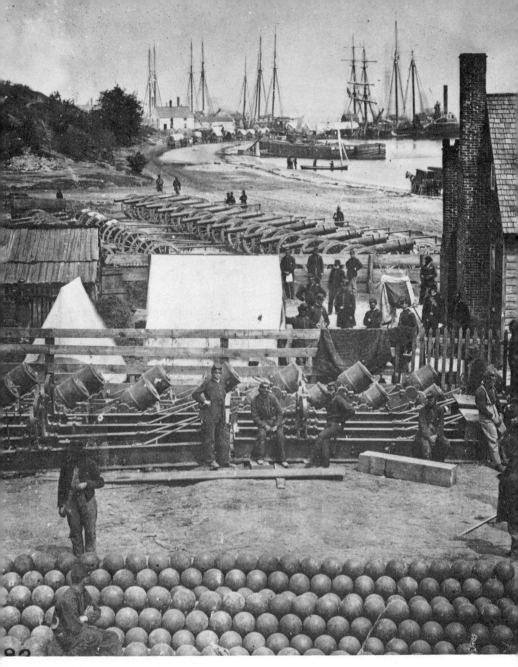

In May 1862 Matthew Brady photographed the beach at Yorktown, which was serving as a staging area for the Peninsula Campaign. Considering the intensity of the activity, there appears to be surprisingly little contamination of the shipwrecks with Civil War period artifacts. (Courtesy of National Archives)

lacking. I presume that she was sunk fully loaded, yet I am inclined to try a new method which should be more successful."[46] Whatever his new method was, it required a substantial amount of equipment. In an account filed at the end of May, there is an entry for nearly 15,000 francs, spent for the purchase of "blocks, tackle and lines necessary to raise the English frigate Guadeloupe."[47] La Villebrune had apparently located a source of equipment in the area, and was continuing in his efforts to raise the most important prize of all the vessels in the harbor.

The persistence with which La Villebrune pursued his objectives was finally rewarded when, on July 1, 1782, a fleet under the command of the Comte de Latouche was sent to reinforce the small squadron at Yorktown. Although no report of the composition of the fleet has been located, it is apparent from the instructions issued to Latouche that he was to take over command of the forces in the Chesapeake, supplement them with his vessels, and thereby free La Villebrune and his leaking ships to return to France for repairs. One of the primary missions of the relief fleet was the raising of the *Guadaloupe*, and it must be presumed that Latouche was better equipped than had been La Villebrune.[48]

This fleet was not destined to rendezvous with the French forces at Yorktown, however. By the time it sailed from France, Rochambeau was in the process of withdrawing the bulk of the French army from Virginia. The troops marched north to Baltimore from Yorktown and Williamsburg on July 1, 1782, leaving behind only a token contingent. The chevalier de La Vallette was left to command the remaining forces, largely militia: "I have the Honour to inform you that the Compte Rochambeau has intrusted to me the Command of the French Troops which he left at York & West Point. . . . Some Detachments of Militia have arrived at York & would be obliged to you to write me the number upon which I may count at present & what I may expect if Circumstances should require a more considerable Reinforcement."[49] While the Virginia militia was moving into the post at Yorktown, it appears that the French naval forces remained in the harbor. On July 16 the governor requested their aid in clearing the Chesapeake of British raiders, most of whom came from the Eastern Shore.[50] This transitional force must have been withdrawn in late August, as a journal of one of the men in the army reported from Baltimore on August 25, 1782, that "shortly before our departure the detachment we had left in Yorktown arrived by sea in the *Romulus* and the *Guadeloupe.*"[51] Obviously, the *Guadaloupe* had been raised without the help of the relief fleet; neither she nor the *Romulus* seems to have gotten the refit they both so badly needed. They were detained in Baltimore for some time, and Rochambeau wrote to La Villebrune on October 13, 1782: "As for your personal destination with the Romulus, I do not believe that it is yet settled, and I believe that you should hold yourself in readiness to put to sea with the Guadeloupe in six weeks, if the circumstances warrant."[52] Without doubt, the *Guadaloupe* was the most difficult and most valuable of those vessels worth salvaging in the York River, and with her recovery, and the departure of the army we must presume that formal salvage operations by the French forces drew to a close. As a consequence of this salvage effort, a fairly large, if indeterminate, number of wrecks were certainly raised. Equally certainly, many were left unsalvaged on the bottom of the river.

7

~~~~~~~~~~~~~

Salvaging the Captive Fleet

WITH THE DEPARTURE of the French forces and the Virginia militia, all formal efforts at salvage presumably drew to a close. There was no lack of interest in the wrecks, however; they would have constituted a considerable economic resource if properly raised. Not only were the Americans interested in them but the British as well. In November 1782 Robert Alexander had made application to Brook Watson, commissary general of the British forces in New York: "In Consequence of the conversation that passed between us yesterday, I now repeat the offer I then made, which is that I will pay you £250 New York Currency for each Vessel of the Number that were sunken or taken at York Town in Virginia, which I shall bring into this port, such payment to be in full for the Right of the Crown to such Vessels."[1] This was Alexander's second offer, and apparently the end of a long negotiation with Watson. The day before he had written a complex proposal that Watson evidently rejected as too risky for the Crown: "As you have not agreed to my proposition, I cannot accept yours. I shall now make one, which I know to be agreeable to the practice of the Court of Admiralty, and I am informed is conformable to the usage of the port of New York— That the Repairs made and Stores procured for the Vessel and the Expense of raising her, shall be valued by the Wardens of the Port, that being fixed, the Vessel or Vessels shall be sold at publick auction, and the sum so ascertained by the Wardens being deducted from the sale, 7/8ths of the Balance shall be paid you as Agent for the Crown."[2] There is no indication that Alexander pursued the project further or that any formal agreement was ever reached. The fact that the British could claim little or no legal interest in the ships, combined with their final withdrawal from New York soon thereafter, makes it seem unlikely that any salvage work was completed.

It is evident, on the basis of the contemporary reports, that the salvage effort undertaken by the French, and whoever may have followed them, was incomplete at best. Yorktown was visited in 1783 by Johann David Schoepf, a German doctor, who wrote:

> *The inhabitants had not yet recovered from the disquiets of the war, and many had not returned to their homes. Traces of the devastation were still everywhere visible, and several families were living at the time in the ruins of buildings that had been shot to pieces. The ships sunk in the river for the protection of the garrison were still in their places, and it is thought not worth while to be at the trouble of raising them, for there is every reason to believe that after two years they will be found so eaten by the worms, (which do much damage in these waters), as to be no longer usable.[3]*

Certainly informal salvage operations must have continued for a while and it must be presumed that the local residents regarded the wrecks as a resource to be tapped. Their economic value, however, waned quickly as they deteriorated.

A spectral quiet hung over Yorktown as it settled back into its former pattern. There was no tobacco trade of note remaining, and the town's economic mainstay was thus lost. Recovery for the war-shattered town was slow and hard, and the populace was quick to grieve over its shell-ridden gardens. When the place was visited in later years, the evidence of the battle was still to be seen. The residents were loath, for sentimental or economic reasons, to repair the damage to their buildings, and travelers occasionally took note of the present condition of the area. In 1796, Benjamin Henry Latrobe recorded: "York town is going very fast to decay. It has an excellent harbor, safe from every Wind, but the East. But of what use is an harbor without a trade. The town is now famous only for the best fish and oysters, and the best tavern in Virginia, and for the hospitality and friendliness of its inhabitants."[4] In addition to his description, Latrobe left several drawings of the area. He neither described nor depicted any wreckage in the river, and it must be presumed that the currents and the weather had obliterated what traces the salvors, both official and unofficial, had left behind.

Formal salvage efforts began again in 1852, based on the evidence of a petition submitted to the Virginia General Assembly by one Thomas Ash, of Gloucester Point, Virginia. The Ash family was relatively well known in the Gloucester area, and their descendants continue to live there today; William Henry Ash was granted the Yorktown-Gloucester Ferry franchise in 1865, and the family operated the ferry as late as 1936.[5] It may be presumed that the petitioner, Thomas Ash, was a waterman as well. In any event, he believed that he knew the location where "an English Frigate of large class was sunk in York River" during the Revolution. "It is supposed that she burnt to the waters edge and then went down in fifteen or twenty feet water, with all her guns and apparel, where the wreck now lies." Ash was convinced that he knew "the exact point of her location, as he has on several occasions fished up from it some small articles of value." His application consisted of a request for the exclusive right of salvage from this wreck, for which project he proposed to acquire a diving bell. Because of the considerable expense involved in such a project, he wanted to be sure that there would be no competition.[6]

The principal weakness of Ash's petition was that he made no mention of a division of the spoils with the state; the surprise, then, is that the General Assembly acted favorably on the petition. On May 1, 1852, the General Assembly passed an act authorizing Thomas Ash "to search for and recover, by diving bells or any other means, the guns and equipments, coin or other article of value, which may have belonged to or have been contained within an English frigate or vessel, which was sunk in York River." The state granted Ash the exclusive right of search and recovery, and relinquished any claim which it might have on the property for a period of ten years. The fact that Ash's petition is dated July 6, 1852, after the above act was passed but is noted as received on February 10, 1852, before the date of passage, may be some indication of his political connections at the capitol.[7]

A small pencil sketch by the marine artist Samuel Ward Stanton shows the tugboat Samuel Gedney. *It was this tug that undertook the salvage of a number of relics from the shipwrecks in 1881. (Courtesy of The Mariners' Museum)*

It is not known to what extent Ash was successful in his attempt to recover material from what may have been the remains of the *Charon*. Once he discovered that the guns were not the bronze ones which he expected, but iron, it seems reasonable to assume that he desisted. An indication that he must have recovered something, as well as a reading on the state of historical awareness in the area at the time, is suggested by a letter written by Edward Dunning, dated Gloucester County, February 16, 1851, to his wife:

I had no idea of Antiquity till I reached Williamsburg & seemed to me there must be a law there against the erection of any thing new. I stoped at an old tavern called the Rawleigh tavern which has the head of Rawleigh carved some hundred & fifty years ago

*still over the door & the accomodations were about equal to its
antiquity. . . . At Yorktown I went over the old fortifications
which are in many places distinctly seen, & took a view of the
position of the two armies at the time of the surrender of
Cornwallis, or "Karnel Wallis" as you will often hear the people
call him here so ignorent are they of the history of those times,
though living within the bounds of his old fort. . . . This is no
fiction but a specimen of the ignorence of people in some parts of
Virginia. I gathered a relick or two at Yorktown a bullet & a
piece of an old bombshel & a splinter of an old Brittish ship sunk
in the river during the siege of Yorktown.[8]*

Whether Ash raised any more than the "splinter" must remain a
matter of speculation. In any event, any such salvage efforts
must have been interrupted by the Civil War, in which
Yorktown played no little role. Although no indication has been
found that any additional vessels were lost during the Battle of
Yorktown in 1862, there is evidence to suggest that the beach
served as a major supply depot for the remainder of the peninsu-
lar campaign. Artifacts from the American Revolution must
have been the least of the many concerns of the day.

Interest in the recovery of artifacts did not wane with the
passage of time. It appears that around the time of the Yorktown
Centennial some recovery work was undertaken in the river. In
1909 several artifacts were donated to the Society of the Sons of
the Revolution, now housed in the Fraunces Tavern Museum in
New York City. They were accompanied by a letter from the
donor, William Lightner Cowan, which stated in part: "The
piece of timber was taken from the wreck of the British frigate
Charon, together with the small piece of copper attached, and
also the two silver coins of the period of George III, and were
brought to Washington, D.C. by the late Captain Jos. R. Spran-
sy, of Washington, D.C., owner of the tug Samuel Gedney, who
assisted in raising the wreck of the Charon, and was by him
presented to William Lightner Cowan, October 20, 1881, who
was at that time a resident of Washington, D.C."[9] A review of
the Norfolk newspapers around the time of the centennial celebration has failed to reveal any account of this operation.
Though the *Samuel Gedney* was in active service for many years,

it is not clear when she might have worked at Yorktown. In addition, Francis Bannerman Sons, dealers in antique weapons, offered for sale for many years an iron cannon said to have been recovered from the river in 1881. It stood at the entrance to their display room in the New York City area until approximately 1970, when it was sold to an individual who proposed to donate it to a museum.[10]

The existence of the material in the York River was not forgotten, largely because oystermen were continually tonging up artifacts of one sort or another. With the Yorktown Sesquicentennial, in 1931, the National Park Service took over the management of the battlefield area, and as a part of its research and restoration program, it decided to investigate the potential of the artifacts on the river bottom. On May 15, 1934, James W. Head, Jr., the assistant engineer at Colonial National Monument (as the Yorktown–Jamestown complex was known at the time), wrote to the superintendent of the monument, B. Floyd Flickinger. In his memorandum he stated that "fishermen, clam dredgers, etc., have come into contact with what appear to be the remains of old ships on the bottom of the York River opposite the foot of Ballard Street. Some of the fishermen have reported bringing guns, blocking, etc., to the surface of the water."[11] He continued that this seemed to be an ideal opportunity to acquire artifacts for the museum at Yorktown and suggested that salvage of the material should be considered. Evidently the project proved of interest to Superintendent Flickinger, since members of the engineering staff did some exploratory dragging toward the end of the summer of 1934. Their technique was relatively simple, towing grappling hooks behind a small boat until obstructions were encountered. In the course of this investigation, several sites were plotted and " a few pieces of ancient appearing wood" were recovered.[12]

Flickinger quickly realized that any salvage of the recently located vessels was far beyond the capabilities of his staff at the park. As a consequence, he took advantage of a social gathering at which Homer L. Ferguson was present to suggest that he might want to participate in such a project. Not only was Ferguson the president of the Newport News Shipbuilding and Dry Dock Company at that time, but he was also president of the

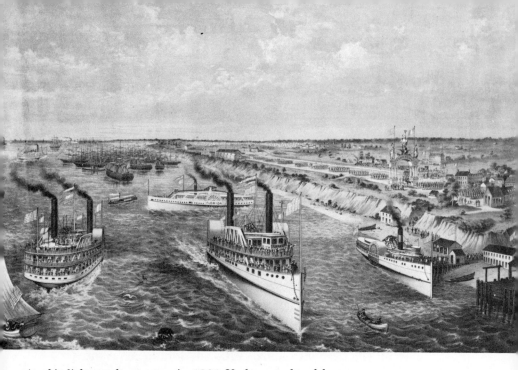

As this lithograph suggests, in 1881 Yorktown played host to large numbers of troops and visitors, as well as excursion boats and naval vessels. Obviously, changes must have been made along the shoreline to accommodate them. (Courtesy of The Mariners' Museum)

newly founded Mariners' Museum. The principal owner of the Shipyard, Archer M. Huntington, had established this museum in 1930, with the hope that it would "make America sea minded." During the following four years, the active collecting of artifacts had taken place on an international scale, under Ferguson's general guidance. He was a man of action, and when the concept of salvaging relics from the river was proposed, Ferguson made immediate arrangements for a tug and diver from the shipyard to explore the site. On October 8, 1934, the search began, as reported by Ferguson to William Gatewood, the manager of the museum: "We located with the tug 'HUNTINGTON' and the diver the wreck of an old vessel, perhaps the British frigate 'CHARON,' off Yorktown starting out today. We had some difficulty in finding the wreck but after finding it discovered the tug to be unhandy from the sweep of the current. After discussion with Mr. Lamphier we decided the best thing to do would be to take a derrick barge for use of diver and gang and fit it with a gasoline driven water pump so as to wash the sand out of the wreckage, sending the men to and from by automobile each day."[13]

In another description, written later, a slightly different version of the first day's enterprise was offered: "The first descent of the diver from a tug was discouraging and produced no results, but later in the day a lead bullet was found on the deck near the spot where the diver took off his suit. The fact that sunken wrecks were in existence and could be located was so apparent that the decision was made to outfit a barge and begin a real effort. A wooden barge 75 feet long by 22 feet wide was equipped with a boiler, a reciprocating fire pump, a winch and derrick and clam shell bucket, diving apparatus, and necessary anchors, small tools, etc."[14] The barge was outfitted by the shipyard, and on October 15, 1934, work began on a regular basis. While the shipyard provided the equipment, the diver and associated crew were paid for by the museum, with unskilled help and small craft provided by the National Park Service, utilizing Civilian Conservation Corps labor.

Apparently it was the initial hope of the parties involved to succeed in raising one of the vessels intact. The Mariners' Museum had been contacted in September 1934 by Ralph E. Chapman, one of the salvors of the sloop *Royal Savage* on Lake Champlain concerning the possibility of adding that hulk to the museum's collection. This vessel was discovered in 1932 by T. F. Hagglund, and raised and brought ashore during the summer of 1934. The flagship of Benedict Arnold's fleet on the lake, she had been lost on October 13, 1776. The *Royal Savage* may be the first vessel of Revolutionary War vintage to have been recovered for historical reasons. Although the museum did not pursue the acquisition of the hulk, or of the gundalow *Philadelphia*, which was discovered and raised the following year, the salvors must have hoped for some similar result at Yorktown.[15] But by November the newspapers were forced to report: "Hope of raising again to the surface the hulk of the British warship Charon, which has lain on the bottom of the York River for 153 years, has been virtually abandoned, B. Floyd Flickinger, superintendent of the Colonial National monument, said last night. . . . Relics found aboard the remains of the vessel, however, together with other data in hand, removed any doubt that the craft really is what is left by time of the Charon, Mr. Flickinger said."[16] If there was doubt as to the feasibility of total excavation, there was no doubt in anyone's mind that the first ship encountered must, of course, have been the *Charon*.

The barge was moored directly over the obstructions that had been located at the foot of Ballard Street, Yorktown, 250 feet offshore in about 50 feet of water. The wrecks were located in the deep water beyond the drop-off, lying perpendicular to the beach on the shelving bank that drops to a depth of nearly 90 feet. There were apparently two wrecks found close together in this area, both of about sixty to eighty feet in length.[17] The decision to clean the artifacts out of the wrecks one at a time was fortunate for later researchers, since it is possible to tie some of the now very miscellaneous artifacts together as having come from one vessel.

The techniques employed by the diver were necessarily limited by the nature of the site, with its turbidity and strong currents, and by the awkward hardhat diving equipment. The following description of the project was provided in a newspaper interview of diver Frank Lange, published in 1938:

> *The mud was from six to 12 feet thick, and a fire hose under 70 pounds pressure was used to jet it away. A 50-pound weight was fastened to the hose behind the nozzle to keep it from whipping around. And the hose itself was tied to a protruding frame of the wreck to prevent the tide from taking it away. Mr. Lange had to brace himself always against the wreck or wedge himself sturdily into the mud in order to maintain his position against the tide. And so he worked, on his knees in the dark, using his hands as feelers, jetting away at the mud (which would settle behind him as he advanced) and pausing whenever he encountered a loose object. He could sometimes hear bottles swishing around in the jet. Small objects he would put in his pockets, then when a larger one came to hand he would place the hose so that the water-stream shot straight up, and signal to the surface for the sling-chain.*[18]

Apparently most of the small artifacts were sent up tied to a rope, while the really large pieces were lifted using the clamshell bucket. The clamshell was not actually used for excavating within the wreck, according to those who remember the project.[19] Under the circumstances of the excavation, it is not surprising that little or no effort was made to note the locations of artifacts as they were recovered or to take down much information regarding the ship itself. In short, techniques that were then standard in dry-land archaeology were not yet applied to an underwater site.

In spite of the lack of documentation, however, some evidence was recorded, though largely of a secondary nature. These were the days when the technical experts stayed topsides and academically untrained divers did the underwater work, so we must look upon the diver's reports with caution. However, a press release issued by Colonial National Monument on December 14, 1934, stated:

> *The two ships explored so far have been definitely identified as war ships. The diver found that the interiors of the hulls were of a finished construction, with lined sides and ceilings, and this was usual only with ships of war at the time. Another interesting check was the discovery of cans and brushes containing a bright red paint, all in good condition. At the time of the revolution it was customary for men-of-war to have their decks painted this bright red color in order that blood would show less plainly and as a consequence the more squeamish of the men would have less excuse for being affected. Still further, the number and types of the gun ports help to identify these vessels as war ships rather than merchant men.[20]*

It is immediately apparent that if the ceiling planking and gunports were still visible, these ships were in far better than average condition. It should be noted, however, that neither red paint nor ceiling planking were found exclusively on warships in the eighteenth century.

The material recovered from this first hull was quite varied, including ships' timbers, cannons and swivel guns, some ceramic ware, shot, and various metallic items. A large quantity of domestic material was recovered, the most dramatic of which were the nearly 200 glass bottles that were discovered in the aft part of the ship. So many of these bottles were found that after several days of sending them to the surface, the diver, Frank Lange, is

The Sesquicentennial celebration in 1931 again attracted numerous vessels to the York River. Among the visitors was the venerable Constitution, *not then confined to her permanent berth in Boston. (Courtesy of The Mariners' Museum)*

reported to have called up through his telephone, "This was no battle ship, it was a bottle ship."[21] The bottles had suffered considerable surface deterioration, giving them an iridescence similar to nineteenth-century art glasses.

By the week of November 19, 1934, it became apparent that everything that could be conveniently removed from the first hull had been recovered. Therefore, the barge was moved to the site of the second wreck, which apparently was immediately adjacent to the first. Since this wreck is often discussed in the same breath with the former one, it must be presumed that they were quite similar structurally. Once again, a cannon was recovered, along with some miscellaneous items, but it soon became too cold to work in the river; operations were suspended for the winter on December 11, 1934. Everyone involved seemed quite pleased with the results of the project, however, and the resumption of work in the spring was planned.

Work did resume on May 15, 1935, apparently on the same wreck. Several more cannon were recovered along with various small artifacts, and on May 22, a large brass bell, which unfortunately was unmarked. Several pieces of lead pipe were brought up, apparently from the bilge pumps and scuppers of the ship. By the end of the month, however, the returns were diminishing; though an anchor was recovered, it was becoming apparent that the ship had yielded most of her artifacts. The diver went off looking for something more productive and on June 4 this report was filed: "Brought up some scraps of timber and iron, found we were on an old ship that was burned and sunk in 1917. Sunk the small gas boat in placing an anchor."[22] This proved sufficiently discouraging that the barge was brought in and secured, while further investigations were undertaken.

It was decided that the most productive procedure would be to move the barge and diver to the Gloucester side of the river and explore the obstructions that had been located there. A wreck was soon found, the only one from this salvage effort that can be accurately located today, based on the bearings which were recorded. This wreck (now known as GL 136) yielded some material, as described in a later report to Superintendent Flickinger:

> The *"mass of molten copper, brass, glass and crockery"* [mentioned in a press release of an earlier date] possibly refers to the material pictured in the enclosed photograph. As the ship was obviously burned, all materials on board were subjected to extreme heat; apparently, as the superstructure and decks burned the cargo fell through to the bottom of the ship, collecing there in heterogeneous fashion. The mass pictured here contained metal, crockery, and glass, and was covered with mud.
>
> The muzzle of the cannon is shown protruding from the side of the salvaged material. These guns were too badly damaged to be of use as a museum exhibit.[23]

It was soon discovered, however, that the area where the barge was working was oyster bottom that had been leased to an oysterman from Gloucester Point, J. H. Jordan. Jordan was afraid that the salvage work would damage the bottom and possibly kill the oysters which were planted on it. He therefore demanded that work be stopped until the legal ramifications of the salvage were considered. Thus, by July 1, 1935, work had been halted on the wreck, while the legal issue was discussed by all parties concerned. It proved impossible to come to any agreement; both the National Park Service and The Mariners' Museum wanted to avoid a lawsuit at all costs, and Jordan was prepared to undertake one to gain recompense. After nearly a month of deliberations, the Newport News Shipbuilding and Dry Dock Company moved its barge back to Newport News on July 24, 1935, and the salvage effort stopped.

That Jordan was not unreasonable in his request is indicated by his subsequent actions; when the barge was removed, he submitted a bill for only twenty-five dollars in personal expenses incurred during the argument. Since almost all of the area on the Gloucester shore which was considered likely to contain wrecks had been leased to Jordan, negotiations were continued with him at a later date. The Mariners' Museum reached an agreement with him whereby salvage operations could have been resumed during the summer of 1937. The Museum was to buy outright all the oysters on the bottom for $900 and further agreed that if any excavations were necessary, these would be refilled with oyster shells. Although it appeared that all of the major hurdles had thus been removed, the operation was not resumed.[24]

It is evident from the correspondence and reports of the period that the persons involved in this salvage effort realized the importance of the venture. Their intentions were of the best, and at every possible juncture they sought expert opinion. Perhaps the best evidence of their good intentions is contained in the minutes of a staff meeting held at Yorktown by the Park Service, on November 6, 1934. With operations just getting underway in earnest, Flickinger reported:

> We feel, in view of what has been brought up, that we are working on a very interesting and important thing, and, in order to handle it properly, we must go about it in a scientific way. The results of the work will make quite a contribution to human knowledge in addition to making interesting exhibits. . . . We want, not only a complete narrative account, but a complete pictorial record, and a complete set of measured drawings, of the important objects we find. We will photograph each piece very

carefully, we will get minute photographs of all objects. . . . We
want to make a chart of the vessel. All of the structural pieces
will be keyed up to the ship.[25]

Although the program Flickinger outlined was an admirable one, it was apparently never realized. Only four measured drawings were made of artifacts recovered soon after the meeting. Though some photographs were taken, the coverage was by no means thorough. Perhaps most unfortunate of all is that no structural records of the ship were made, or at least none survive. The conservation of the artifacts proved to be a task for which neither The Mariners' Museum nor the National Park Service was equipped, in addition to the fact that the science of conservation was not so advanced as today. The problem of the deterioration of the artifacts was recognized early, as suggested by a press release issued November 23, 1934:

After so long an immersion in sea water and consequent corrosion
from acids many of the substances, apparently in good condition
when found, crumble and deteriorate rapidly on exposure to the
air. The Mariners' Museum and Colonial National Monument
technicians are trying every preservative or similar treatment
that might help, but progress along this line is developing slowly.
Cast iron contains a relatively small amount of iron and this in
almost every case has rusted and left the graphite which has
cracked and crumbled when dried out. Wooden objects, too,
wither and split up rapidly as they dry out.[26]

In spite of these well-intended efforts, many artifacts were lost or seriously altered due to an imperfect understanding of the damage they had sustained. During the period when the artifacts were being recovered and preserved, they were housed in a building in Yorktown. As they were mixed together in this situation, there was little chance of keeping records of the provenance of any single artifact. It has been reported that the resident watchman, whose task was the safeguarding of the collection, had his problems as well. Apparently he was in the final stages of a heated courtship and found scant time to spare on his task of guarding moldering artifacts. As a consequence, a number of the excavated artifacts did not end up in the museum collections.[27]

A series of photographs of the 1931 celebration was taken from a dirigible. This view of the waterfront at Yorktown shows the temporary pier that was erected for the event, very near the location of the two wrecks excavated in 1934 and known today as YO 85 and YO 86. The presence of timbers from old docks makes the study of the wrecks more complex. (Courtesy of The Mariners' Museum)

All was not disaster, however, and both The Mariners' Museum and the National Park Service were able to preserve a large number of artifacts. Most of the wood and iron which survived was treated by wax impregnation, a process that seems to have been relatively effective. The oxidation of the bottles seems to have stabilized without treatment, and the ceramics were unaffected by their submersion. The pewter was cleaned by abrasion and now seems to have stabilized. Perhaps the largest problem of all was encountered in preserving the cannons; virtually every conceivable method was tried, generally with less than perfect results. Like all iron cannons after being under saltwater, these began to flake and crumble upon drying. The larger guns were apparently impregnated with various compounds, probably oils and varnishes, but to no good effect. It was finally decided to sandblast them, and miraculously the damage sustained was not what might have been expected, as the markings remain legible on some. Unfortunately, the swivel guns were not treated, and they have virtually crumbled away, with a very small amount of iron remaining. Certainly, the organizations involved are not to be condemned, considering the state of preservation technology at the time; rather, they should perhaps be praised for having saved anything. The collections which resulted from this pioneering effort in underwater archaeology have been of central importance to the exhibits of the two sponsoring museums since the excavations were completed.

8

~~~~~~~~~~~~~~~

Preservation
of the Site

IN SPITE OF the setbacks occasioned by problems with J. H. Jordan and his oyster leases and the disrupting influence of the Second World War, interest in the Yorktown shipwrecks did not cease. The Mariners' Museum had established the artifacts recovered from the wrecks as one of its central exhibits, located in the main room of that institution. The National Park Service gave similar prominence to the material it had received in the division of the artifacts. During the latter part of the 1930s, the Park reconstructed a section of the gun deck and the captain's cabin from H. M. S. *Charon*. This reconstruction was based on the plans of the vessel held by the National Maritime Museum, Greenwich. Only a profile view was available, however, and a number of liberties were taken in the layout; also, the overhead was raised at least one foot to accommodate modern visitors. This, along with many artifacts which were displayed inside the cabin, in the gun deck, and nearby, became a popular exhibit at Colonial National Historical Park, where it was installed in the stable behind the reconstructed Swan Tavern. With these constant reminders, there was continuing interest in the possibility of further excavation of the vessels.

In 1949 the U.S. Army diving unit attached to Fort Eustis undertook renewed exploratory efforts at Yorktown. The dive team at Fort Eustis was headed by CWO Eugene "Mike" Moran, who seems to have been the inspiration for this venture. In the fall of 1949 Moran was engaged in a search for a body in the York River when he stumbled onto a partially buried timber protruding from the bottom. His curiosity was piqued, and he wondered about the presence of wreckage in the area.[1] Whether due to

prodding from Moran or The Mariners' Museum, the army recognized the possibility of good publicity resulting from the exploration of the sunken fleet. A cooperative venture was
launched that ultimately involved representatives of the museum, the National Park Service, and the army, as well as J. H.
Jordan, of Gloucester Point. In late December 1949 the army
sent the dive team and a support barge to Yorktown to make an
exploratory dive. The main purpose of the exercise was to provide material for a series of radio programs, "Time for Defense."

The barge set out for the Gloucester side of the river with a
full complement of dignitaries on the first day's operations. Jordan apparently suggested a likely spot to dive, and the hardhat
divers were sent over the side. A frustrating day was spent on
the site, with no results. The next day Jordan volunteered to
find the location of a wreck, an offer which was quickly accepted. While the barge waited in deeper water, he searched the bottom with the Virginia waterman's classic remote sensing device,
his oyster tongs. Very familiar with this piece of bottom, he was
able within minutes to locate a large hole, which he said was left
after the 1935 excavations on the site. With the barge anchored
over the site, it was not long before the diver sent down had
located evidence of the wrecked vessel. Moran went down to
assist and shortly thereafter brought to the surface a large chunk
of wood with copper sheathing, apparently part of the vessel's
bottom. Having recorded the "voices from the deep," the press
men were content and the operation was concluded. The recovered wood fragment was taken for analysis by The Mariners'
Museum, and several labs worked on small pieces. Although
there is no further record of the army's involvement, Moran
must have had occasion to come back to the area on training
missions; in 1954, he was quoted as saying that he had located
eleven separate hulks on the Gloucester side, some in a very
good state of preservation.[2] It is perhaps fortunate that further
work was not undertaken, in view of the attitude taken towards
the excavation: "Moran, displaying Irish confidence in his organization, has stated that he can clear the wreck inside of two
weeks, if allowed to continue the operation."[3]

Although formal operations by the involved institutions
drew to a close, public awareness of the wrecks continued, and
the desire to work on them did not slacken. In the very early

*The diving barge deployed by the Newport News Shipbuilding
and Dry Dock Company for the excavations undertaken in 1934
and 1935. (Courtesy of The Mariners' Museum)*

days of sport diving, these wrecks were targets of considerable interest. In 1953 The Mariners' Museum was contacted by the president of the Undersea Explorers Club of Richmond, to the effect that "several experienced divers associated with this organization have expressed a desire to investigate the site." He continued to advise that "our divers are equipped with the Cousteau-Gagnan autonomous type of underwater respirators." In spite of modest encouragement from the museum, little seems to have come of the venture in terms of formal work.[4] Similar contacts were made in 1956, when a group from Washington, D.C., calling itself the Underseas Laboratory, contacted the museum. The correspondence with the Underseas Laboratory broke down when it became evident how much support equipment and funding would be required. Another diver, Ray Hyde, of Petersburg, Virginia, did make at least one dive. He found a modern bottle, and seems to have been somewhat discouraged by the difficulties which he encountered as he was not heard from again. The interest of both Hyde and the Underseas Laboratory centered on the site which had been partially excavated in 1935 and on which the army had recently worked. It was from this general vicinity that Hyde recovered his bottle.[5]

It was not until 1961 that any expression of renewed institutional interest in the study of the site was demonstrated. On October 30, 1961, the director of The Mariners' Museum, Rear Adm. George J. Dufek, USN (Ret.), wrote to Stanley W. Abbott, superintendent of Colonial National Historical Park. He stated that it had been "suggested that The Mariners' Museum investigate the possibility of continuing the salvage of relics from the bottom of the York River." Abbott responded enthusiastically, and a meeting of the concerned parties was held on November 17, 1961. The representatives of the Park Service doubted that any separately appropriated funds could be made available for the project, though they thought that some miscellaneous funding might be diverted into it. They expressed the opinion that it would not be worthwhile to undertake a continuation of the project if the artifacts to be recovered would duplicate those raised in the thirties. Their primary interest centered on the location and excavation of the warships, particularly the *Charon* and the *Guadaloupe*. Finally, for the first time, concern was expressed that "agreement should be reached with the state of Virginia on the finder's claim to relics or other valuable objects."[6] It was agreed that further study was needed to ascertain whether the project was viable. Various military agencies were contacted for support, and the Virginia Fisheries Laboratory (now the Virginia Institute of Marine Science) and the Virginia Fisheries Commission (now Virginia Marine Resources Commission) were contacted concerning possible conflicts with oystermen. J. H. Jordan was contacted by the Museum, and he expressed willingness to allow excavations on his leasehold if the bottom could be returned to its original configuration when the work concluded. He confirmed the statement of the state agencies that the area was not actively used for oyster culture at that time, because of the disease MSX that had decimated the oyster population. Robert H. Burgess, then the curator of exhibits at the museum, even contacted a commercial diving firm in Norfolk and obtained prices for the use of divers and equipment in the project. It soon became evident, however, that the cost would be prohibitive, that the Park Service was not in a position to provide financial support, and that the odds were very much in favor of obtaining only duplicate artifacts. In consequence, the project was dropped following a negative report issued to the museum trustees on January 18, 1962.[7]

With the growth of sport diving during the 1960s, there was increasing interest in the wrecks at Yorktown. Several guides to diving spots mentioned the site, and the combination of a pretty beach with relatively shallow water and easy accessibility led to considerable activity. At least two excavations by sport divers are known to have taken place during this period. In 1968 Herndon Jenkins, formerly of Yorktown, submitted a small collection of artifacts to the National Park Service for examination. He had recovered these from a wreck located off the Yorktown Beach (now YO 85), using a small airlift on several dives. The wreck had a stone ballast pile with large timbers protruding, and the material which he recovered consisted of small pieces of glass and ceramic fragments and several buttons. In particular, there were three pewter buttons marked "USA," probably of Revolutionary date, a pewter button marked "37," which seems to have belonged to the 37th Foot Regiment, and one marked "76," which seems to have belonged to the 76th Foot (Highland) Regiment.[8] Sometime in 1969 a second investigation by a sport diver took place in the same area. Harry Wilburn Comett, of Richmond, collected a number of ceramic and tile fragments from the "burned wrecks of some ships in the shallows on the upstream side of Cornwallis Cave." He turned over the bulk of the artifacts to the newly formed Virginia Historic Landmarks Commission, but retained for his personal collection perhaps the most unusual item recovered. A photograph owned by the Landmarks Commission shows what appears to be a pewter teapot, spherical in form with a shaped foot and a straight tapering spout. One might normally expect such a form to date from the mid-eighteenth century. The straight spout, neoclassical in form, may, however, be a replacement on a pot which had been in use for many years, since the more typical examples of this form have curving spouts. Unfortunately, it is difficult to be certain from the photograph, and the location of the original is no longer known.[9]

*The air hose is manned by one of the dive tenders during the
1934 excavation. (Courtesy of The Mariners' Museum)*

In late 1971, while seeking a topic for study as a thesis for
the Winterthur Program in Early American Culture, the author
contacted Ivor Noël Hume, director of archaeology at Colonial
Williambsburg. Noël Hume suggested that the collection of artifacts recovered by The Mariners' Museum and the National
Park Service in the thirties might well warrant reexamination
and study. At about the same time Noël Hume was contacted by
Norman Scott, of Expeditions Unlimited Aquatic Enterprises,
of Pompano Beach, Florida, concerning the possibility of undertaking an intensive study of one or more of the wrecks at

Yorktown. Scott had been interested by a reference to the site in
the book *Here Lies Virginia.*[10] Scott had previously been involved
in the excavation of the sacred cenote at Chichén-Itzá, in the
Yucatan, and in 1971 was involved with the Smithsonian Institution in a project intended to raise the U.S.S. *Tecumseh* from Mobile Bay. He proposed to undertake the excavation and possible
recovery of one or more of the wrecks, in exchange for the media
rights to the undertaking. By this time it was apparent that the
Virginia Historic Landmarks Commission was the state agency
responsible for the preservation of historic material on property
owned by the state. Consideration was given by the Landmarks
Commission to Scott's proposal, which was regarded as timely in
light of the upcoming bicentennial celebrations. Considerable
concern was expressed during these discussions for the need to
follow accepted archaeological practice in the excavations, as
well as to make provision for the conservation and preservation
of the artifacts recovered. It was generally agreed that a preservation facility equal to this task did not exist in Virginia at that
time. No formal agreement was reached with Expeditions Unlimited concerning the project.

In the meantime, the author proceeded with a study of extant artifacts from the thirties excavations and a brief review of
the history of the site.[11] While this study was being undertaken,
the Virginia Historic Landmarks Commission decided to move
to protect the site from future encroachment. On February 20,
1973, the "Yorktown Wrecks" were nominated to the National
Register of Historic Places by Junius R. Fishburne, Jr., then
director of the Landmarks Commission. The York River thus
became the first underwater archaeological site to be included on
the National Register. Not only was damage from federally
funded projects thus forestalled, but the way was opened for
future federal funding for site development. With this increased
activity, and the approach of the bicentennial, there was renewed interest by the institutions which had over the years been
involved with the site. Consequently, on May 30, 1973, an organizational meeting was held, with representatives from The
Mariners' Museum, the Virginia Historic Landmarks Commission, Colonial National Historical Park, the Virginia Institute of
Marine Science, Jamestown Foundation, and the U.S. Navy at-

tending. The participants agreed that work at Yorktown was warranted and should commence in an exploratory fashion. Dr. William J. Hargis, Jr., director of the Virginia Institute of Marine Science, informed the group that his agency had already undertaken several experimental tests with a magnetometer in the area and was attempting to establish a grid that would be suitable for accurate locationing. William D. Wilkinson, director of The Mariners' Museum, stated that his staff had been engaged in some preliminary historical research. It was agreed by the group that an ad hoc committee of the interested parties should be formed to further this research, with Dr. Hargis serving as chairman. Although this informal consortium did not result in any productive work at the time, the contacts were to prove useful in later years when other work did begin.

In the spring of 1975 the author, then on the staff of The Mariners' Museum, was contacted concerning the excavation of one of the wrecks by sport divers. Since at least the beginning of the year, a group of six divers belonging to the Undersea Explorers Club of Richmond had been diving regularly on a newly exposed wreck. Although it was later claimed by other divers that the existence of this wreck had been known for years, this was the first concerted effort at excavation. On July 3, 1975, the author was given the opportunity to examine the recovered artifacts and make an inventory. A truly remarkable array of material had been recovered in an extremely good state of preservation. There were a number of domestic items, including a pewter spoon, ceramic fragments of jugs, pans, and plates, and a complete earthenware oil jar identical to those recovered in 1934. The most impressive group of materials, however, consisted of ships' fittings. There were blocks and sheaves in all sizes and shapes, as well as deadeyes and tools for shipboard use. The wood was very well preserved after its years on the bottom. It was still possible to make out the broad arrow, symbol of British naval ownership, stamped on many of the fittings, along with what were evidently size designations for the various blocks. Because of the cooperative attitude shown by the divers involved, the lack of a public agency which was able to undertake an excavation on its own, and the absence of legislation directly restricting such activities, the decision was made to work with the group

Nearly two hundred bottles were recovered during the excavations in 1934 and 1935. They exhibited a remarkable variety of forms, given the fact that they were all recovered from the same location. (Courtesy of The Mariners' Museum)

as far as possible. In this fashion it was expected that the material recovered could at least be examined, inventoried, and presumably kept as a fairly cohesive group.

There was an understandable reluctance by the group to reveal the location of the wreck, but it soon became evident from the activity in the area that it was located offshore from the Cornwallis Cave. Later in the summer, weekend visits to the beach in that area suggested considerably increased diving activity, by no means limited to the relatively small group from the Undersea Explorers Club. It was apparent that more than simple surface collecting must be underway, since a wide range of re-covered artifacts was visible on the shore. In addition to the usu-al miscellany, such artifacts as a portion of a baluster from a stairway, elaborately carved with acanthus leaves, had been re-covered and subsequently disappeared. It further became evi-dent that a number of divers from out of state were regularly represented at the site, and, with at least twenty divers working every weekend, the integrity of the site was severely threatened. Any control that might have been expected through the limita-tion of recovery to a small group had obviously been lost.

In the face of this dilemma, more information was needed about the wreck in question, and the site in general, before ef-forts could be made to control the recovery of artifacts. At the urging of John D. Broadwater, a sport diver from Richmond who had been involved in several archaeological surveys, a vol-unteer group formed to investigate the wreck. Support was of-fered by the Virginia Institute of Marine Science, which provid-ed a boat, The Mariners' Museum, which covered some of the expenses of the participants, and the Virginia Historic Land-marks Commission, which sent an archaeologist as observer. The North Carolina Department of Cultural Resources kindly allowed Gordon P. Watts, Jr., the underwater archaeologist for that state, to participate. During the period October 15 to 19, 1975, an investigation was made of the wreck, which by that time had been dubbed the Cornwallis Cave wreck (now YO 12), and the immediate surrounding vicinity. It had been hoped that it would be possible to undertake a magnetometer survey of the shallow area off the Yorktown beach, but the equipment availa-ble for this purpose proved too insensitive for the task. In conse-quence, the survey was limited to a visual search of a section of the river bottom and an intensive examination of the Cornwallis Cave wreck itself. A swimline survey was undertaken from the foot of Nelson Street to the foot of de Grasse Street. With four divers spaced along a forty-foot line, and visibility limited to about two feet, a comprehensive search was not possible. No indications of wreckage were observed, however, except for the Cornwallis Cave wreck, and some timbers immediately down-

A heavily encrusted cannon being recovered gave no hint of the remarkable state of preservation of the barrel within. (Courtesy of The Mariners' Museum)

stream from that site which had been marked the day before by a cooperating local diver, Milford Kennedy. In consequence, the remainder of the survey was devoted largely to the examination of the Cornwallis Cave wreck.

The wreck was located and buoyed, and the site was surveyed with rough coordinates so that it could be relocated easily. The stem of the vessel was sticking out of the bottom, and the area around it was considerably disturbed. As it was not intended to undertake any excavation work during the course of this survey, it was only as a result of the previous disturbance by sport divers that the hull could be examined. Measurements were taken of the exposed timbers and of the transverse bulkhead that was discovered approximately thirty-five feet aft of the stem. A base line was erected so that measurements could be taken in the forward area, and was extended aft by probing for remains, to a length of thirty-three meters, with remains continuing. Probing was also undertaken to ascertain the extent of hull remains in the forward part of the vessel. The Undersea Explorers Club group had stated that the bulk of their artifacts were recovered from this forward area. As boatswain's stores frequently were stowed in the lower forward hold, this seemed a reasonable statement. In spite of the fact that they had only been digging by hand, the sport divers had disturbed the bottom to a depth of several feet. It was the opinion of the survey team that approximately eight feet of the hull remained at the bow, with the likelihood of better preservation at the stern, where the overburden covering the site was deeper. Based on the results of this survey, a preliminary verbal report was given to the Virginia Historic Landmarks Commission, and a written report was submitted later.[12]

Recognizing the possible significance of the wreck and the Yorktown site in general, as well as the danger which uncontrolled diving represented, the Virginia Historic Landmarks Commission moved to protect the site. An opinion was requested from the State Attorney General's Office concerning the rights and interest of the Commonwealth of Virginia in the wrecks and the possibility of protecting that interest. This opinion was submitted to the Landmarks Commission in a memorandum dated November 7, 1975. It outlined the legal precedents which applied, and confirmed that the wrecks were properly considered the property of the Commonwealth of Virginia. The basis for this statement was the common law right of the Crown to abandoned property on the seas, a right that had devolved upon the Commonwealth of Virginia. In seeking some means to protect this property, a number of options were explored, and the final choice relied on the state's ownership, not of the wrecks, but of the river bottom. "The bottom lands in which these ships now lie are sovereign lands of Virginia. . . . The Virginia legislature has made it unlawful for anyone to trespass upon or over or take or use any materials from the beds of rivers which are the property of the Commonwealth, unless pursuant to a permit of the Marine Resources Commission."[13]

Organic preservation at the site was very good, as is suggested by this Manila hawser recovered in 1934. Note also the condition of the iron guns at the bottom of the picture; unfortunately, without treatment they soon began to deteriorate. (Courtesy of The Mariners' Museum)

On the basis of the state's right to protect the river bottom and the responsibility of the Virginia Marine Resources Commission to provide that protection, the Landmarks Commission requested aid from the Virginia Marine Resources Commission even before the formal opinion was issued. On the weekend of October 18 and 19, 1975, a patrol vessel belonging to the Virginia Marine Resources Commission was stationed over the site to oversee diving. Although it was not possible to prohibit diving, divers were warned that should they disturb the bottom, they would be subject to charges of a misdemeanor. Recovery of an artifact from the river would be regarded as evidence of having disturbed the bottom. The presence of the patrol vessel, and the ensuing news coverage, resulted in an immediate decrease in the number of persons diving in the area. No summonses were issued that weekend or on the following weekends that the boat was in place. The point was made, however, and with the onset of cold weather the free-for-all was under control. There was a considerable backlash from the sport diving community as a result, and a number of letters appeared in the newspapers pro-

The chief diver during the excavations in 1934 and 1935 was a professional hard-hat diver named Frank Lange. (Courtesy of The Mariners' Museum)

testing the action and the tone of the press coverage. The divers objected not only to the infringement of their "right" to recover artifacts from the wrecks but to the use of the term *looting* to describe the activity. In an effort to cool heated tempers and continue the dialogue face to face rather than in the press, a meeting was scheduled between members of the diving community and the various historical agencies involved. When it became evident that little progress could be expected from such a public meeting, it was canceled in favor of informal gatherings with smaller groups. Recognizing the need for a more formal legal basis for the protection of underwater antiquities, the

Landmarks Commission encouraged the amendment of the Virginia Code to accomplish this goal. A bill was submitted to the House of Delegates on February 2, 1976, and passed several months later. In addition to defining underwater historic property, it provided for a permit system which would allow for the controlled recovery of that property under the supervision of the Virginia Marine Resources Commission and the Virginia Historic Landmarks Commission. It cannot be said that there was ever any satisfactory resolution of the complaints of the sport diving community, but the great debate finally settled down.

Recognizing that legal action was simply a stopgap measure in the effort to provide protection for the wrecks, the Virginia Historic Landmarks Commission sought to provide for an active investigation and excavation of the site. William Kelso, chief archaeologist, and Junius Fishburne, director of the Landmarks Commission, spearheaded a campaign for a special legislative appropriation to fund exploratory work. With the backing of Lewis McMurran, chairman of the Virginia Bicentennial Commission and a member of the state legislature, and others, an appropriation of $15,000 was approved. Recognizing that such an appropriation was a possibility, Ivor Noël Hume had taken advantage of a chance meeting with Dr. George Bass of the American Institute of Nautical Archaeology to invite him to consider working on the project. Encouraged by his interest, a formal invitation was issued by the Virginia Historic Landmarks Commission, and a contract was drawn up with the American Institute of Nautical Archaeology for a preliminary investigation of the Cornwallis Cave wreck. Several organizational meetings were held during the spring of 1976, and it gradually developed that the excavation crew and the accompanying field school would be housed by the Virginia Institute of Marine Science, which would also provide logistical support.

Work began on the project on May 6, 1976, with George Bass as project director, Paul F. Johnston, assistant field director, Donald H. Keith, chief diver, and J. Richard Steffy, ship consultant. Members of the thirteen-man expedition were housed aboard the *Retriever*, a converted landing craft belonging to the Virginia Institute of Marine Science. It had originally been thought that it would be possible to moor the *Retriever* directly

One of the few recovered artifacts having a name associated with it is this bottle marked "Edward New"; unfortunately, New has not yet been identified. (Courtesy of The Mariners' Museum)

*Confident of the identity of their discovery, the salvors of the
1934 excavations arranged the bottles they had recovered to spell
"1781" and chalked "H.M.S. Charon 1781" on the board in the
background. It is now clear that this material did not come
from the* Charon, *though there is no reason to doubt the date.
(Courtesy of The Mariners' Museum)*

over the excavation site on a permanent basis, but this did not
prove possible. As a consequence, initial work had to be undertaken from various small craft made available by the Virginia
Institute of Marine Science. This initial investigation immediately revealed to the excavators the hostile nature of the site.
With practically zero visibility, strong and continuous currents,
hard-packed layers of sharp oyster shells, and an abundance of
stinging nettles, it was far different from the Mediterranean sites
which the American Institute of Nautical Archaeology had
worked in previous years. Recognizing the difficulties which
would be entailed in pursuing such an excavation, Bass devoted
substantial energy to the design and construction of a floating

cofferdam to be used for water clarification. A large wooden framework was floated over the site, surrounded by a plastic membrane, with a canvas skirt weighted to the bottom. It was intended that a commercial-size swimming pool filter would be used to clarify the water contained within this device. When the cofferdam was deployed, however, strong currents in the area made it virtually impossible to guarantee the integrity of the skirt's seal with the bottom, and unclarified water seeped in constantly. Further, it finally became clear that the *Retriever* would not be available for use as a diving platform on the site. In consequence, the use of the cofferdam, which depended heavily on the lifting boom of that vessel, had finally to be abandoned. With a good part of the planned two-month excavation season gone, efforts turned to a more traditional excavation of the site to the extent possible under the conditions. Two locally owned crab boats, the *Kingfish* and the *Georgie E.*, were chartered in succession, to serve as the excavation platform. Work went slowly owing to continuing logistical problems, the difficulties of working from the cramped deck of the crab boats, and bad weather. In consequence, the excavation was extended until July 24, although a part of the team had to go on to Maine to work on the American Institute of Nautical Archaeology's excavations on the site of the *Defense* in Penobscot Bay.

The principal goal of the excavation was to determine the state of preservation of the hull and the overall dimensions of the ship and to decide whether further excavation was warranted. Because only very limited facilities were available for the conservation of any artifacts recovered, the work was intentionally concentrated in the bow area, which was known to have been heavily looted already. A grid was placed over the area to provide horizontal coordinates, but it was decided that vertical coordinates would not be useful or informative, in view of the disturbed nature of the site. An effort was made to locate the stern and ascertain its condition under the heavy layer of overburden; toward the conclusion of the excavation, this was done, with somewhat disappointing results. The hull at the stern had deteriorated almost to the keelson, with only minimal framing and planking visible. It did, however, prove possible to identify the aftermost part of the keel of the vessel, which allowed specula-

Of the cannon recovered in 1934, the National Park Service installed three in its recreation of the Charon's *gundeck. Contrast the surface of the tube after forty years with its appearance immediately after recovery. (Photo by the author)*

tion as to its overall dimensions. The length of extant keel was 111 feet 9 inches, suggesting a length on the main deck, considering the probable stern overhang, of about 118 feet. The beam measured in the excavations at the bow was 28 feet 9 inches, which was projected to an approximate total beam of 32 feet. The ship was roughly estimated at 550 tons burthen. She was, in summary, a large, heavily built vessel, in all probability an armed merchantman. Although she was certainly a part of the line of vessels scuttled by Cornwallis along the shore to defend the beach, no indication was found of her name, and no speculation as to her identity seems warranted at this time.[14]

The answer to the principal question, Does the wreck warrant continued excavation? was a qualified probably. There was considerable disappointment at the degree of hull deterioration, the extent to which the artifacts had been disturbed, and the difficulty of conducting the work under the diving conditions which the river offered. On the other hand, it was generally believed that the hold of the ship, aft of the forward bulkhead, was largely undisturbed and might offer a considerable collection of artifacts in a very good state of preservation. Further, there was general optimism concerning the possibility of improving the diving conditions through the use of water clarification and a permanent diving structure. This seemed especially promising in view of the shallow water on the site (about fifteen feet). The budget which had been prepared in preparation for a full excavation of the wreck over a three-year period came to about $360,000, a not inconsiderable sum. In view of the high costs involved, and the apparent uncertainty concerning the ultimate value of the site, the Virginia Historic Landmarks Commission decided to postpone efforts to fund a full excavation of the Corn-wallis Cave wreck. Instead, efforts were to be directed toward the completion of a full survey of the entire York River site, with the goal of selecting a hull for excavation. Whether there were hulls which were better preserved and less disturbed by looting was for the moment an open question.

9

Remote
Sensing Surveys

THE IDEA OF undertaking an electronic survey of the shipwrecks in the York River dated back several years. In the summer of 1972 the Virginia Institute of Marine Science, at the urging of its director, Dr. William J. Hargis, Jr., had experimented with a magnetometer in the vicinity of Gloucester Point. After locating and recovering a large, modern, yachtsman-type anchor, the project was dropped, however. There was little doubt, based on the historical record, that a number of wrecks remained to be located, but limitations of funding, personnel, and equipment had precluded a detailed search.

When the brief survey of the Cornwallis Cave wreck was undertaken in October 1975, it became increasingly evident that the nature of the site required the use of some form of remote sensing equipment. A swimline survey along the Yorktown shore had been attempted, but with only marginal success. For the first time, however, the possibility of undertaking such an electronic survey was at hand. Gordon Watts had been largely responsible for the location of the wreck of the U.S.S. *Monitor* off Cape Hatteras, and during that survey he had developed several contacts which were to prove useful. Although the *Monitor* was located by the Duke University research vessel *Eastward* on August 27, 1973, two parallel searches were underway at about the same time. As a part of Project Cheesebox, a student project at the U.S. Naval Academy, an airborne magnetometer survey was made in an effort to locate the remains of the *Monitor*. This effort was undertaken by the Magnetics Branch of the David W. Taylor Naval Ship Research and Development Center, Annapolis, under the leadership of William J. Andahazy. The other search was undertaken by Underwater Archaeological Associates, a private nonprofit group, in the vicinity of the Cape Hatteras lighthouse, utilizing various navigation and sensing systems over the course of the summer. John Broadwater, who had worked on the survey of the Cornwallis Cave wreck, was in charge of the technical aspects of that survey.[1] Gordon Watts offered to contact Andahazy concerning the possibility of undertaking a survey of the wrecks at Yorktown, an offer enthusiastically accepted by the Virginia Historic Landmarks Commission. Formal contact was made during the fall of 1975, and official approval was granted for the project on December 12, 1975. The U.S. Navy agreed to contribute the use of the magnetometer equipment, with the personnel donating their own time. In the face of these developments, the Virginia Historic Landmarks Commission requested that John Broadwater serve as technical advisor to the project, a post he agreed to assume.

An organizational meeting was held in Annapolis, on January 11, 1976, to plan the details of the survey. In addition to William Andahazy, Douglas Everstine and Bruce Hood of the Magnetics Branch participated. Virginia was represented by the author, John Broadwater, and David Hazzard, survey archaeologist for the Landmarks Commission. It was decided that the optimum time for the initial survey was during either April or May 1976. The team from the Magnetics Branch was to take full responsibility for the acquisition and interpretation of magnetic data on the site. Support facilities were to be provided by the Landmarks Commission, with boats provided by the Virginia Institute of Marine Science. The principal outstanding problem was the need for a precise navigation system, with the capability of accurate site relocation (repeatability). Because of his experience with the Teledyne Hastings-Raydist system at Cape Hatteras, John Broadwater proposed that it be used on the project. It was known that the Virginia Institute of Marine Science then had one of the Raydist receivers in service, and it seemed likely that it could be used.

A second meeting was held on March 4 in Virginia for the purpose of settling the details of the navigation system and checking the background magnetic noise at Yorktown. Representatives of the Hastings-Raydist Corporation were present to discuss the use of the system. They generously offered to lend a full complement of equipment to the project for the duration of the survey and to provide area grid overlays for the system. It had originally been thought that to achieve good system accuracy, it would be necessary to establish two temporary transmitter stations for the Raydist at Yorktown. It was the opinion of the Raydist firm, however, that the extant stations providing coverage of the entire Chesapeake Bay would be more than adequate for the purpose. As a consequence, plans to establish a separate and temporary grid were abandoned.

The survey was begun on April 30 and continued through May 2, 1976. Because the study of the Cornwallis Cave wreck by the American Institute of Nautical Archaeology was scheduled to start soon thereafter, there was considerable interest in completing the magnetic study expeditiously. Although the American Institute of Nautical Archaeology work was intended to focus on the one wreck, it was hoped that the time might be found to examine some of the magnetic contacts. The survey vessel was a thirty-five-foot Bruno and Stillman fiberglass workboat, the *Captain John Smith*. She was modified to accommodate the Raydist equipment by James Whitcomb, who operated the Raydist system in use by the Virginia Institute of Marine Science. The operational concept of Raydist is similar to that of a Loran system. A permanently installed "T" system, consisting of four transmitter stations, provided an overlay of hyperbolic radio signals on the Chesapeake Bay. The shipboard receiver read these signals passively, and by noting the changing values of the two coordinates, a precise position with respect to the transmitters could be ascertained. By setting in the coordinates of a known landmark at the beginning of the survey, it was possible to achieve repeatability to within three feet during the course of the survey. This was judged to be of extreme importance because of limited underwater visibility, and the consequent need for divers to be dropped directly over any magnetic anomaly that might be discovered.

It was originally thought that it would be possible to use a line follower for navigational positioning during the survey. This device makes it possible to run along one radio coordinate while simply noting the other coordinates as they pass by. In this fash-

Magnetometer experts William Andahazy and Bruce Hood consult with James Whitcomb, of the Virginia Institute of Marine Science, concerning the installation of the equipment. The projection off the stern of the vessel is the sensor head of the magnetometer equipment, which must be kept removed from any ferrous metal. (Photo by the author)

During the magnetometer surveys, lanes of uniform width were traversed down the York River. An effort was made to maintain constant depth over the course of any one run, so that the sensor head would be roughly the same distance from the targets encountered. (Photo by the author)

ion it is possible to ensure thorough coverage of the bottom without major overlaps. Unfortunately, it was discovered that both the red and green coordinates of the system were oblique to the shoreline. Following either of these coordinates would have necessitated operations in constantly changing water depths. This was unacceptable, given the nature of the magnetic sensing equipment. Lanes were therefore run on the basis of visual positioning and compass courses, a less accurate but satisfactory system. Had time and funding permitted, this problem could have been overcome through the installation of temporary stations so positioned as to provide the desired radio transmission characteristics.

The navy provided two magnetometers, a Schonstedt high-balance gradiometer and an AN/ASQ 81 magnetometer. Tests had been made in the laboratory and on the water to determine which unit was best suited for which task. The results suggested the gradiometer as the most suitable instrument for use in shallow water, the first area to be considered:

> *It was calculated and demonstrated operationally that the gradiometer was more effective for the shallow-water survey (less than 10 meters) because it offered an improved signal-to-noise ratio and provided additional spatial information. Since a large portion of the noise is spatially coherent over the base length of the gradiometer, it is cancelled by the opposing sensor elements. The scalar magnetometer does not have this capability and will experience a degradation of the benefits of a larger peak signal. Moreover, the magnetic signal from a given source measured by a gradiometer changes spatially at a faster rate than that measured by a scalar magnetometer, enabling the magnetic center of a shipwreck to be localized with greater accuracy.[2]*

The sensor head for the gradiometer was mounted as a "stinger" on the stern of the survey vessel. A wooden mount was constructed, using nonmagnetic fastenings, and suspended about eight feet off the transom. Considerable care was taken to ensure that the sensor was kept dry, since it was not designed for submerged operation.

The survey was conducted in the areas of the river that were less than ten meters deep. Survey runs were made parallel with the shoreline in order than a more or less uniform water depth

George Bass, of the American Institute for Nautical Archaeology, supervised the excavation work on the Cornwallis Cave Wreck (YO 12) during the summer of 1976. (Photo by the author)

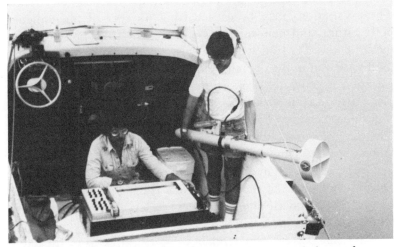

The sensor head of the Klein side-scanning sonar is lowered overboard by John Broadwater, while Garry Kozak monitors the equipment. (Photo by the author)

would be encountered throughout a single run. The areas covered during the period included the shoreline along the Yorktown beach and that along the Gloucester Point beach, both above and below the highway bridge. When a magnetic anomaly was noted, an event number was assigned and a permanent digital printout was made on the Raydist printer to establish the location. Though it had originally been intended that buoys would be placed when an anomaly was noted, this was discontinued early in the survey; visual positioning proved sufficient from return visits. There was difficulty placing the buoy accurately with the sensor head mounted on the stern, difficulty keeping it in place because of the strong current, and some concern about marking the newly discovered locations on a weekend with a crowded beach full of observers. The primary reason for marking the sites was to allow diver examination while the electronic gear was on location. It soon became evident that this was both impractical and inefficient, since the equipment stood idle while the site was being visited by a diver. In consequence, the entire period was devoted to electronic surveying, with on-site investigation left until a later time. Even at a fairly fast rate of surveying, roughly five knots, it took almost three days to cover the shallow areas scheduled for examination.

Both the magnetometer and the gradiometer work on the principle of detecting variations in the earth's magnetic field. These variations may be caused by a number of phenomena, both natural and man-made, one of which is the presence of a piece of iron. As iron will deflect a compass, so will it cause a local variation in the overall field of the earth's magnetism. This variation is generally proportional in strength to the size of the piece of iron, but it decreases geometrically with the distance. Since most shipwrecks of the historic period contain iron in some quantity, they may frequently be detected with this equipment. Obviously, the same may be said of any iron or steel trash that may have accumulated on the bottom of the river over the years. During the course of the seventy-one transits made during the survey, 189 magnetic anomalies were observed. Not all of these represented separate occurrences since there were a number of revisits, and there was a tendency for readings from the same target to be seen on parallel tracks. A substantial number of targets were indicated, however, with particular concentrations along the beach at Yorktown, as might have been expected. Large areas of the bottom downstream from Gloucester Point were barren, and there was only one target upstream from the point. There were only a few targets upstream from the bridge on the Yorktown side, though one gave a very strong indication, suggesting a sizable deposit of iron. Efforts were made on the last day of the survey, and during the subsequent week, to identify several of the targets, but without success. In those cases which were investigated, the causes of the anomalies seem to have been buried beneath the bottom and thus were not readily visible.

Because of the diversion which the exploratory excavation of the Cornwallis Cave wreck entailed, and other demands on the time of the navy personnel, it was not possible to resume the magnetometer survey immediately. Pending renewed efforts with the magnetometer in the deeper waters of the river, an effort was made to test the feasibility of using a sub-bottom profiling sonar on the site. A Raytheon RTT 1000 sonar, owned by Virginia Institute of Marine Science, had been installed for geological survey work on board the *Captain John Smith*. While it was being tested in October 1976, it was taken over the known Cornwallis Cave wreck. Although the unit worked well in deep water, the noise caused by the shallower water, and possibly by the composition of the bottom, gave negative results. Although the excavation left by the American Institute of Nautical Archaeology was clearly visible, it was impossible to detect any indication of wreckage beneath the bottom. A run was made along the Yorktown beach, with similar results. This unit was operating at seven kilohertz, and it was suggested that a lower frequency might result in greater penetration, though loss of resolution could be expected. As equipment of this type was unavailable at that time, it could not be tested.

It was finally possible to undertake the remainder of the magnetometer survey on October 22, 1977. Using the AN/ASQ 81 magnetometer, the deep-water areas of the river were searched. The Raydist positioning system was used once again, but was backed up by two transits mounted on the shore. Working from an established base line, these transits were able to pro-

A side-scan sonar trace shows the remains of the colonial wharf and the Cornwallis Cave wreck (YO 12). The boat's path of travel is the double black line in the center, with the river bottom depicted on either side. (Courtesy of the Virginia Historic Landmarks Commission)

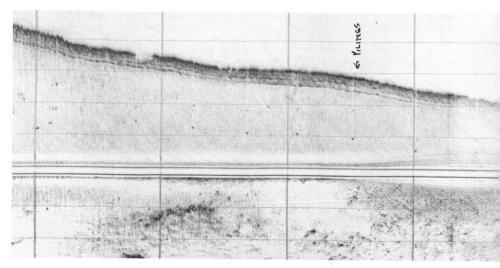

A side-scan sonar trace which shows the beach at Yorktown, the pilings offshore which mark the swimming area, and several areas of bottom disturbance. Investigation revealed that the two black clusters were shipwrecks (YO 85 and 86), while the large gray area represented a natural deposit of oyster shells. The small double circle in the center proved to be a set of railroad wheels, an unexplained intrusion. (Courtesy of the Virginia Historic Landmarks Commission)

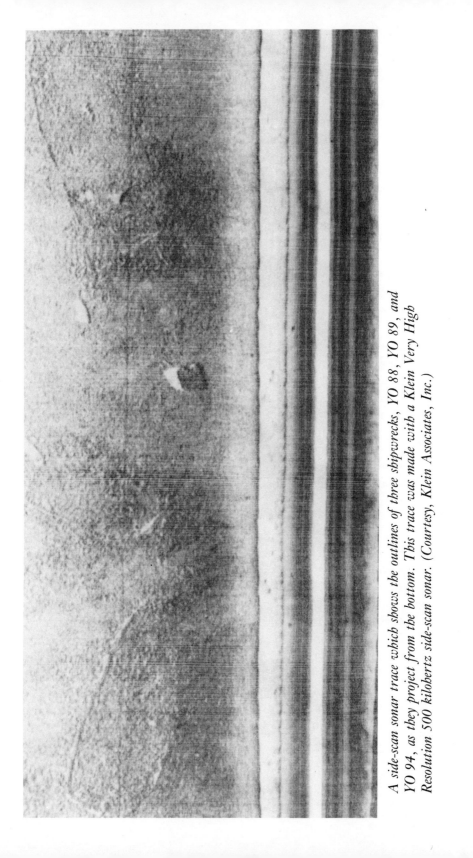

A side-scan sonar trace which shows the outlines of three shipwrecks, YO 88, YO 89, and YO 94, as they project from the bottom. This trace was made with a Klein Very High Resolution 500 kilobertz side-scan sonar. (Courtesy, Klein Associates, Inc.)

vide accurate positioning information to corroborate the data obtained from the Raydist unit. They were in constant radio contact with the survey vessel, which they tracked. Instead of seeking the constant positioning that had been attempted on the first survey, only the locations of the individual targets were sought. These were marked by buoys, a process that was facilitated by mounting the sensor head on the bow of the vessel; this gave more time to drop the buoy and provided less interference with the equipment. A second boat followed to pick up the buoys, once they had been shot in; because of the strong currents, their position was only reliable for a very brief interval. Although problems were encountered with the Raydist system, the back-up provided by the transits allowed accurate positioning. In spite of the need to limit the work to one day, it was possible to cover the area downstream from the bridge quite thoroughly and to get broad coverage above the bridge. The search upstream confirmed the results of the earlier survey, which had indicated minimal remains in this area. A number of widely scattered targets, most fairly large, were encountered below the bridge. Eighty-eight events were recorded, most of which represented targets of some substance. A recording fathometer was run in parallel with the magnetometer, and in several cases indicated a hump on the bottom in the vicinity of the magnetic target.

Following the American Institute of Nautical Archaeology excavation at the Cornwallis Cave wreck, an application had been submitted by the Virginia Historic Landmarks Commission to the National Endowment for the Humanities for funding for a three-year excavation of the site. After the decision was made to undertake serious survey efforts before initiating any further excavations, the application had been withdrawn. A similar application, which envisaged an extensive survey effort during the first year, was submitted for funding during fiscal year 1978, to be followed by two years of excavation. This project received partial funding, with the first year's survey work approved. Based on that encouragement, the Landmarks Commission hired John Broadwater as the state's first nautical archaeologist. His initial project was to be the survey of the Yorktown site, and facilities were established at Yorktown to undertake the project. Equipment and personnel were gathered, with work to start in June 1978, but completion of the electronic surveys remained the first priority. A sonar survey of the bottom was a necessary preliminary to any on-site diver investigation of the targets indicated during the magnetometer survey.

It was felt that both side-scanning sonar and sub-bottom profiling sonar should be tried on the site in an effort to gather as much information as possible through remote means. In consequence, Klein Associates of Salem, New Hampshire, was contacted, and the firm agreed to participate in a survey to be undertaken June 19 to 25, 1978. Their HYDROSCAN 530 sonar was used, which has both side-scanning and sub-bottom profiling capabilities in the same unit; it was operated by Garry Kozak of the Klein staff. A small research vessel was provided by the Virginia Institute of Marine Science, but Raydist equipment was not available for the project. In view of the problems which had developed with the electronic navigation system on the last magnetometer survey, and the relative success of the transit system, transits were employed once again. However, since the side-scanning sonar provides a picture of the bottom on either side of the boat rather than readings of discrete targets, it was thought necessary to have location information for the entire survey run. Consequently, survey runs were made parallel to the shore as before, but locations were taken at one-minute intervals. In this fashion it was possible to interpolate between events and ascertain the location of any significant target. This proved to be a tiring process for the crews manning the transits, but provided good results, especially in the areas relatively close to the transit stations. The sub-bottom profiling feature of the equipment, in spite of an output frequency of only 3.5 kilohertz, proved no more successful than what had been attempted two years before. Consequently, the bulk of the survey was run using only the side-scanning aspect of the unit. Sixteen sites were indicated as being of primary interest, with thirty-five secondary ones; these were distributed in both deep and shallow water. In some cases, there seemed to be correlation with the magnetometer readings, but in other instances the targets were independent. The two surveys thus served to complement each other, rather than duplicate earlier work.

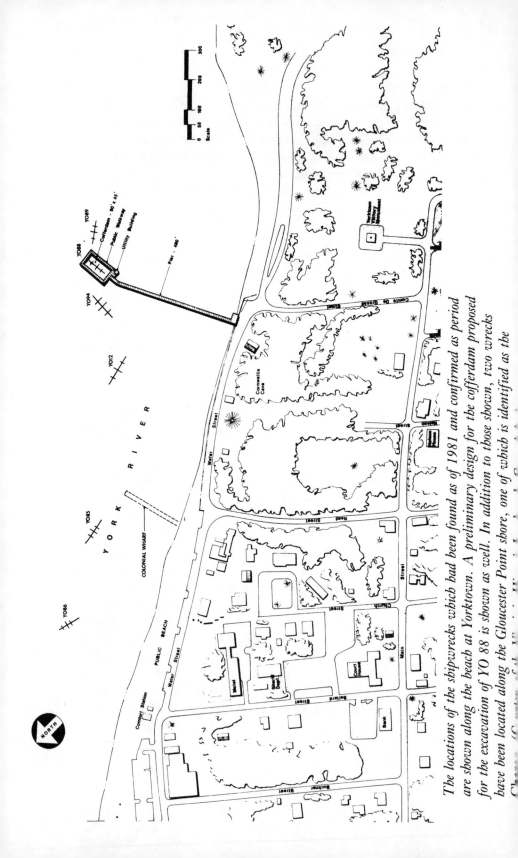

The locations of the shipwrecks which had been found as of 1981 and confirmed as period are shown along the beach at Yorktown. A preliminary design for the cofferdam proposed for the excavation of YO 88 is shown as well. In addition to those shown, two wrecks have been located along the Gloucester Point shore, one of which is identified as the

As a result of the three remote sensing surveys, a large number of possible wreck sites were located, requiring confirmation by on-site examination. The combination of the magnetometer equipment with the sonar equipment provided more detailed information than either system alone was able to indicate. Had funding and scheduling been no hindrance, it would have been most efficient to have had both systems on the survey vessel at once in order to undertake real-time analysis. Some correlation that might then have been evident between the various readings was undoubtedly lost in the process of charting and recording over two years. Navigation proved to be a constant problem during these surveys. If time is not a factor, the Raydist system seems to offer the most promise for precise positioning and good repeatability. The system requires time to set up and test, however, and too many problems were encountered to make it entirely reliable. For hastily organized surveys in a limited geographical area, the use of transits seems to provide adequate information with fewer problems. It has the added advantage that the relocation of a specific target at a later date does not require the use of a complex electronic system that is frequently unavailable when needed. Taken together, the three surveys provide an extensive data base for future investigations of the entire site.

With the conclusion of the remote sensing surveys, a formal on-site survey program was undertaken by the Virginia Historic Landmarks Commission. With the funding from the National Endowment for the Humanities, John Broadwater assembled a team of divers and began work in May 1978. The results of that project, and the detailed analysis of the wrecks that have been located, are beyond the scope of this study. They fall more properly into the area of a detailed archaeological analysis of the individual wrecks and their associated artifacts. A brief outline of the results is given here, however, to clarify the results of the electronic survey and the ways in which these results can be correlated with information gathered on the site. The sites are described by their official state numbers, and may be located by reference to the map reproduced herein. Technical details concerning size, water depth, extent of remains, and the like have been assembled in Table 1.

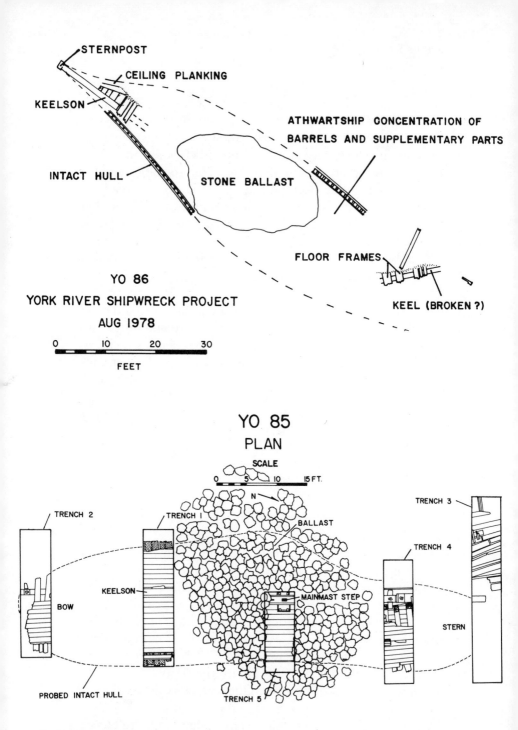

Preliminary survey excavations of two wrecks, YO 85 and YO 86, undertaken in 1978, yielded considerable information. It is thought these may have been partially excavated 1934 and 1935. Damage caused by those excavations, as well as by the hostile riverine environment, had made it difficult to fully comprehend the exact configuration of some portions of the wrecks. (Courtesy of the Virginia Historic Landmarks Commission)

YO 12

The history of the discovery and partial excavation of this wreck, otherwise known as the Cornwallis Cave wreck, has been detailed in chapter 8. Lying parallel to the shore with the bow pointing downstream, the wreck has an exposed ballast pile and some timbers protruding from the bottom. This bottom disturbance is clearly visible on the sonar record. The magnetometer readings on the site suggest a dispersed deposit of iron throughout the hull, probably centered in the vicinity of the ballast pile, with a reading in excess of 10 gammas. There is an additional indication of a large single piece of iron off the bow of the vessel, producing a sharp dipolar reading of 7.5 gammas. Though it has not yet been identified, this suggests the possibility of an anchor or a cannon in that area.

YO 85

This wreck lies parallel with the Yorktown beach, with its bow downstream. This site, in about twenty feet of water, was partially excavated by Herndon Jenkins in 1968, as outlined in chapter 8. A large ballast pile is evident on the bottom and is visible in the sonar record. In addition to this stone ballast, considerable timber survives. The keelson is intact, with frames remaining on both sides; ceiling and exterior planking are both in evidence. A structure around what appears to be the mainmast step is evidently a pump box, for the base of the bilge pumps. The starboard side of the vessel, complete at least ten feet out from the keelson, has collapsed onto the bottom. The wreck was first recorded in July 1978 and at that time appeared to be threatened by possible erosion of the riverbank. In 1979 extensive test excavations were conducted to record the vessel in case of destruction. Four major trenches were cut across the site to obtain cross sections at the bow and stern, as well as two in the center. Artifacts recovered included creamware fragments, bottle fragments of the period circa 1780, a cufflink with a glass "jewel," and a pewter spoon. There is considerable wood stored in the vessel, in log form, length about five feet, apparently for use as dunnage.

YO 86

This wreck lies off Ballard Street, with its bow downstream in about forty feet of water. There is a large pile of stone ballast in place which is visible on the sonar record. The sternpost of the wreck is visible, and the frames and planking appear to be intact and in place in the after part of the ship. It is not clear how well preserved the hull may be at the bow, for the timber becomes quite confused; it has been suggested that there may be another wreck overlying the first in this area. To date few artifacts have been recovered from this site; a few bottle fragments of the period and pieces of a barrel which apparently contained coal are the major items. This is explained in part by the belief that this site is one of those which were excavated in 1934 by the National Park Service and The Mariners' Museum. The wreck is not completely barren, however; a strong but mixed signal of over 11 gammas, suggesting scattered iron debris, was obtained during the second magnetometer survey.

YO 88

This wreck lies almost perpendicular to the shore, with the bow downstream and toward the middle of the river. There are frames projecting from the bottom around 80 percent of the vessel, their angle suggesting that as much as eight feet of the depth of the hull may survive. The stumps of two masts are visible, as well as both stem and sternpost; several knees and a deck beam are visible in place. Although nothing was evident in the sonar record produced during the 1978 survey, a visit in 1979 with a high-resolution Klein sonar revealed the outline of the wreck. A test excavation was made in the after part of this vessel in 1978. A test pit was dug next to a bulkhead about seven feet forward of the sternpost, and taken all the way to the bottom of the hull. A number of period artifacts were recovered, including bottle fragments, redware fragments, a decorated pipe bowl, wooden pins for sheaves in blocks, and an intact window pane. There were indications of several different patterns of wood moldings in the concretions which were recovered. This site and the adjacent wreck (YO 89) gave a continuous signal during the magnetometer survey, making it impossible to distinguish the two. It would

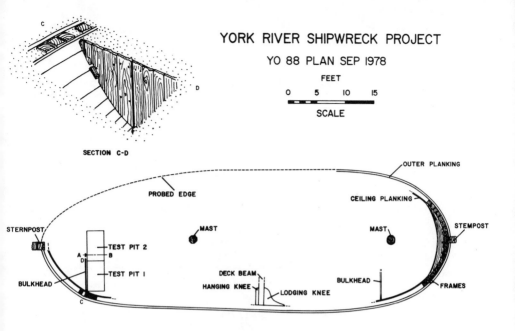

YORK RIVER SHIPWRECK PROJECT

YO 88 PLAN SEP 1978

FEET

SCALE

SECTION C-D

OUTER PLANKING

PROBED EDGE

CEILING PLANKING

STERNPOST

MAST

MAST

STEMPOST

TEST PIT 2

TEST PIT 1

DECK BEAM

BULKHEAD

FRAMES

BULKHEAD

HANGING KNEE

LODGING KNEE

The best-preserved wreck located to date is YO 88, and it is this vessel which is slated for full excavation. A preliminary excavation suggests preservation of the hull as far up as the first deck level. (Courtesy of the Virginia Historic Landmarks Commission)

appear that a field strength in excess of 10 gammas was recorded over the extent of the two vessels, however. A full excavation protected by a cofferdam is planned.

YO 89

This wreck lies parallel to the shore, with its stern only thirty feet from the bow of YO 88, and its bow downstream. It seems evident that the vessel was connected in some manner to YO 88, presumably when the line of ships was scuttled during the battle. There are frames visibly protruding from the bottom, and probing suggests that six feet or more of the hull may survive. As in the cases of YO 94 and YO 88, no sonar trace was visible without a high resolution unit of 500 kilohertz. No excavations have been undertaken on this site to date.

Table 1. Survey results Yorktown shipwrecks

Site no.	Length (feet)	Width (feet)	Est. % remains
YO 12	115	29	20
YO 85	90+	28	5–10
YO 86	88	24	5
YO 88	72	25	40
YO 89	94	29	30
YO 94	110	26	35
YO 222	—	—	—
GL 106	90	25	15
GL 136	112	30	10

YO 94

This wreck lies off the foot of Comte de Grasse Street in about twenty feet of water, with its bow pointing downstream. Although nothing was evident on the sonar record produced during the first survey, a brief visit to this site in the fall of 1979 with a Klein 500 kilohertz side-scanning sonar revealed the outline of the wreck, and of the two adjacent wrecks (YO 88 and 89). Portions of the hull are visible several inches above the bottom, and a breasthook is a place in the bow. The hull is roughly 45 degrees to the beach, with the bow downstream. Although no excavations have been undertaken, a large group of hemp cables is visible coiled in the hull, varying in diameter from two to six inches. Magnetometer readings indicate a diffused mass of iron over a length of about 160 feet, with the highest signal in excess of 10 gammas.

YO 222

During operations in the fall of 1980, what appeared to be the wreckage of an eighteenth-century vessel was located in deep water off the Yorktown Beach. Because the water depth was in excess of 80 feet, and the visibility was zero and the currents were strong, it was not possible to positively confirm that the wreck was period. If this is the case, it represents the first of several wrecks presumed to exist in the deeper water of the river.

Water depth (feet)	Shore distance (feet)	Condition	Bal-last
15	340	good	stone
18–25	280	fair	stone
20–45	280	fair	stone
18	490	excellent	—
20	535	excellent	—
20	400	good	—
80+	500+	—	—
20–25	1,200	fair	—
10–15	1,500	fair	flint

GL 106

This wreck is located in about twenty feet of water on the Gloucester Point side of the river. It was located by chance with a simple white line recording fathometer and is marked by a hump in the bottom. Frames and ceiling planking are visible, which have the appearance of having been charred. The hull is sheathed in wood, a practice which was not uncommon on naval and merchant vessels with worm problems. Fragments of a small oil jar and of red-bodied lead-glazed earthenware have been recovered. There were only minor readings in this area during the magnetometer survey, yet it was from this site that an iron cannon was recovered on October 10, 1978. The gun appears to be a 6-pounder, length overall 58¾ inches; the tube is unmarked, and to date no identical example has been found.

GL 136

This wreck is the one on which the National Park Service and The Mariners' Museum were working when they were forced to stop in 1935. This is the only wreck worked at that time for which coordinates were recorded, and it lies today, as it did then, on the Jordan family's oyster grounds. About 20 percent of the perimeter of the vessel is marked by exposed frames, which rise nearly one foot off the bottom. In addition, there is copper sheathing visible on the bottom, even though in some cases the planking has been destroyed. There are large concretions in this wreck, which, on the basis of one recovered in 1935, appear to be the result of a fire. Ballast on the site consists of large rectangular iron pigs and small stones, probably flint, about two inches in diameter. Artifacts taken from the site have included fragments of slipware and white salt-glazed stoneware, portions of the vessel's chain and reciprocating pumps, as well as several swivel guns recovered in 1935.

Excavations were undertaken on this site for a five-week period commencing June 9, 1980, in an attempt to identify this wreck. The excavation was a field school in nautical archaeology, sponsored by the Anthropology Department of Texas A&M University and headed by J. Richard Steffy. Although a full report on the excavation will be prepared, preliminary indications definitely point to the firm identification of the site as the wreck of H.M.S. *Charon*. Scantling dimensions, length of the keel, and a number of other significant measurements, as well as the placement of features such as the bilge pumps and the mast steps, correlate well with surviving plans of the ship. There is widespread evidence of a massive fire, including ballast rock which has been cracked by heat, and portions of the copper sheathing which have melted. Of all the sites at Yorktown, then, this is the only wreck to which a name can safely be attached.[3]

To date, nine shipwrecks of the period of the Battle of Yorktown have been located and examined. Their location conforms well with the distribution pattern that might be expected from the historical record. The two vessels on the Gloucester Point side of the river seem to have been burned, which might be expected since the *Charon* and the transports which burned with her finally sank on that side. The ships which are located in the shallow area off the beach at Yorktown are all more or less parallel to the shore, all have their bows downstream, and are all in a fairly uniform depth of water. This certainly suggests that they were, in fact, hauled into shallow water, in an orderly fashion, and scuttled. That the line of ships is not complete is more likely the result of subsequent salvage efforts than of any lacunae in the line of defense. In general, it appears that the wrecks located upriver, and nearest the channel, are the least well preserved.

Those further downstream are not as close to the channel and may have been protected by the extensive shoals on which they rest.

It is not suggested that nine shipwrecks represent the entirety of the fleet sunk at Yorktown. A count of the vessels mentioned in the Catalogue reveals sixty-nine vessels involved in some way in the battle, with only thirty-five subsequently accounted for in the records. Even allowing for the recovery of unidentified vessels by the French and the possibility of gaps in the historical record, it seems reasonable to assume that several more wrecks remain to be located. Attention to date has obviously centered on the wrecks located off the beach at Yorktown, since they are both the most numerous and the most accessible. The results of the remote sensing surveys suggest little likelihood of finding wrecks on the upstream side of the Coleman Bridge. They do, however, indicate several promising sites in the deeper water of the river, in mid-channel. Swift currents and lack of visibility have prevented the examination of these targets, several of which may well prove to be wrecks of the 1781 period. Certainly the historical record would lead one to believe that by the end of the battle, there were ships sunk in the deeper water. The nine wrecks which have been discovered to date, nonetheless, present an unparalleled opportunity for the study of the ships and artifacts of the late eighteenth century.

10

~~~~~~~~~~~~

Conclusions

SEA POWER PLAYED a significant, even critical role in the Battle of Yorktown. The involvement of naval forces was immediate and direct in the strategic planning which led up to the battle, in the attempts by the British to save Cornwallis, and in the tactical development of the battle itself. The historical record sheds considerable light on the general development of this campaign and on the specifics of this naval involvement. The archaeological work which has been undertaken in conjunction with the project has shed further light on the subject.

Throughout the American Revolution, the British forces in North America were critically dependent on support from the sea. They were fighting in hostile territory, removed by the barrier of the Atlantic Ocean from supplies, reinforcements, and support of all kinds. This was the first war in the history of the British Empire that was fought on such terms and on such a scale. The logistical implications of the project were immense and only gradually appreciated. Not only was it necessary that naval ships, themselves in short supply, be provided, but large quantities of transport ships had to be bought or chartered and convoyed to the theater of operations. The importance of this support effort was emphasized by the strategic decision to pursue the war from the South northward, a decision that dated from 1778. Emphasis was placed on the acquisition of seacoast strongholds along the southern coast. They were to serve the dual purpose of providing a base for troops making raids into the interior and a base for the naval forces that would control the navigation and trade of the area. These bases were, in fact, established by 1781, at Savannah, Charleston, Wilmington, and Portsmouth. Properly supported and defended, they might well have served the purpose for which they were intended. The extent of the support they would require was significantly underestimated, however; there was little anticipation that the countryside would be as inhospitable, or the inhabitants as hostile, as they proved to be. The consequence was that the British forces in the South required constant support by sea, and convoys were frequently moving between these forces and the bases of supply in New York, Halifax, and England. Symbolic of the size of this effort is the group of ships which Cornwallis finally found under his control at Yorktown. Although that fleet numbered over sixty ships, of which only five were naval, Cornwallis was neither oversupplied nor able to move his forces in one body. The magnitude of the logistical problem faced by the British army in North America may never have been fully recognized in ministerial circles in Britain.

Because of the dependence of the British forces on this support, it was vitally important that control of the seas be retained. None of the posts was so well supplied or manned that it could afford to be cut off for very long from the regular flow of men and materials. By 1778 the British had little to apprehend from the American navy, but the new alliance with France raised the specter of a French fleet on the American coast. In point of fact, when a French fleet under d'Estaing did arrive in North America, it failed to have the effect which had been anticipated. At Savannah, at Philadelphia, and at Newport, the lack of both decisive action and coordination with the land forces prevented a major victory for the Americans. The lessons of failure were well learned, however, and the coordination of forces at Yorktown can only be described as amazing for the times. The fleet under Admiral de Grasse, though only on the American coast for two months, severed the connection with New York and enabled the land forces to reduce Cornwallis. It is important to note that de Grasse finally recognized, as d'Estaing had not, that the most significant object of his attentions was not the enemy's fleet but his army. By holding the Chesapeake until Cornwallis was reduced, he prevented any possibility of relief from New York. To his credit, it must be said that Washington was

responsible for persuading de Grasse to remain anchored in the
Bay, rather than patrolling off its mouth. The result was all that
might have been hoped.

The shipping under the command of Lord Cornwallis, in
addition to its principal supply role outlined above, played a tactical role in the battle. The ships at his disposal enabled Lord
Cornwallis to act more boldly than he might have otherwise. His
move to occupy Yorktown was sudden and unexpected by the
American forces, a move undertaken totally by water. The control of the harbor and the York River enabled Cornwallis to occupy successfully both sides of the river. This was vital both to his
defense of the post and the protection of a fleet, the primary
reason that Yorktown was chosen in the first place. The French
never did succeed in directly attacking the water side of the post
at Yorktown, though this should theoretically have been extremely vulnerable to such a superior fleet. In addition to the
implied obstacles of the batteries which faced the river, there was
a very real obstacle to a naval assault in the presence and positioning of the captive ships. The sinking of a considerable number of ships in front of the beach at Yorktown was a direct effort
to prevent an assault up the river by the French at that vulnerable point. Until the last day of the battle, the captive fleet continued to pose a threat to the success of the siege. It was a weak link
over which Washington had no control, notwithstanding his efforts to neutralize the force. Cornwallis maintained, through his
ships, control of the river for many miles above Yorktown, and it
was a very real possibility that he might have effected an escape
by that route. That this was not simply an imagined threat is
indicated by the escape attempt of October 16. That attempt was
only foiled by the shortage of small craft still afloat at that time, a
shortage which necessitated several trips across the river. Had
the effort been made sooner in the siege, or had the weather held
on October 16, the implicit tactical importance of the captive
fleet might well have been realized.

The history of the shipwrecks since the time of the battle is
revealing, suggesting a change in attitude toward the resource
over the years. Immediately following the battle, the wrecks
were little more than an economic asset to the French, to be
mined to the extent that it was practical. By 1851, however,
there was beginning to be an awareness of the historical value, or

at least the relic value, of the wrecks. Even then, however, the wrecks were the subject of an economically motivated salvage effort by Thomas Ash. With the passage of time, the relic value came to outweigh any direct salvage value the wrecks might have had. Even through the 1960s, however, they continued to be regarded as sources of "relics of the revolution," rather than as archaeological sites to be studied as an entity. With the recognition that it was important to protect the archaeological integrity of the site as an entirety, and of each individual wreck, a new approach has had to be taken toward the site.

It has been manifestly evident that passive efforts at preservation and protection are not effective on underwater sites, at least in the populous Northeast. Nomination of the site to the National Register of Historic Places had no immediate effect in the effort to preserve the site. Passage of an underwater antiquities law by the state has had little effect on the protection of other sites in the state, and has only been effective at Yorktown because of an active and ongoing effort to suppress looting. It would appear that there is some hope for the education and persuasion of the sport diving community regarding the significance of shipwrecks and their preservation, but this will be a slow process. In the meantime, underwater sites will continue to suffer the indiscriminate looting which has been documented at Yorktown.

The archaeological survey work undertaken on the York River site has had a threefold purpose. First, although there were indications in the historical record that there were a number of shipwrecks and that their distribution might be expected to parallel that outlined in contemporary maps, this was by no means a certainty. Whether the line of scuttled ships along the beach at Yorktown actually existed, and its extent if it did, was unknown. Contemporary accounts were both vague and conflicting, and many of the details of the tactical aspects of the battle were thus unconfirmed. Second, if efforts at protection were to be made, they required a base of information, lest they be as random and indiscriminate as the actions of the often uninformed sport divers. It was unknown how many wrecks might be at Yorktown, how many might be in any condition to warrant preservation, and where they were located. The National Register boundaries were intentionally drawn to encompass a much larger area than actually included wrecks, as far as anyone knew. To protect such a large area, where both swimming and diving continued to be within the rights of the citizen, posed a severe problem. Finally, if any rational attempt was ever to be made at site excavation on one or more of the wrecks, a basis was required for the selection of the site. All of the sites excavated in 1934, 1949, and 1976, had been dug because the wrecks were located by chance. With considerable funds involved in a full excavation, it was important to be able to state that the most significant and best preserved wreck was to be excavated. Without a survey, there was no way to make this statement on rational grounds.

The survey itself is of interest from a technical viewpoint, as it is one of the earlier efforts at the in-depth survey of an underwater archaeological site of such size and variety of topography. Because of the hostile conditions posed by the currents, water depth, lack of water clarity, and bottom conditions, it seemed that a remote sensing survey was the only practical approach to the problem. The technical aspects of the survey have been reported in considerable detail because of the novelty of the project and the variety of techniques which were employed. It is to be hoped that some of the lessons learned from the effort, which was undertaken on a shoestring, will be of use to future researchers. The location and identification of nine shipwrecks has essentially fulfilled the original goals of the survey. The disposition of the ships which was indicated in the historical record has been confirmed. The site has clearly been shown worthy of protection and further study. Several wrecks have been located which are far better preserved than any which had been known before the survey, and excavation efforts will center on them.

The shipwreck remains from the Battle of Yorktown constitute one of the most diverse and extensive deposits of shipwrecks in North America dating from the colonial period. Including both naval and merchant vessels, of varying size, with considerable supporting documentation available, it is an unparalleled resource for the study of eighteenth-century shipping and life. Having established the site's historical context and significance, it is to be hoped that continued efforts will be made to preserve, excavate, and document these survivals from the birth of this nation.

Catalogue of Ships
at Yorktown

Catalogue of Ships at Yorktown

A PREREQUISITE for any archaeological study of the ships at Yorktown is a detailed knowledge of the ships involved, not just in general terms, but as specific a reconstruction as is possible from the surviving documents. Without the knowledge of which ships were present, which were lost, which were salvaged, and which are likely to still rest on the bottom of the river, any excavations will be lacking in pedigree and hence lose meaning. Unfortunately, the surviving documents are not always as complete as one might wish.

There are two lists of the shipping in the York River, both made immediately after the battle, which are of primary importance. The first is contained in a letter sent by Captain Symonds, of the *Charon*, the ranking naval officer in Yorktown, to Rear Admiral Graves, in New York, his commanding officer. It not only contains a description of the fate of the naval vessels in the harbor but also includes a list of transports, prepared by the British agent of transports, Lieutenant General Robertson. The other list, somewhat more complete, is included in a letter from Admiral de Grasse to George Washington, sent October 24, 1781. Apparently, the source of de Grasse's information is the series of reports submitted by Captain Granchain. Though these reports have not been located, it appears that de Grasse sent an accurate rendition of them. This "List of Vessels Seized or Destroyed at York, Virginia" served as the basis for the official inventory that was reported to Congress and printed in the *Pennsylvania Packet* of November 6, 1781. In the midst of his attempt to salvage some of the vessels which lay in the York River, Villebrune submitted a list of vessels which were afloat in May 1782. This, along with his financial accounts, gives a more accurate, if less complete, picture than the lists which were compiled immediately after the battle.

The list of shipping submitted by Captain Symonds indicates that of the thirty-two transports and victuallers in the harbor, only two were still afloat at the conclusion of the battle. This grim picture of destruction may be somewhat overcolored, since the reports of the French are not so pessimistic as one might expect in the face of a completely destroyed fleet. Certainly, the British captain had something to gain in representing his fleet as destroyed, while the French had little to gain through overoptimism. That at least a portion of the shipping was still afloat and usable is indicated by the announcement made by Washington on October 25, 1781, in his general orders. "It having been represented that many Negroes and Mulatoes, the property of the Citizens of these States have concealed themselves on board of ships in the harbor," he cautioned his troops and guards to be on the lookout for these escapees.[1] This order tends to confirm the picture of very lax security that prevailed on board the vessels during the transition to French ownership. We are forced to take the report of Captain Symonds at face value, though in recognition of his position, moderate skepticism is in order.

Insofar as it is presently possible, the following is a ship-by-ship analysis of individual involvement in the battle and the ultimate fate of the vessels.

AGNESS

The *Agness* was a horse transport chartered by the Quartermaster General's Department for £71.10.0 per month. A schooner of 110 tons, she was commanded by Nathaniel Proctor. She was reported in Virginia as of August 17, 1781, and it is presumed that she was still there at the time of the battle. Her fate is unknown.[2]

ALDBOROUGH

The *Aldborough* was a ship-rigged transport of 261 tons, draft fifteen feet, which had been sent to Virginia from New York in

June 1781 with troops on board. She was owned by her former captain, Williams Clark, and chartered to the government; she had been built in 1765 in Philadelphia and was previously known as the *Speedwell*. She mounted eight 3-pounders, had undergone thorough repairs in 1773 and 1775, including sheathing in 1775, and was highly rated by Lloyd's in 1781. Following the destruction of the *Vulcan* in the raid of September 22, she was converted by Captain Symonds to a fire ship. Her captain, Lionel Bradstreet, was replaced by a naval officer, Lieutenant Edwards, first lieutenant of the *Charon*. Although there were several other transports converted to fire ships as well, they were never used, and it must be presumed that they were scuttled. The *Aldborough* is listed as "Sunk" by Symonds after the battle. No further mention of her has been found.[3]

ANDREWS

The *Andrews* was a transport of 259 tons and mounting six guns. She was commanded by Francis Todring, and was still afloat at the conclusion of the battle. She was one of the vessels used by the French to carry paroled British army officers to New York, and left on that service November 5, 1781.[4]

ARNO

The information about the *Arno* comes entirely from the letter of Granchain dated October 21, 1781: "As to the cargo of the Arno, it should be returned to the shipowner according to the terms of the Capitulation; but the ship with her rigging and fittings belongs to us. I imagine that the owner, Guilchrist, will be well prepared to redeem her; you could propose to him that this ship should be worth at least one thousand guineas to him. While waiting you could always take the brass and tar which she has on board and send it to the fleet as soon as you can." It seems likely that the vessel referred to is the ship of 200 tons listed in *Lloyd's Register*. She was built in Exeter in 1765, mounted four 4-pounders, and is listed as owned by J. Baring & Co. She was engaged in private trade on the North American coast in 1780 and 1781.[5]

ARNOLD

The *Arnold* was a horse transport chartered by the Quartermaster General's Department for £82.4.6 per month. A brig of 126½ tons, she was commanded by William Young. She was reported in Virginia as of August 17, 1781, and it is presumed that she was still there at the time of the battle. Her fate is unknown.[6]

BELLONA

The *Bellona* was a ship-rigged transport of 350 tons, drawing fifteen feet. In addition to her single deck, she had open or unfloored transverse beams in her hold, which could be covered to form a deck if required. She was fitted with at least 153 beds for troops. She was commanded by John Ward and chartered to the navy by her owner Charles Jackson through the transport agent William Wilkinson. She had been taken into service in December 1777, immediately after her construction in Whitby, and she had been in North America for at least three years by the summer of 1781. She had carried troops to Virginia in a convoy of June 1781. Still afloat at the conclusion of the hostilities, she was designated as one of the three ships which carried paroled British naval officers back to England. On that voyage she was commanded by Capt. Hugh Robinson, formerly of the *Guadaloupe;* following her arrival in Portsmouth on December 19, 1781, she was sent on to Brest with exchanged French prisoners. Within six months the ship had been recaptured by H.M.S. *Queen,* though there was some initial difficulty in demonstrating that the retaken ship was the same as that lost at Yorktown. A model in the J. Templeman Coolidge Collection of the Boston Museum of Fine Arts represents a *Bellona* of about that period and size. It came from an unidentified English collection, and it is conceivable that it represents this ship, probably after her recapture from the French.[7]

BETSEY

The *Betsey* was a schooner of thirty tons, commanded during the battle by John Younghusband, though she was earlier commanded by James Ballingtine. She was chartered from Peter Butt, apparently of New York, for £46.10.0 per month. Her charter was paid from the accounts of Lord Cornwallis only through August 31, 1781, but she was reported by Symonds as having been sunk in the battle.[8]

BONETTA

H.M.S. *Bonetta*, 307 tons, was a ship of the sixth rate, mounting
fourteen 6-pounders and fourteen swivel guns. She was built on
the Thames by Perry and Hankey between June 1778 and April
1779. After her launching she was taken to Woolwich for fitting
out and coppering. Her captain was Ralph Dundas, of Edin-

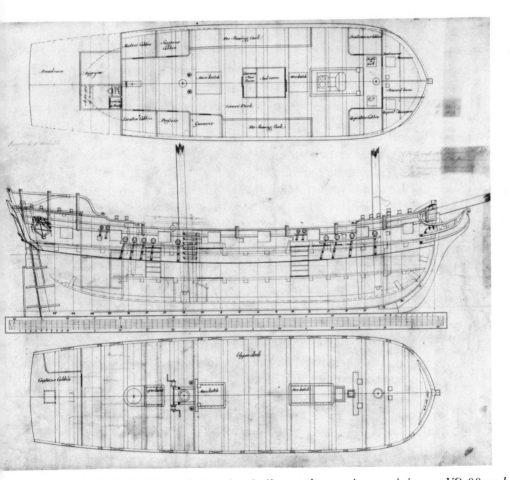

The plan of H.M.S. Dispatch *is quite similar to the remains surviving on YO 88 and
may give an idea of the configuration of the original vessel. Note that while this is a
square-sterned vessel, the underbody draws in to a point at the sternpost, explaining the
initial appearance that YO 88 is double-ended. (Courtesy of the National Maritime
Museum, London)*

burgh, who supervised her construction and fitting out. He described the day of her launch in a letter to his brother: "Last Friday she was launched and made a very fine one. J. G. accompanied me to the Exibition we dined with the Builder who gave a very good feed upon the occasion but not like a Scots one for we got much more Meat than Drink. She was conveyed away as soon as Launched from Blackwall to Woolwich." The ship was ninety-six feet, seven inches on her gun deck, seventy-nine feet, three inches on her keel, beam twenty-seven feet and draft twelve feet, ten and a half inches. When Dundas finally took the ship across the Atlantic, he was ordered to New York but eventually made port in the West Indies. Describing the voyage, he wrote, "From the Day we left Spithead we had almost a continual Hurricane during which we lost our Boats, Guns, Anchors, Masts &c. & when we got in were in every other respect a Meer Wreck." She participated in the siege of Charleston and in the early phases of the Virginia campaign.

The role the *Bonetta* played in the battle itself is very poorly documented. In fact, she probably did little, if anything, as far as actual fighting was concerned, though she certainly acted as a deterrent. Most of the maps of the battle show her riding on the Gloucester side of the river and slightly upstream of the point. In fact, this is the only position in which she could have survived the battle in usable condition. Her role in subsequent events has been discussed in chapter 6.[9]

CESAR

The *Cesar* was a horse transport chartered by the Quartermaster General's Department for £71.10.0 per month. A sloop of 110 tons, she was commanded by a man named Balfour. She was reported in Virginia as of August 17, 1781, and it is presumed that she was still present at the time of the battle. Her fate is unknown.[10]

CHARM

The *Charm* was an American schooner which was discovered near Yorktown and seized on August 26, 1781. She was put in the hands of Lieutenant James, of the *Charon*. He used her between September 9 and September 11 to reconnoiter the French fleet, in which duty he narrowly avoided capture. Becalmed and chased by the French as they returned to the bay, James abandoned the vessel and fled upriver in the tender he was towing. It is presumed that she was taken by the French.[11]

CHARON

H.M.S. *Charon*, 891 tons, was a ship of the fifth rate, mounting forty-four guns. She was built between January 1777 and October 1778 by John Barnard of Harwich and then moved to Sheerness for fitting out and to Chatham for coppering. She was 140 feet, 3 inches on the gun deck, 116 feet, 1 inch on the keel, drew 16 feet, 4 inches, and carried a complement of 300 men. Under the command of Thomas Symonds, she sailed from Cork on August 12, 1780, with a convoy of 100 ships for North America.[12] The log of H.M.S. *Fowey* records on November 10, 1780, while on guard duty off Sandy Hook: "Arrived here 9 Sail of transports & Victuallers from Corke under convoy of His Majesty's Ships Charon & Hussar."[13] She left New York almost immediately as a part of the convoy carrying Benedict Arnold to Chesapeake Bay in late December 1780. With Symonds in command, she was the largest naval vessel at the time of the French attempt to seize control of the Bay in March 1781. She convoyed empty transports back to New York after reinforcements had been landed in Virginia, and came back to Portsmouth with a group of transports when Clinton demanded the return of troops upon learning that Cornwallis had come to Virginia. She arrived in Portsmouth on July 12, escorting eight transports and four horse vessels.[14] With the change in plans and the choice of Yorktown as a post, the *Charon* joined in the movement of troops to that town.

Admiral Graves originally intended to have the *Charon* sent back to New York as an escort for the troop convoy Clinton had requested; this plan was abandoned. The *Richmond*, Captain Hudson, until that time the flagship of the naval forces in the area, left instead for New York, leaving Captain Symonds in command.[15] Before this departure, the *Charon* and the *Richmond* had been moored above Yorktown in a position to flank the enemy should they attack from that sector. Guns from both ships had been landed for the construction of the sea battery at

Yorktown, and apparently all of the *Charon's* 18-pounders had been removed from her lower deck.[16] Captain Symonds, in writing to Admiral Graves on September 8, 1781, stated that "most of the Cannon and Ammunition of the *Charon* are landed and great part of the Crew in Tents and employed in enlarging the Sea Battery, and assisting the Army."[17] After the departure of the *Richmond*, the *Guadaloupe* took her place, and the *Charon* remained in her original position, though she actually had little armament on board. That she was a relatively ineffective deterrent is indicated by the fact that complaints by the forces in the French Trench were primarily directed at the *Guadaloupe*, actually the smaller of the two, but apparently the better armed at that time.

The *Charon* had only a skeleton crew, and on the night of October 10, when the French began to fire red-hot shot, she could not withdraw along with the *Guadaloupe;* the consequences were disastrous for the British. The ship took fire and burned the whole night. Descriptions lead one to believe that the destruction must have been complete, that she burned to the waterline.

Several reports state that the weather on this evening was calm, and this is confirmed by the logbook of Admiral de Grasse, which stated on October 10, "Vents de l'Est au Sud, petit frais, presque calme."[18] Had the ship simply broken loose from her moorings and drifted in the breeze, it is likely that she would have come ashore near Gloucester Point. This seems to have been the case, as indicated by the report of Lieutenant James, who had served on board the *Charon:*

She was set on fire at half-past six o'clock in three different places, and in a few minutes in flames from the hold to the mastheads. From our being quartered at the guns in front of the army, that timely assistance could not be given her which was necessary to extinguish the fire, and she broke adrift from her moorings and drove on board a transport to which she also set fire, and they both grounded on the Gloucester side, where they burnt to the water's edge. The loss of our things in the Charon are so very trivial when compared to the more distressing scenes of the garrison, that I shall say no more on this head, than that we saw

*with infinite concern one of the finest ships in the navy of her rate
totally destroyed on this day.*[19]

It was, therefore, a reasonable assumption that the wreck of the
Charon was to be found on the Gloucester side of the York River.
Further, one might have presumed the presence of one or more
burned transports in the same area. Excavations undertaken on
site GL 136 during the summer of 1980 have demonstrated, in
fact, that it is the wreck of the *Charon.* Further details of the
wreck may be found in chapter 9.

It is conceivable that the French undertook salvage efforts
on the wreck of the *Charon* after the battle in an effort to recover
some of her guns. In 1783, the French frigate *Danae* was forced
to jettison her guns in a storm, and later sought to replace them
in Philadelphia. Seventeen 18-pounders were located in the arse-
nal at Philadelphia and were given to the French on the basis of
their having come from the *Charon.* They were thus rightfully
French property as a part of the naval prizes of the battle. Later,
five more of the *Charon's* 18-pounders were located at Head of
Elk; these, too, were put on board the *Danae.* It seems most
likely, however, that these twenty-two guns represented the armament from the gun deck of the vessel which had been unloaded before the battle. They presumably were removed by the
American land forces after the capitulation.[20] This supposition is
further supported by the fact that the *Charon* could accommodate twenty cannon on her gun deck, which leaves two 18-
pounders for stern chasers.

Profile plans of the *Charon* survive in the collection of Admiralty draughts in the National Maritime Museum, Greenwich.
Further, an Admiralty-type model was built by Maj. Raban Williams during the 1930s; it is today a part of the Doughty collection, exhibited in the Welholme Galleries, Great Grimsby, England.

Some insight into the character of Captain Symonds is
given by the narrative related by Col. Ethan Allen in January
1776, when he was held prisoner on board the *Solebay,* at that
time commanded by Symonds:

*When we were first brought on board Capt. Symonds ordered all
the prisoners, and most of the hands on board, to go on deck, and*

*caused to be read, in their hearing a certain code of laws, or rules
for the regulation and ordering of their behaviour; and then, in a
sovereign manner, ordered the prisoners, me in particular, off the
deck, and never to come on it again; for, said he, this is a place
for gentlemen to walk. So I went off, an officer following me,
who told me, that he would shew me the place allotted for me,
and took me down to the cable tire, saying to me, this is your
place.*

. . . . .

*However, two days after, I shaved and cleaned myself as
well as I could, and went on deck. The Capt. spoke to me in a
great rage, and said, "did I not order you not to come on deck?"
I answered him, that at the same time he said, "that it was the
place for gentlemen to walk," that I was Col. Allen, but had not
been properly introduced to him. He replied, "G--d damn you,
sir, be careful not to walk the same side of the deck that I do."
This gave me encouragement, and ever after that I walked in the
manner he had directed, except when he, at certain times
afterwards, ordered me off in a passion, and I then would directly
afterwards go on again, telling him to command his slaves; that I
was a gentlemen, and had a right to walk the deck; yet, when he
expressly ordered me off, I obeyed, not out of obedience to him,
but to set an example to his ship's crew, who ought to obey him.*[21]

Though Captain Symonds was obviously no lover of Americans,
it cannot be said that he was much different from many captains,
British and American, of the period.

COCHRAN

The *Cochran* was a privately owned ship-rigged vessel of 247
tons, commanded by T. Bolton. Built in Whitby in 1770, she
mounted 22 guns originally and was copper sheathed, a rarity for
a merchant vessel. She was one of the vessels which carried the
paroled British officers to New York on November 5, 1781, and
the ship on board which Lord Cornwallis sailed. Upon her return to the York River, she was rearmed by the French and employed in the defense of the Chesapeake Bay. In 1782 her owner,
William Cunningham of Glasgow, was allowed nearly £600
damages for stores removed from the vessel during the battle.[22]

This model of the Bellona *is thought to date from the late 18th century. Apparently of French origin, it is possible that it represents the vessel of the same name captured at Yorktown. If so, the model must have been built in Brest during the six months that the French held the ship before she was recaptured by the British. (Courtesy, Museum of Fine Arts, Boston)*

CONCORD

The *Concord* was a transport commanded by Andrew Monk which was reported sunk during the battle. She is presumably the same vessel, of 251 tons, which was in Charleston on March 21, 1781, in use as a prison ship. She may have been one of the group of ships which sailed from Charleston to Jamestown as cartels, in a fruitless effort to exchange prisoners during the summer of 1781.[23]

CONVERT

The *Convert* was a hired schooner, presumably in use as a transport in the Quartermaster General's Department. Her hire was paid through October 18, 1781, and the owners were allowed £410 for her value, suggesting that she was captured, and possibly sunk, during the battle. A subsequent account suggests that she may have been put back in service as £31 were paid to "Captain William Peacock of His Majesty's Ship Carysfort Salvage for the Sloop Convert retaken by the said Ship."[24]

DEFIANCE

The brig *Defiance*, attached to the Quartermaster General's Department, mounted fourteen 18-pounders and two 9-pounders. She was commanded by Joseph Nash and survived the battle. She was used by Villebrune to defend the lower Chesapeake Bay, during which time she mounted fourteen cannon and was commanded by M. de Chabon, an Ensign.[25]

DELIGHT

The *Delight*, a sloop of forty tons, was commanded by John Kerr. She was one of the vessels carrying paroled British officers to New York after the battle. It is uncertain whether she was British or American, but she evidently did not suffer appreciable damage during the battle.[26]

DIANA

The *Diana*, a sloop of 137²/₃ tons, commanded by John Perkin, was apparently a multipurpose vessel in the hands of the British. She was under charter to the Quartermaster General's Department for £89.9.8 per month and served in a number of different roles. On June 30, 1781, she was described as an "Army victualler"; on August 17, 1781, as a "horse vessel"; and in between, from July 17 to August 4, 1781, she had carried 310 men from Portsmouth to Yorktown. This was substantially in excess of the usual loading allowance of a ton and half per man. She was reported sunk in the battle.[27]

DUNDAS GALLEY

The *Dundas Galley* was one of the several dispatch boats which regularly carried messages between Yorktown and New York. Her last trip out of the York River was made around October 1, when she encountered "3 Rebel ¼ Galleys, one of which blew up in firing." After this narrow escape, the *Dundas Galley* seems to have remained in New York.[28]

ELIZABETH

The *Elizabeth*, 400 tons, was chartered to the government as a navy victualler. She was built at Whitby in 1765, was ship-rigged, wood-sheathed, and drew sixteen feet. Her owner filed a claim with the Commissioners of the Navy following her loss: "Mr. Joseph Holt of Whitby, Owner of the Ship Elizabeth, Levi Preston Master, Chartered to you, by his Agents Messrs. Wilkinson, on the 13th of January 1781, having rec'd information that his Ship had by the orders of Admiral Graves, been applyed for the use of Government as a Fire Ship, has directed me to request you would give directions for payment of the twelve months certain Freight, convenanted by the Charterparty." Several fire ships had been fitted out in New York during the fall of 1781, but it is presumed that the *Elizabeth* may have served as a replacement for the *Vulcan*. She was reported sunk during the battle.[29]

EMERALD

The *Emerald* was a transport of 215 tons commanded by William Tindall; she had carried troops to Virginia in early June 1781. The ship was reported sunk in the battle, but may have been raised, as Rochambeau used an *Emeraude* in his departure from Boston, October 1782.[30]

FAVOURITE

The *Favourite* was a ship-rigged troop transport of 221 tons, commanded by Joseph Willson. She was owned by one Thomas Fisher and chartered to the government through the transport agent John Wilkinson. She was reported sunk in the battle, and following her loss, her owner appealed her low valuation to the Navy Board. In his letter he outlined the history of the ship, and his expenses associated with her. She was built at Workington in May 1775, at an initial cost of £2,544. She was twice chartered as a troop transport to Quebec, in 1776 and 1777. On March 13, 1778, she was chartered for a third time, and carried troops to America; she remained in North America until her loss at Yorktown. During that time she was damaged in a gale and barely escaped capture by a privateer. She was armed in 1776 with six 4-pounders and six swivels, and it must be presumed that she continued to carry this armament. Although Fisher's petition for a higher valuation was denied, the ship may have survived the battle after all. On August 7, 1782, Rochambeau sent his dispatches home to France on board a ship named *Favorite*, an admittedly common name. The ship was apparently used during the battle as a prison ship, judging from a request by Major McHenry, aide-de-camp to Lafayette, to free one of the men held on board her by Cornwallis.[31]

FIDELITY

The *Fidelity* was a transport of 262 tons, but she was in use as a cartel ship during the summer of 1781. She had carried prisoners from Charleston to be exchanged at Jamestown, but the exchange apparently did not take place. She was therefore returned to Portsmouth, where she participated in the transfer of troops from that post to Yorktown carrying Negroes and baggage. As a cartel, she was unarmed. She was commanded by Robert Pilmour, and was reported sunk during the battle.[32]

FORMIDABLE

The *Formidable*, a sloop of eighty tons attached to the Quartermaster General's Department, mounted twelve 18-pounders and two 12-pounders. She was commanded by Nathaniel Horton and was one of the vessels which Clinton intended to use for the transportation of the troops he had requested of Cornwallis in June 1781. The troops never left Virginia, however, nor did the *Formidable*. At Yorktown she was positioned with the *Guadaloupe* and the *Charon* to help defend the Fusilier's Redoubt. As in the case of the *Guadaloupe*, she was driven back from that position when the French opened fire. She did survive the battle afloat, however, and was used by La Villebrune in the summer of 1782 to carry supplies to Baltimore.[33]

FOWEY

H.M.S. *Fowey*, 513 tons, was a ship of the sixth rate, mounting twenty-four guns. She was 113 feet, 2¾ inches long on the gun deck, and 93 feet, 3 inches on the keel. Launched by Moody Janvrin at Beaulieu on July 4, 1749, she had a beam of thirty-two feet, two inches, and drew eleven feet, one-half inch while carrying 160 men.[34] Her captain at Yorktown was Peter Aplin. The *Fowey* was by no means unknown to Virginians, since it was to her that Governor Dunmore had retired when the rebellion broke out in Williamsburg in 1775. He did not leave the area immediately, but rather maintained a force in the rivers of Virginia, periodically attacking one town or another; the *Fowey* must have been a familiar sight indeed when she returned to Yorktown in 1781.

The logbooks of the *Fowey* survive in the Public Record Office and can give us some insight into the nature of the vessel and her armament. On December 8, 1777, the ship was in New York and was surveyed; some of her sails and rigging were apparently condemned at that time and were sent to the storekeeper to be replaced. In January of 1778, the main- and fore-masts were removed and sent to the yard for repairs while the ship was recaulked. In May 1778 the carpenters of the yard worked for six days to replace a rotten plank in the side of the ship. This was very obviously a ship which was feeling the weight of her years at sea. On May 26, 1778, the *Fowey* received on board an 18-pounder for river service, larger than one might expect to find on a ship that normally mounted 6- and 9-pounders.

In September of 1779, the *Fowey* was involved in the attack on Savannah by the French and Americans, an engagement that proved to be a very difficult defense. She landed a considerable part of her guns and ammunition for the use of the garrison, but presumably they were returned after the battle. She and the other British ships in the harbor were forced to withdraw up the river for protection, and even so the *Fowey* sustained some damage, principally in the stern and quarterdeck sections, including the loss of her mizzenmast. She was not rendered unfit for service, however, and on April 29, 1780, she reported firing a 6-pounder at a schooner to bring her to. Further, on May 18, 1780, she received two 9-pounders from the British sloop *Loyalist*, apparently to augment or replace her own supply of armament. In September 1780 she returned to New York for another refit, at which time she was again rerigged and caulked. On October 10, 1780, she was back in service, since she reported firing a 4-pounder loaded with shot; beginning in November 1780 she was on guard duty off of Sandy Hook, New York. While there, she

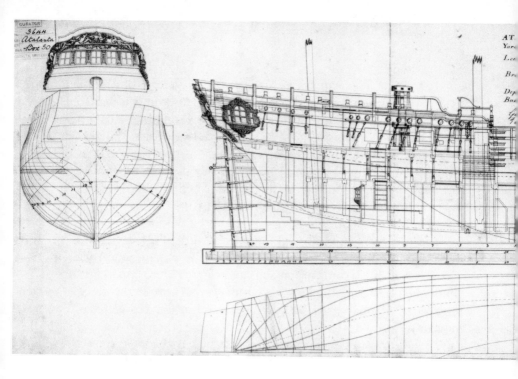

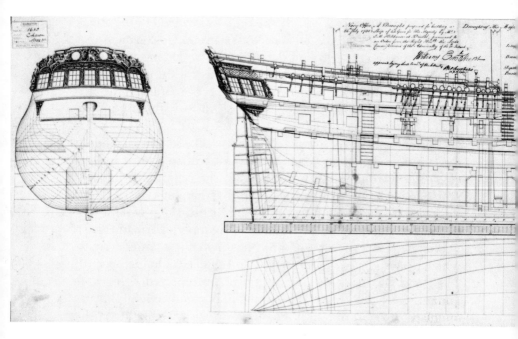

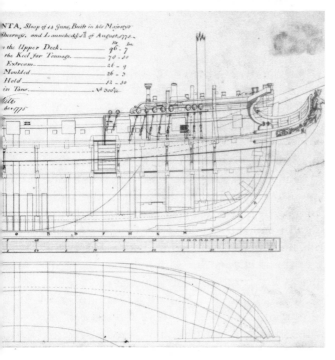

Plans of the Atalanta, which was of the same class as H.M.S. Bonetta. The Bonetta was the only naval vessel to survive the battle unscathed, and gained considerable notoriety when she was allowed to sail to New York without inspection. (Courtesy of the National Maritime Museum, London)

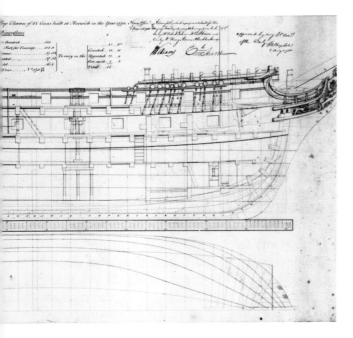

A contemporary plan of H.M.S. Charon. The ship herself was burned early in the battle. Note the pumps and shot lockers in the vicinity of the mainmast, as well as the stanchions under the capstan. All of these features were revealed during the excavation of the wreck and helped to confirm its identity. (Courtesy of the National Maritime Museum, London)

reported firing two 6-pounders and two 9-pounders, both to bring ships to. It will be seen by these references that the *Fowey* carried at various times a considerable assortment of guns. Old and decrepit though she was, she must have mounted a formidable array of firepower.

The *Fowey* sailed as an escort with the expedition under Benedict Arnold, leaving New York December 22, 1780. She remained in Portsmouth and the James River until the withdrawal to Yorktown. She was left to cover the embarkation of troops from Portsmouth and did not leave for Yorktown until August 20, 1781. She must have continued to deteriorate, as the report on the state of the fleet filed by Admiral Arbuthnot on June 2, 1781, lists her as "irreparable." The ship was moored off the shore at Yorktown, with cables fore and aft; on September 3, the crew "unmoor'd ship and hove close in shore and moor'd." A tent was erected for the storage of her provisions, and these, with her gunner's stores, were taken ashore. During the first half of September her crew was employed getting her ammunition on shore and helping with the erection of the town's defensive works. On September 5 they struck the yards and topmasts of the vessel. On September 16 through 18 they sent ashore twenty-four 9-pounders and two 6-pounders, virtually the entire armament of the ship. On September 20, three of her crew members received one dozen lashes each for attempting desertion, and two others one dozen each for theft. On September 30 the log records "a large party of the French advancing to the Right of our works we kept up a Constant fire on them which drove them back into the woods with great slaughter." For the next three days the vessel continued to fire on the troops digging the trench opposite the Fusilier's Redoubt, presumably in concert with *Charon* and *Guadaloupe*. Following this, on October 6, the *Fowey* "got on board the best Bower anchor in order to heave of into the Stream but the Tide being low did not Float." It was not until the next day that she was able to get off and anchor in the channel; this movement accounts for her survival when the *Charon* was burned several nights later. She must have then hauled into shallow water once again for the crew was employed in unrigging the ship, especially the foremast, and sending the rigging ashore. On October 13, 1781, the log records, "P.M. bored holes under the Starboard fore chains to sink the Ship pr. order from Captain Symonds. A.M. at 7 two shells fell into the Provision Tent, which destroy'd one Puncheon of [Rum] 4 Barrels of Flour 27 Pieces of Beef and 6 firkings of Butter allso the Ships and Warrant Officers Books they being put there for safety." With that, the ship joined the scuttled fleet lined up along the Yorktown beach. Even with the bulk of her guns removed, she must have been the keystone of that line of defense.[35]

The fact that the ship was bored has a bearing on her subsequent history. De Grandchain wrote on October 21, 1781, "The agent of the transports . . . has promised to give me a report of those transports which have been sunk by boring and which not, and consequently, could be raised easily."[36] The difficulty of raising a bored ship, combined with the age and condition of the *Fowey*, suggests that she was not salvaged by the French. We have some indication of her location on the beach, as well. A manuscript map of the battle drawn by John Hayman and now in the British Museum appears to be accurate in all its details save one. It shows H.M.S. *Fox*, of twenty-four guns, sunk off Yorktown, approximately at the foot of Ballard Street. There was no *Fox* at the battle, though there was one in commission at the time. She was a frigate mounting thirty-two guns, commanded by Capt. George Stoney, and served in the West Indies during this period; she continued to be mentioned well into 1782. It must be assumed, then, that either the maker or the copier of the map, since it is a copy, made an error, writing *Fox* when he should have written *Fowey*, which did indeed mount twenty-four guns. It is interesting to note that it is this area that was excavated in 1934–1935. A deck plan of the *Fowey* survives in the collection of Admiralty draughts, National Maritime Museum, Greenwich.

GENERAL REIDSEL

The *General Reidsel*, of 150 tons, was chartered by the Quartermaster General's Department; she was commanded by William Boyes. She had proceeded to the Chesapeake with a passport issued by General Washington on December 9, 1780, under a flag of truce. She was carrying supplies and clothing to the Hessian troops held prisoner at Charlottesville; however, through a

long and complicated series of events, the supplies were never
delivered and the ship was trapped in the Chesapeake during the
battle. The deputy quartermaster general in charge of the delivery of these supplies sought a new safe conduct from Washington on October 20, 1781, so that he might proceed to New York,
where the troops had since been quartered. The implication of
this is that the vessel was still afloat after the battle.[37]

GUADALOUPE

H.M.S. *Guadaloupe*, 586 tons, was a ship of the sixth rate,
mounting twenty-eight guns. She was built at Plymouth between 1759 and 1763, and was 118 feet, 4 inches on the gun
deck, 97 feet, 3½ inches on the keel. With a beam of 33 feet, 8
inches, she drew 10 feet, 6 inches, carried 200 men, and was
commanded at the Battle of Yorktown by Capt. Hugh Robinson.[38] The *Guadaloupe* joined the forces in Virginia with the reinforcements which were sent to Arnold in late March 1781. She
assisted in the move to Yorktown, both carrying troops and
standing guard during the destruction of the works at Portsmouth.[39] On August 29, 1781, she was sent by Lord Cornwallis
to carry dispatches to Charleston and to convoy supplies and
convalescents back to Yorktown. She never made it out of the
Chesapeake, however, having encountered the French fleet at
Cape Henry and scurried back into the York River.[40]

Soon after this she was moored above Yorktown in a position to enfilade the valley and marsh behind the Fusilier's Redoubt, through which the road to Williamsburg passed. It was
from this position that she harassed the troops constructing the
French Trench, and it was from here that she withdrew in the
face of red-hot shot on October 9, 1781. She moved to a position
on the Gloucester side of the river, apparently below Gloucester
Point. Presumably in this same position, she was scuttled on
October 17 to prevent capture.[41]

Captain Robinson sank the *Guadaloupe* in accordance with
an order received from Captain Symonds of the *Charon*, dated
October 15, 1781: "Whereas I think it absolutely necessary for
the benefit of His Majestys Service to prevent His Majestys Ship
under your command (from being burnt or otherwise falling into
the hands of the Enemy) that you should Scuttle and Sink her,

after landing such provisions Stores &c. as you possibly can."[42] Writing after the battle, St. George Tucker reported "the Guadeloupe sunk to the Waters Edge"; it is presumed that she had water up to her gunwales and that her decks were awash.[43] However, as has been indicated in chapter 6, she was finally salvaged by the French and apparently without the aid of the fleet sent to assist in the project. It was the intention of M. de La Touche, in command of that relief force, to arm the vessel by impressing armament, presumably from the land forces, and to place M. du Quesne, a lieutenant, in command of her.[44] But the departure of the forces from Yorktown before his arrival forced Villebrune to use the vessel less than fully equipped, as indicated by a letter of Rochambeau, written on October 5, 1782, from Boston: "With regard to the vessels to carry myself and the other officers and general staff, and the intendant and his staff, to France, I believe that the Emeraude and the Gloire, which I beg you to give me, [will be sufficient, along with] the Romulus and perhaps the Guadeloupe, if you like, which we could arm sufficiently for our baggage."[45] Presumably a large portion of the *Guadaloupe's* armament had been offloaded either before or during the battle, thus accounting for her condition. Plans of the *Guadaloupe* survive in the collection of Admiralty draughts, National Maritime Museum, Greenwich, as does an Admiralty model.

HARLEQUIN

The *Harlequin*, a victualler, was commanded during the battle by Thomas Skinner and was one of the vessels intentionally scuttled to form the defensive line along the beach. The accounts of the deputy quartermaster general in Cornwallis's army are debited as follows: "William Skinner for the hire of the Schooner Harlequin from the 1st to 19th of October 1781 £49-8-0, and for the Value of the said Schooner sunk by order of Earl Cornwallis at the Stockade in York River £446-5-0." There were several *Harlequins* in service at this time, and it is difficult to be certain which was involved here. There was a forty-ton sloop by the same name carrying wood to the troops in New York at the time of the battle. There had been a privateer *Harlequin* operating off the Capes of Virginia around 1778, and this might be related. Finally, there was a forty-ton schooner of that name captured by the *Swift* in 1779 and sold in New York. She was en route from Port au Prince to Virginia and had been built in 1778 in Gloucester County, Virginia. Her original port of registry was Yorktown; there would be a fitting symmetry if this were the vessel lost two years later.[46]

HARMONY

The *Harmony*, a brigantine of 258 tons, was commanded during the battle by John Duffield. She was chartered as a transport May 13, 1780, had come to Virginia with Arnold in January 1781, and carried a second contingent of troops south in June 1781. Although she was sunk during the battle, she was subsequently raised by Villebrune.[47]

HORSINGDON

The *Horsingdon* was a transport of 235 tons, a British brig built in 1773, wood-sheathed and drawing thirteen feet. She mounted six guns, was owned by Jackson & Company, and was commanded by Christopher Jobson. She had apparently sailed from Cork late in 1778 and had come from New York to Virginia with the reinforcements of late March 1781, under General Phillips. During the trip from New York she had run afoul of another ship and had to be towed for a good part of the trip. She was reported sunk in the battle.[48]

HOUSTON

The *Houston*, a transport of 258 tons and mounting six guns, was commanded by Robert MacLeish during the battle. During the move from Portsmouth to Yorktown, she carried baggage; she was sunk in the battle.[49]

JOHN

The *John* was a horse transport chartered by the Quartermaster General's Department for £69.6.8 per month. A sloop of 106²/₃ tons, she was commanded by Edward Welchford. She was reported in Virginia as of August 17, 1781, and it is presumed that she was still there at the time of the battle. Her fate is unknown.[50]

LEENDERT & MATTHY'S

The *Leendert & Matthy's* was a privately owned Dutch vessel which had been taken prize by the privateer *Goodrich* and brought into Portsmouth May 19, 1781. Because she was not then in good condition, the master of the *Goodrich*, John Buchanan, was unable to find a convoy to New York for her and was forced to leave her in Virginia. She followed the British forces to Yorktown and sought a convoy to New York from there. When Captain Hudson sailed with dispatches for New York, he "would not take under His Convoy, nor give Sailing Instruction to, nor wait for the Ship Leendert & Matthy's, as she appeared to be a dull or heavy sailor." The ship remained in the York River, and following the destruction of the *Charon*, withdrew to the Gloucester side of the river. Although some stores were requisitioned from her, she was left reasonably intact after the battle. Her cargo en route from Curacao to Amsterdam consisted of sugar, coffee, hides, indigo, cocoa, dyewood, and miscellaneous merchandise. It was of considerable value and of interest to both the Americans and the French. The bulk of it was finally allowed to the French and sold at a considerable profit in Philadelphia.[51]

LORD HOWE

The *Lord Howe* was a transport commanded by Thomas Woodhouse; there were at least two vessels by this name in the transport service, and it has not been possible to distinguish between them. She was reported sunk in the battle.[52]

LORD MULGRAVE

The *Lord Mulgrave*, 324 tons, was commanded at the time of the battle by Andrew Easterby. He had brought the ship from Leith, Scotland, to New York with nearly 200 men of the Eightieth Regiment of Foot (the Royal Edinburgh Volunteers). The ship had sailed March 15 and arrived August 27, 1779. Presumably Symonds was in error when he noted that she was sunk in the battle, for she was one of the ships designated by Washington to carry the paroled British officers back to New York. She departed on November 5, 1781, but, unlike the others, did not reach New York. She was blown south and eventually made port at Charleston. Her paroled officers were exchanged for French prisoners, and she sailed back to the Chesapeake in the fall of 1782. She was not destined to serve the French, however, for she went ashore on Willoughby Spit in Norfolk and was thought to be a total loss.[53]

MACKERAL

The *Mackeral* was a chartered transport of 191³⁵/₉₄ tons, commanded by William Fraser (or Farrer). She was reported sunk in the battle.[54]

MARIA

The *Maria* was a sloop used as a dispatch boat by the Quartermaster General's Department. She mounted two 9-pounders, four 3-pounders, and two swivels; she was commanded by Peter Stark. She had served between Virginia and New York during the early part of the summer of 1781, arrived in New York on July 14, 1781, and may have returned to Virginia in time for the battle.[55]

MARY

The *Mary* was a schooner used as a dispatch boat operating between New York and Yorktown. She was evidently captured, and her owners were paid for her value, £360, though she seems to have been taken not at Yorktown but en route to New York. Cruising with the fleet under Admiral Graves off the Capes of the Chesapeake, Clinton received this information on October 25, 1781: "A Boat going from Lord Cornwallis to New York was taken but the Letters were in Cypher. That Captain Carey in a large Boat with 30 Oars he believes sailed on Friday morning. This Man originally belonged to the Lapwing Dispatch Boat & knew the Schooner to be the Mary as soon as he saw her."[56]

MARY ANN

The *Mary Ann* was a horse transport chartered by the Quartermaster General's Department for £93.12.0 per month. A brig of 144 tons, she was commanded by Alexander Morrison. She was reported in Virginia as of August 17, 1781, and it is presumed

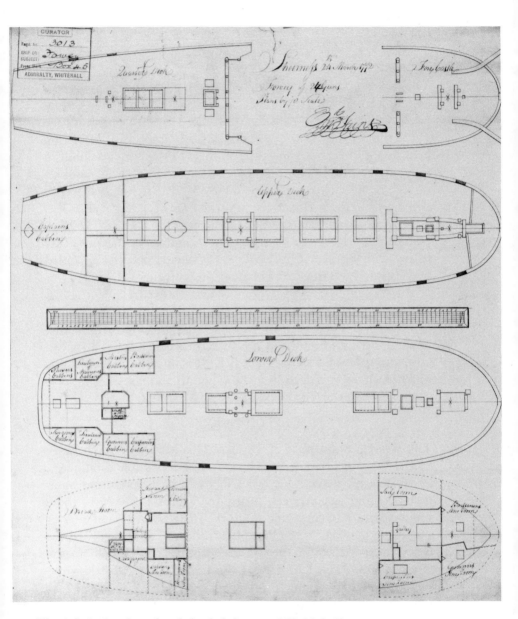

The Admiralty draught of the deck layout of H.M.S. Fowey. Unfortunately, hull lines of the Fowey do not survive, though her general type is documented. (Courtesy of the National Maritime Museum, London)

that she was still present at the time of the battle. Her fate is unknown.[57]

MERCURY

The *Mercury* was one of the ships detained by Leslie when the annual victualling fleet called at Portsmouth, en route from Cork, via Charleston, to New York. The fleet had called in June 1781, and on July 17 the *Mercury* and the *Ocean* were still being held in Virginia with their provisions. The *Mercury* was built in 1771, apparently in Newburyport, Massachusetts. She was ship-rigged, mounted six guns, was owned by J. Ritchie, was wood-sheathed and drew fifteen feet. At the time of her arrival in Virginia she had on board over 230,000 pounds of flour, 165,000 pounds of pork, 35,000 pounds of beef, and miscellaneous other stores. She was listed by Symonds as having been commanded by Arthur Ryeburn, and as having sunk during the battle.[58]

MOLLY

The *Molly*, a sloop of forty tons, was commanded by Samuel Hicks. She was the fifth of the vessels carrying paroled British officers to New York after the battle. It is uncertain whether she was British or American, but she evidently did not suffer appreciable damage during the battle.[59]

NANCY

The *Nancy*, commanded by Robert Hoaksley, appears to have been a sloop of thirty tons. There are three possible candidates, all of the same name. One was a dispatch boat, mounting six 3-pounders and two swivels, in use in August 1781. Also, there was a *Nancy*, of twenty-nine and three-fourths tons under charter and "carrying baggage &c. to the diff. posts." And finally, there was a sloop *Nancy*, of thirty tons, captured by Arnold in the affair at Osborne's Landing on the James River. She does not seem to have been sent to New York for sale. The *Nancy* was reported sunk in the battle.[60]

NEPTUNE

The *Neptune* was a store ship of 395 tons, commanded by John Atkinson. She had been built in Scarborough, England, in 1777, and was owned by W. Sutton. She was built with a single deck with open transverse beams below, drew sixteen feet and mounted four 6-pounders and three 4-pounders. She had sailed from Spithead soon after March 8, 1779. Though reported sunk during the battle, she was included by La Villebrune in the list of three-masters which were raised.[61]

NONSUCH

The *Nonsuch* was a small coasting schooner of about twenty tons, laden with tobacco and flour, which was captured in the Chesapeake Bay by the barge *Resolution*, apparently a privateer. She was taken into Portsmouth in July 1781, and eventually moved to Yorktown. She was sold there, complete with cargo. It is not clear to whom she was sold or whether she was present for the battle.[62]

NORTH BRITON

The *North Briton*, a private vessel of 208 tons, was under charter to William Chisholm at the time of the battle. He was evidently a loyalist and had chartered the vessel to carry a cargo from his Virginia plantation, Pettenweem. She had on board 50,000 feet of mahogany and 20 tons of Brazeletto wood, all of which, with the vessel, was taken over by the French at the end of the battle. Chisholm, having lost his vessel, bought a large schooner from Captain Dundas of the *Bonetta*, in which he sailed with other loyalists to Charleston. The *North Briton* was sold to American owners and fitted as a Letter of Marque under the name *Jolly Tar*. Mounting fourteen carriage guns, she was nevertheless recaptured by H.M.S. *Jason* on September 28, 1782, and taken into New York for condemnation.[63]

OCEAN

The *Ocean* was a ship-rigged victualler of 280 tons which was commanded by John Walker. She had been built in Ipswich in 1774, drew fifteen feet, mounted six 6-pounders, and was owned by T. Beswick. She was wood-sheathed in 1780 and sailed soon thereafter for America. She was one of the ships detained by Leslie when the annual victualling fleet called at Portsmouth, en route from Cork, via Charleston, to New York. On July 17 the

Ocean had on board almost 300,000 pounds of flour, over 122,000 pounds of pork, 35,000 pounds of beef, and miscellaneous other stores. Though she was reported sunk, she was among the three-masters which were raised by La Villebrune during the following year.[64]

PATRIOT

The *Patriot* was a pilot schooner in the service of the Virginia State Navy. Commodore James Barron, the younger, described her capture on April 8, 1781, in the James River:

> We saw the schooner Patriot in chase of the suspicious sloop, and as we supposed fast coming up with her. Here Capt. Starlins, (for so our African called himself,) allowed his patriotism to get the better of his judgment, and gave free utterance to the most extravagant expressions of joy—at the same time hopping about with uplifted and clapping hands,—in the hope, which indeed we all indulged, that we should soon see both vessels changing their course and going up the river, instead of down to the Roads. But now for the end . . . up jumped fifty Marines with their officers, who had hitherto not been seen; —and the capture of the Patriot was but the work of a minute. And what now was the dismay of our thunder-struck group, at this sudden disappointment of all our hopes. . . . The Patriot was afterwards taken round to York Town with the British fleet that attended Lord Cornwallis's army when he established his head quarters in that place, and when he afterwards surrendered to the combined armies, she fell into the hands of the French, according to the terms of the capitulation, and the last that we heard of her was that she was carried to Cape Francois, and there employed as a government packet.

There is a chance of confusion with regard to this vessel, since she was soon replaced by the Virginia forces with another of the same name.[65]

PEGGY

The sloop *Peggy* was sent out from Yorktown in early September 1781 under a passport from Captain Symonds to carry the slaves and property of certain residents of Yorktown to the Rappahan-

nock for safekeeping. It is not clear where she came from originally, but it is presumed that she was a captured local vessel. As
of October 12, 1781, she had not been permitted to return to
Yorktown, and her commander, William Hannah, filed a protest
with Governor Nelson. It is not known whether her return was
permitted or whether she survived the battle.[66]

PORTSMOUTH

The *Portsmouth* was a schooner hired as a transport from William
Malcolm, who received £204 for the period from July 1 to September 30, 1781. He was also granted £280, "more to him for the
value of the said Schooner expended as a fire vessel against the
french vessels at the Mouth of York Town River as by Certificate
of two Ship Masters and foreman of the Ship Yard appears."
Presumably, the *Portsmouth* was included in the raid of September 22, since those fire vessels fitted out after that date were
never used.[67]

PRESENT SUCCESSION

The *Present Succession* was chartered to the government as a troop
transport in January 1779 by her owner, John Reed. At 286 and
89/94 tons, she was built in 1772 at Whitby, was wood-sheathed
and drew fifteen feet. Ship-rigged, she mounted six guns. Notwithstanding a dispute over the rate at which she was hired, the
ship continued in service and was inspected at Portsmouth dock-
yard on December 28, 1780. She was declared refitted and ready
for service; on January 19, 1781, she embarked 172 men at Portsmouth, men who disembarked June 20, 1781, in Portsmouth,
Virginia. She also carried 190 men from Portsmouth to
Yorktown and must have been among the last to leave that town,
on August 20, 1781. She was commanded by William Chapman
and was reported sunk in the battle.[68]

PROVIDENCE

Two vessels named the *Providence* may have been at Yorktown.
The first, a transport of about 400 tons, was commanded by
Benjamin Huntley. Owned by G. Ware and chartered to the
government, she had been built in 1764 in Stockton, England.
Ship-rigged and wood-sheathed, she drew fifteen feet and

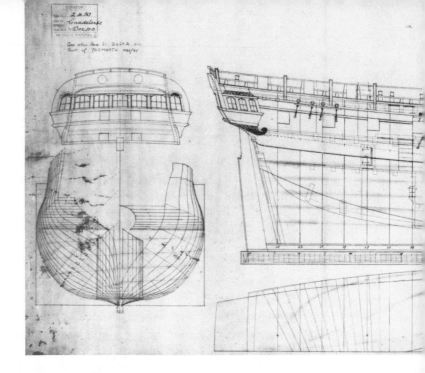

mounted two 4- and six 3-pounders. She had sailed in convoy with the *Roebuck* from New York in May 1781. She must have been speedy, since the *Roebuck's* log records on May 17, "At 7 fired 2 shot at the Providence to make her bear down." She was reported sunk in the battle. The second *Providence* was a schooner which Cornwallis's quartermaster general manned. From June 20 to August 26 her master was James Tait, and she had a crew of six seamen. He may well have returned to New York on board the *Richmond*, which sailed that date, since from then until October 19 her master was Alexander Murray, with no crew listed. Her fate is unknown.[69]

PROVIDENCE INCREASE

The *Providence Increase* was a ship-rigged vessel of 234 tons which had been built in Scarborough, England, in 1756. Notwithstanding her age, she received a high rating from Lloyd's, presumably because of repairs undertaken in 1776, 1778, and 1779. During her last repair she had been wood-sheathed; with a draft of fourteen feet, she mounted one 3- and five 4-pounders. She was commanded by Thomas Berryman, was in Portsmouth on June 30, 1781, and was reported sunk in the battle.[70]

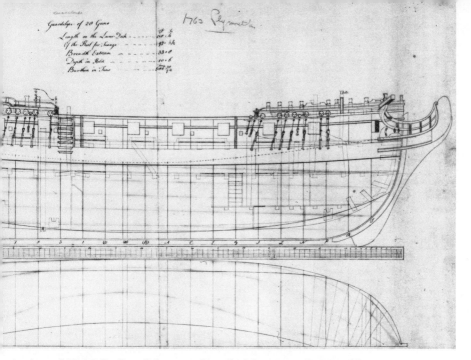

A *plan of H.M.S.* Guadaloupe, *launched in 1763. It was this vessel which the French labored so long to raise after the battle, with eventual success. (Courtesy of the National Maritime Museum, London)*

RACEHORSE

The *Racehorse* was a transport of 231 tons, commanded by Christopher Chisman, who was part owner with his father George and a Mr. Coombes. She is listed as built in France in 1775, and she may have been a captured French vessel that had been renamed. She was a snow, a variant of the brig, drawing fourteen feet and mounting eight 4-pounders; she had been wood-sheathed in 1779. During the move from Portsmouth to Yorktown, she carried baggage. She was reported sunk during the battle, and is not to be confused with the "Race Horse Schooner" mentioned in the dispatches of Lord Rodney in May 1782.[71]

RAMBLER

The *Rambler*, a brig attached to the Quartermaster General's Department, was listed in the records as mounting sixteen 6-pounders. Whether she had that many at the time of the battle is problematical. In a gale of December 26, 1780, while convoying Arnold to Portsmouth, the *Rambler* was forced to jettison some of her guns. Whether they were replaced is unknown, as is her fate in the battle; she is presumed to have been sunk.[72]

RANGER

The *Ranger* was chartered by the Quartermaster General's Department for £76.4.3 per month. A brig of 117¼ tons, she was used as a horse transport and was commanded by Michael Neal. She was reported in Virginia as of August 17, 1781, and it is presumed that she was still there at the time of the battle.[73]

ROBERT

The *Robert* was a chartered transport of 235 tons, commanded and partially owned by Jonathan Moore. She was launched in April 1777 at Whitehaven, England, and was built with a single deck with transverse beams for bracing below. She was snow-rigged, wood-sheathed, drew thirteen feet, mounted six 4-pounders, and was one of the few vessels at Yorktown to carry an A1 rating from Lloyd's. She carried provisions in the move from Portsmouth and was reported sunk in the battle.[74]

ROVER

The *Rover* was a victualler commanded by John Beveon and was reported sunk in the battle.[75]

SALLY

There were two vessels at Yorktown by the name of *Sally*. The first was a transport of about 330 tons, ship-rigged, which had been built in America in 1760. She had been lengthened and substantially rebuilt in 1777 and had undergone thorough repairs in the springs of 1779, 1780, and 1781, all in New York. She was a single-deck vessel with additional transverse bracing in the form of open beams below, was wood-sheathed, and drew fourteen feet. The ship mounted six 6-pounders, was commanded by Arthur Elliott, and was owned by John Liddell. This must have been a multipurpose vessel. As of April 9, 1778, she had been issued 184 beds, suggesting use as a troop transport. When Arnold sailed to Virginia in December 1780, he stated that the

"Sally, or Ordnance Ship, was very near foundering." She was reported sunk in the battle.[76]

The second *Sally* was a schooner of sixty tons hired by the deputy quartermaster of the army under Cornwallis, at the rate of £23 per month. She was seized at the end of the battle, and her owner was paid her full value, £280. She had been used to carry dispatches from Clinton to Cornwallis and had been trapped at Yorktown. Her master thought that he had a buyer for the vessel when, on October 16, the sails were taken by the Quartermaster General's Department for use as tents on shore. In consequence, the vessel was not able to escape and was captured when Yorktown fell.[77]

SELINA

The *Selina*, a brig of 221 tons, was a transport commanded by John Croskill. Carrying a crew of fourteen and mounting six guns, she drew thirteen feet and had a single deck with transverse beams below. She was wood-sheathed, and had been built of fir in 1777 in Finland; she carried an A1 rating from Lloyd's, unusual in the case of a foreign-built ship. On a voyage from Germany in May 1779 she had carried baggage amounting to twenty-one casks and five cases. She was last surveyed in Cork in 1779 before sailing to America. She was reported sunk in the battle.[78]

SHARP

The *Sharp* was a three-master of about 250 tons which was listed by La Villebrune as having been afloat after the battle. But she was still lacking sufficient sailors, sails, and cordage to be of use when Rochambeau was evacuating Virginia in 1782.[79]

SHIPWRIGHT

The *Shipwright* was a chartered transport of 301 tons, ship-rigged, which was commanded by Thomas Kaye. She had been built in 1774 at Hull, England, had been wood-sheathed in 1778, and mounted six 6- and six 4-pounders. She was owned by T. Wilton & Company and was reported burnt during the battle. Whether she was one of the fire ships of September 22 or one of the ships that burned with the *Charon* is unknown.[80]

SPITFIRE

The *Spitfire*, a brig attached to the Quartermaster General's Department, mounted eight 12-pounders and four 6-pounders. She was commanded by Richard Pindar and her fate in the battle is unknown. It seems possible that she was scuttled, since her captain was acting for the land forces on October 16. The master of the *Sally* reported: "Richard Pindar Commander of the Brigantine Spitfire employed in the Quarter Master General's Department in an arbitrary and forcible manner without any authority took from the said Schooner Sally her Mainsail, Foresail, Jibb and Square Sail." The sails were used ashore for tents for the sick and wounded.[81]

SUCCESS INCREASE

The *Success Increase* was a brig of about 300 tons, commanded by John Saunderson. Built at Whitby in 1772, she was owned by a Mr. Cockerill; she drew fifteen feet and mounted six 4-pounders. The vessel was reported sunk during the battle; it is not clear whether she is the same vessel that was listed by La Villebrune as a three-master named the *Success*, which was raised. The difference in name and rig, as well as tonnage, make it unlikely.[82]

SUSANNAH

The *Susannah* is apparently the same vessel as the *Suzanne*, a private vessel which originally mounted at least fourteen 4-pounders. A brief history of the vessel is related by Boulainvilliers, who took command of her after the battle: "I have the honor to report to you that the Count de Grasse has agreed in granting me, after the taking of York, the command of the brig Suzanne, mounting sixteen cannons of four. This vessel was scuttled by the English the day of the capitulation but happily she sustained very little damage and I had her afloat again several days later." This vessel was one of the mainstays in the small fleet of prizes which attempted to protect the navigation of the Chesapeake after the battle.[83]

SWIFT

The *Swift* was a schooner mounting two 4-pounders and four swivels. She was owned by John Dixon and was commanded in August 1781 by James Ridley. Her hire was paid through September 30, 1781, but, unlike other vessels of her type, there is no indication of a payment for the value of the vessel due to loss. Since she was in use as a dispatch vessel, it seems possible that she may have made good her escape from Yorktown. She is not to be confused with the *Swift* sloop of war that helped convoy Arnold in December 1781 and remained in the Chesapeake until August. On her voyage back to New York she proved so leaky that the crew had to bail at the hatches the entire trip, and she was condemned as unfit for service in September 1781.[84]

TARTAR

The *Tartar*, in all likelihood, was the same vessel as the *Tarleton*. Little is known about her, and it is tempting to connect her with the vessel of the same name owned by the Virginia State Navy. That vessel was in the Chickahominy state shipyard, stripped down for sale, at the time of Arnold's raid there, in late April 1781. There is an earlier reference to a *Tartar*, however: "The Ordnance Ship Tartar shall cover the left Flank [of the Portsmouth fortifications] as you desire with Ten nine pounders." In consequence, it seems likely that there was a *Tartar* in Virginia not associated with the state navy. If this was the same vessel as the *Tarleton*, she was fitted out by La Villebrune with twelve 4-pounders and used in the defense of the Chesapeake after the battle.[85]

THREE SISTERS

The *Three Sisters* was a small coasting schooner of about twenty tons, laden with tobacco and flour, which was captured in the Chesapeake Bay by the barge *Resolution*, apparently a privateer. She was taken into Portsmouth in July 1781, and eventually moved to Yorktown. Being unfit for sea and therefore unable to reach New York, she was sold in Yorktown. Having been captured and sold with the *Nonsuch*, the two vessels realized £516 together. It is not clear to whom she was sold or whether she was present for the battle.[86]

TWO BROTHERS

The *Two Brothers* was a ship-rigged troop transport of 359 tons, chartered to the government by Francis Hall. She had been built at Whitby in 1774, lengthened in 1776, and wood-sheathed at that time. Carrying six 4-pounders, she drew sixteen feet. She had been fitted with 189 beds for the accommodation of troops. Her commander, Magnus Mariners, had the most fitting name of the entire campaign. Though she was reported as sunk in the battle, the *Two Brothers* was one of the ships sent to Europe with English sailors who were to be exchanged. She was commanded on that voyage by Captain Symonds, formerly of the *Charon*. Following her arrival in England, she was sent on to France with exchanged French prisoners. She went ashore as she left Plymouth Harbor, however, and was presumed lost.[87]

VULCAN

H.M.S. *Vulcan*, 291 tons, was purchased by the Royal Navy in 1777, and it has been suggested she was formerly the *Lord Camden*, built in Philadelphia in 1775. A fire ship, she mounted eight 6-pounders, was ninety feet, ten inches long on her gun deck, and seventy-two feet on her keel. With a beam of twenty-seven feet, six and three-fourths inches, she drew twelve feet, three and one-half inches and carried forty-five men.[88] She was commanded during the battle by Capt. George Palmer.

The *Vulcan* was the main fire ship sent to attack the French blockade on September 22, 1781. She was accompanied by four converted sloops and schooners whose identities have not been clearly established. A strong wind was blowing downriver at the time of the attack, and a current running in addition. Fired too early, the fire ships were avoided by the French and drifted harmlessly by. Although two of the French ships of the line were run aground, they sustained no damage, and the attack was a failure. The attacking ships were said to be visible for the whole of the next day as they burned themselves out; whether anything of consequence remains of the *Vulcan* is questionable. It must be assumed that the ship was substantially stripped before she was dispatched on her incendiary duty, and that the guns would certainly have been removed. In Captain Palmer's formal statement at his court martial, he reported that having set fire to his ship, "the Two French Line Battle Ships ran on shore as did the Vulcan in Flames close to them." Presumably whatever remains of the vessel is to be found in about twelve feet of water near the mouth of the York River.[89]

Fire ship duty was hazardous in the extreme, and special

incentives were introduced to encourage the crew to undertake
these missions. Cash bonuses of considerable size were to be paid
to the captain and crew of a fire ship, in the event they succeeded
in destroying an enemy ship, and in proportion to the size of that
ship. They were also offered priority reassignment to other
ships, so that their careers would not be checked. Similar incentives were offered to the masters and crews of private vessels
used for this service, and the full value of any vessel thus con-
sumed was promised to its owners. A description survives of the
outfitting of a group of temporary fire ships, and the provisions
must have been similar on a formally designated fire ship:

> *With Ruff Ordinary Deal Inclosed the hatchways and built
> bulkheads and battend seams to Inclose the fire room, fire spouts
> made in the form of V fitted 3 ft. 4 in. under the Deck one Tier
> of each side, with cross spouts and paid with Pitch and Tarr . . .
> Tarr Barrells and faggotts dipt placd on board of them also Read
> made into Bundles and Dipt in Tar lasht in the fire spouts,
> Strowed over with brimston, the under side of the Deck and Side
> of the Vessells not paid, fitted fire Iron to the Lower Yards, Iron
> Barrs with Locks to the fire scuttles and Fire Trunks &
> hatchways.*

One can well imagine the devastating effect of a vessel thus
equipped with her rigging slung in iron to avoid burning down,
and her hatches barred and locked so that the fire couldn't be
extinguished once lit.[90]

A profile view and deck plan of the *Vulcan* survive in the
National Maritime Museum, Greenwich, England.

WORTLEY

The *Wortley* was one of four cartel vessels sent from Charleston
to exchange prisoners at Jamestown. The exchange did not take
place, and the ships were added to the fleet under Cornwallis for
the move from Portsmouth to Yorktown. The *Wortley* was captured by the French fleet under de Grasse on August 30, 1781,
before she could reach Yorktown. Cornwallis protested this
action and requested the return of the ship and the release of the
crew. The vessel was not returned, as both Lafayette and de
Grasse pointed out irregularities in her papers and the cargo of
the vessel.[91]

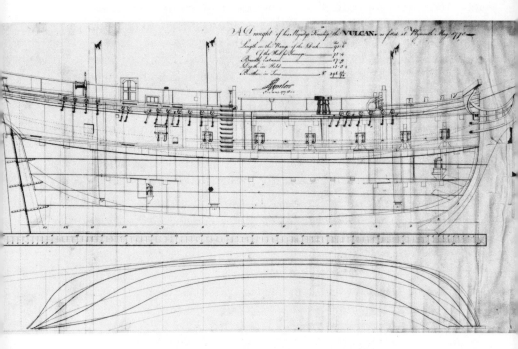

Plans of H.M.S. Vulcan, *the fireship lost on September 22, 1781. Note the deck plan which shows the configuration of the fire spouts fitted to carry combustibles and spread fire out the ports. (Courtesy of the National Maritime Museum, London)*

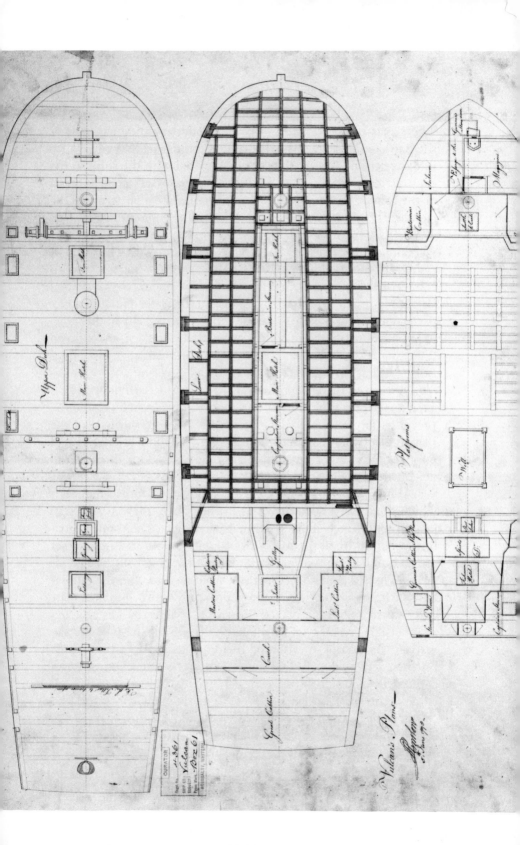

UNNAMED SMALL CRAFT

There was unquestionably a large assemblage of small craft at the Battle of Yorktown. Boats present in the town were swept up into the action, as were the boats associated with the ships in the captive fleet, and the boats built especially for service in support of the army. There is little documentation on small craft of the eighteenth century, and records concerning the number or type of vessels which were at Yorktown do not appear to have survived in any quantity. For the most part, such boats were sufficiently inconsequential that they did not merit listing on the official records. There are mentions in the documents of "Boats and Batteaux," especially used by the Quartermaster General's Department, "Troop Boats," and "Horse Boats." In addition, a number of boats were taken from the local populace, including a "petit augre," which was a form of dugout canoe, a "Schooner Boat," and a "30 hogshead Flat with sail covering anchor & cable." What the British could not use, they apparently destroyed, as suggested by the claim of one John Robinson, who lost "One very fine large six Oared Cypress petty Auger burned by the British troops under the command of Col. Dundass, after I had put her under Guard two miles from the River. One three Oared do. burned by do."[92]

While we can only hypothesize about most of the small craft which must have been involved in the battle, there is one segment about which more is known. Benedict Arnold, after analyzing the nature of the war he was going to fight in Virginia, set out to build a group of barges to use on the rivers of the Chesapeake. He had experienced considerable success with the gundalows he had built on Lake Champlain years before, and he apparently saw a role to be played by such a boat here. The shifting channels and numerous shoals of the rivers on the Chesapeake made it hazardous to attempt their navigation in naval ships. Further, it was both impractical and uneconomical to tie up a contingent of naval ships to support what would eventually become a sort of local police force. If permanent control of the countryside was to be achieved, it would require a resident, highly mobile force, able to move quickly to counter any rebel activity. The extensive rivers of the area provided a virtual highway system to effect this program, with the right boats. In consequence, Arnold wrote to Clinton concerning "Light Boats (of which I propose to build Fifty)." He gave further details concerning the plan: "The Boats which I propose to build will carry about eighty men, row with Twenty four, draw 12 inches water, and move up and down any of their Rivers with ease, one hundred miles in twenty four hours; they will also carry Cavalry horses, Artillery and provisions."[93] He proposed to utilize the carpenters and laborers who were available locally, and apparently received authorization from Clinton to go ahead. By February 25 he had twelve boats that would be finished shortly, if he received the nails which he had requested from New York. It seems that he was able to complete at least twenty-four before he returned to New York, with ten more still under construction. Clinton, in requesting the return of men and material to New York in June 1781, asked Cornwallis to forward him "the 24 Boats built by General Arnold. . . . it is probable the ten which I understand are now building in Chesapeak will be sufficient for your Lordship's Purposes." Later he again requested the twenty-four boats, and referred to certain of them which had "platforms, to have Cannon mounted in them, and compleatly fitted."[94]

Regardless of how many of the boats Arnold succeeded in building, they may not have proved as successful as he had hoped. Having taken over the force, General Leslie wrote to Cornwallis from Portsmouth on June 10, 1781, "Six of the new Boats are sent up the River. I hope they may answer, I doubt it much myself, if ever they Ground, they must get out of order, the Expence of building them is very great." Whether this refers to the original group of boats built or the later ones which were under construction is not clear. In any event, not all the boats available to Cornwallis were faulty, as became evident when he embarked his troops for the move to Yorktown: "Most of the new boats here are reported to me to be unserviceable. I have therefore thought it necessary to order up six of those boats which are with the Fleet, in order to carry the 80th regt. to Glocester. As that regt. will employ eight boats, I shall be much obliged to you if you will please to order fifty six Seamen to man them, at the rate of seven to each boat." It is apparent that a number of the boats were moved to Yorktown, for on October 10 eighteen barges were assembled to carry troops upstream, but were dispersed by fire from the allied cannon mounted on the Gloucester Point side. One of the boats was captured and was found to mount a brass 4-pounder field piece. When Cornwallis eventually tried to cross to the Gloucester side on October 16, with only sixteen boats, he had to attempt the move in three waves. It must be presumed that many of the boats at Yorktown had fallen victim to the allied cannonade.[95]

It is not entirely clear what the barges built by Arnold looked like. There is a surviving sketch and some dimensions, apparently in his hand, dated May 3, 1776, which outlines his concept for the boats built on Lake Champlain. The length of the keel was forty-five (possibly forty-eight) feet, beam sixteen feet, and draft three feet six inches. He specified a deadrise of four inches, which suggests that he did not intend to build a flat-bottomed boat such as eventually resulted. Given the ease of flat-bottomed construction, and the success which he had experienced with the gundalows like the *Philadelphia*, it seems not unreasonable that he might have adopted that form in his later boats in Virginia. There was a tradition of constructing barges of approximately these dimensions in the Chesapeake. In August 1781 a private group offered to sell a barge to the state of Maryland; its dimensions were fifty-four feet on the keel, fourteen feet beam, and three feet draft. If Cornwallis and Leslie had reservations about the boats which Arnold had constructed, Arnold himself harbored no such doubts. Upon his arrival in New York in August 1781, he immediately set to work to construct more and even proposed to Clinton that some of the skilled builders from the Chesapeake be brought to work on the project. What effect these may have had on the fleet's operations at New York is suggested by a report filed with the Navy Board in February 1782, by the agent for transports in New York: "Captain Tonkin has represented the Flat Boats are unfit for Service & not worth repairing and that the Batteaux built by the Quarter Master General answer the purposes wanted better and desire he will please to consult with the Commander in Chief of the Troops at New York relative to the future use of the Flat Boats and if they are not wanted or worth repairing that he will order them to be broke up, that the materials may be applied to such works in the

Yard as they may be fit for." We can only wish that we had a clearer idea of the design characteristics of these boats.[96]

There is little likelihood that it will be possible to determine with any certainty the exact number of small craft Cornwallis had or the number that survived the battle. Certainly, as outlined in chapter 6, there was a very real shortage of boats following the battle. In all probability many of the boats present were destroyed, either intentionally or by accident. Some may have been scuttled and not salvaged, and may be preserved under the bottom of the York River today. Unfortunately, small craft generally have no ballast to push them into the protective mud, and consequently are more likely to be destroyed by worms and current. Further, if they are present, they do not lend themselves to location with the remote-sensing devices presently available. They are not massive enough to leave a mound on the bottom, and they probably carried insufficient iron to be noted on the magnetometer readings. Barring a chance discovery, then, it is doubtful that the York River will yield up a hull of the caliber of the *Philadelphia*.

Notes
Bibliographical Essay
Bibliography
Index

Notes

~~~~~~~~~~

Preface
[1]George Washington to Noah Webster, 31 July 1788, "Documents Relating to the Siege of Yorktown, 1778–1788," J. Pierpont Morgan Library, New York City.

Chapter 1
[1]George Germain to Sir Henry Clinton, 7 March 1781, Benjamin Franklin Stevens, ed., *The Campaign in Virginia, 1781*, 2 vols. (London: B. F. Stevens, 1888), 1:335.

[2]John C. Fitzpatrick, ed., *The Diaries of George Washington, 1748–1799*, 4 vols. (Boston: Houghton Mifflin, 1925, 2:208.

[3]This plan is laid out in an untitled paper written by William Knox, undersecretary of state for America, circa 1778, William Knox Papers, 9, no. 21, William L. Clements Library, Univ. of Michigan, Ann Arbor.

[4]Germain to Clinton, 8 March 1778, CO 5/95, folios 35–49. Public Record Office.

[5]Richard Oswald, "General Observations Relative to the Present State of the War, London, August 9, 1779," folio 60, and "Thoughts on the War between Great Britain & America wrote in Septr. & October, 1776 and Thoughts on same Subject wrote Feby., 1778," Clements Library, Univ. of Mich., Ann Arbor.

[6]Oswald, "Observations," folios 63–64.

[7]"Observations on the Trade of America & Its Effects in the Present Rebellion," May 1779, George Germain papers, Clements Library, Univ. of Mich., Ann Arbor.

[8]Clinton to William Phillips, 11 April 1781, Letterbook, "Correspondence with Phillips, March 10–April 30, 1781," Sir Henry Clinton Papers, Clements Library, Univ. of Mich., Ann Arbor.

[9]Germain to Clinton, 27 September 1779, Germain Papers.

[10]Clinton to Marriot Arbuthnot, 5 July 1780, CO 5/100, folio 293, P.R.O.

[11]George Brydges Rodney to Germain, 22 December 1780, Germain Papers.

[12]Clinton to Arbuthnot, 26 August 1780, CO 5/100, folio 296, P.R.O.

[13]Germain to Clinton, 4 October 1780, CO 5/100, folios 249–55, P.R.O.

[14]Arbuthnot to George Gayton, 2 September 1780, ADM 1/1839, "Gayton," P.R.O.

[15]Clinton to Lord Cornwallis, 20 September 1780, Clinton Papers.

[16]Clinton to Alexander Leslie, 12 October 1780, Clinton Papers.

[17]Lord Rawdon to Leslie, 24 and 31 October 1780, Clinton Papers.

[18]Gayton to Philip Stephens, 31 December 1780, ADM 1/1839, "Gayton," P.R.O.

[19]Clinton to Leslie, 12 November 1780, Clinton Papers.

[20]Leslie to Clinton, 19 November 1780, Clinton Papers.

[21]Germain to Clinton, 3 January 1781, 30/55, folio 3266 (3), P.R.O.

[22]Germain to Knox, 29 December 1780, Knox Papers.

[23]Germain to Knox, 1 January 1781, Knox Papers.

[24]Germain to Clinton, 3 January 1781, 30/55, folio 3266 (5), P.R.O.

[25]Clinton to Benedict Arnold, 14 December 1780, 30/55, folio 3204, P.R.O.

[26]Arnold to Clinton, 21 January 1781, Letterbook, "Clinton/Arnold Correspondence," folio 4, Clinton Papers.

[27]Arnold to Clinton, 23 January 1781, Clinton Papers.

[28]Further details on this group of boats are provided in the Catalogue of Ships under the heading "Unnamed Small Craft."

[29]Arbuthnot to Germain, 19 December 1780, Germain Papers.

[30]Chevalier Destouches to unknown, 31 March 1781, Fr. N. A. Margry 9420, folios 75–76, Bibliothèque Nationale, Paris.

[31]Hayes to Mellish, 18 March 1781, Charles Mellish of Hodstock Papers, Department of Manuscripts, MSS 171–111, Nottingham University, Nottingham, England.

[32]Clinton to Arnold, 18 February 1781, Letterbook, "Clinton/Arnold Correspondence," folio 33, Clinton Papers.

[33]Arnold to Clinton, 8 March 1781, Letterbook, "Arnold/Clinton Correspondence," folio 36, Clinton Papers.

[34]Arnold to Clinton, 12 March 1781, Letterbook, "Arnold/Clinton Correspondence," folio 39, Clinton Papers.

[35]Arbuthnot to Stephens, 20 March 1781, ADM 1/486, folios 575–86, P.R.O.

[36]Clinton to Phillips, 14 March 1781, Stevens, *Campaign in Virginia*, 1:352.

[37]Germain to Clinton, 2 May, 1781, ibid., p. 464.

Chapter 2

[1]Marriot Arbuthnot to Philip Stephens, 30 March 1781, ADM 1/486, folios 625–26, Public Record Office.

[2]Sir Henry Clinton to William Phillips, 10 March 1781, Benjamin Franklin Stevens, ed. *The Campaign in Virginia, 1781,* 2 vols. (London: B. F. Stevens, 1888) 1:347–50.

[3]"Substance of several Conversations had with Major General Phillips on the subject of operations in the Chesapeak before his enbarkation on his Expedition thither, 26 April 1781," Lord Shelburn papers, 68, folios 63–67, William L. Clements Library, Univ. of Michigan, Ann Arbor.

[4]Benedict Arnold to Clinton, 12 May 1781, Sir Henry Clinton Papers, Clements Library, Univ. of Mich., Ann Arbor.

[5]Phillips to Clinton, 15 April 1781, Letterbook, "Correspondence with Phillips, March 10–April 30, 1781," folio 65, Clinton Papers.

[6]Phillips to Clinton, 29 March 1781, Clinton to Phillips, 5 April 1781, Letterbook, "Correspondence with Phillips, March 10–April 30, 1781," folios 17, 59, Clinton Papers.

[7]Clinton to George Germain, 30 April 1781, Stevens, *Campaign in Virginia,* 1:447.

[8]"Deposition of Benedict Arnold, 10 November 1781," HCA 32/442, bundle B, Prize Papers for *Renown,* P.R.O.

[9]Alexander Leslie to Clinton, 29 May 1781, Clinton Papers.

[10]Clinton to Lord Cornwallis, 1 June 1780, 30/11/2, folios 68–73, P.R.O.

[11]Clinton to Cornwallis, 6 November 1780, 30/11/4, folios 35–38, P.R.O.

[12]Cornwallis to Clinton, 10 April 1781, Clinton Papers.

[13]Ibid.

[14]Clinton to Cornwallis, 13 April 1781, 30/55, folio 3446, P.R.O.

[15]Phillips to Cornwallis, 6 May 1781, Clinton Papers.

[16]Marquis de Lafayette to George Washington, 4 July 1781, Lloyd W. Smith Collection, no. 166, Morristown National Historical Park, Morristown, N.J.

[17]Lafayette to Thomas Jefferson, 31 May 1781, CO 5/102, folio 521, P.R.O.

[18]Clinton to Germain, 5 April 1781, 30/55, folio 3436, P.R.O.

[19]Stephens to Arbuthnot, 5 April 1781, Main Papers, 4 March 1782, House of Lords Record Office, London.

[20]Noah Webster to Washington, 14 July 1788, "Documents relating to the Siege of Yorktown, 1778–1788," J. Pierpont Morgan Library, New York City.

[21]Washington to Webster, 31 July 1788, "Documents relating to the Siege of Yorktown, 1778–1788."

[22]Clinton to Germain, 18 May 1781, 30/55, folio 3517, P.R.O.

[23]Cornwallis to Clinton, 26 May 1781, CO 5/102, folio 329, P.R.O.

[24]Clinton to Cornwallis, 8 June 1781, Clinton Papers.

[25]"Minutes of a Conversation," 17 June 1781, Letterbook, "Correspon-

dence with Admirals," folio 207, Clinton Papers.

[26]Clinton to Cornwallis, 19 June 1781, Stevens, *Campaign in Virginia*, 2:27.

[27]Cornwallis to Clinton, 30 June 1781, Clinton Papers.

[28]Germain to Clinton, 2 May 1781, Clinton Papers.

[29]Cornwallis to Leslie, 20 July 1781, 30/11/88, folio 40, P.R.O.

Chapter 3

[1]Lord Cornwallis to Sir Henry Clinton, 27 July 1781, Benjamin Franklin Stevens, ed., *The Campaign in Virginia, 1781*, 2 vols. (London: B. F. Stevens, 1888), 2:104.

[2]Thomas Graves to Cornwallis, 12 July 1781, 30/11/88, folio 51, Public Record Office.

[3]Lt. Alexander Sutherland, Engineer's Report on Old Point Comfort, 25 July 1781, Main Papers, 18 February 1782, House of Lords Record Office, London.

[4]Cornwallis to Clinton, 27 July 1781, Stevens, *Campaign in Virginia*, 2:107.

[5]Cornwallis to Charles Hudson, 27 July 1781, 30/11/88, folio 54, P.R.O.

[6]Hudson to Graves, 27 July 1781, ADM 1/489, folio 411, P.R.O.

[7]Marquis de Lafayette to Nathanael Greene, 31 July 1781, "Documents Relating to the Siege of Yorktown, 1778–1788," J. Pierpont Morgan Library, New York City.

[8]Cornwallis to Clinton, 12 August 1781, Sir Henry Clinton Papers, William L. Clements Library, Univ. of Michigan, Ann Arbor.

[9]Johann Ewald, *Diary of the American War: A Hessian Journal*, trans. and ed. Joseph P. Tustin (New Haven: Yale Univ. Press, 1979), pp. 319–20.

[10]Ibid.

[11]Unknown to Colonel James Innes, 27 June 1781, John Page Papers, Duke University Library, Durham, N.C.

[12]Lafayette to George Washington, 6 August 1781, *Memoirs, Correspondence and Manuscripts of General Lafayette, Published by His Family* (London: Saunders and Otley, 1837), p. 425.

[13]Lafayette to Washington, 21 August 1781, ibid., p. 427.

[14]Hudson to Graves, 12 August 1781, ADM 1/489, folio 413, P.R.O.

[15]Charles O'Hara to Cornwallis, 5 August 1781, 30/11/70, folio 12, P.R.O.

[16]O'Hara to Cornwallis, 11 August 1781, 30/11/70, folio 18, P.R.O.

[17]Josiah Parker to Greene, 19 August 1781, "Documents Relating to the Siege of Yorktown, 1778–1788."

[18]Graves to Philip Stephens, Secretary to the Admiralty, 20 August 1781, ADM 1/489, folios 409–10, P.R.O.

[19]Ibid. An extended discussion of the causes and ramifications of this problem may be found in Robert Greenhalgh Albion, *Forests and Sea Power: The*

Timber Problem of the Royal Navy, 1652–1862 (Cambridge, Mass.: Harvard Univ. Press, 1926).

[20]"Disposition of H. M. Ships under Admiral Arbuthnot, 12 June 1781," Main Papers, 1 March 1782, no. 29, House of Lords Record Office.

[21]Affidavit of Protest filed by John Buchanan, master of the *Goodrich*, 1 November 1781, HCA 42/134, P.R.O.

[22]Cornwallis to Nisbet Balfour, 27 August 1781, 30/11/89, folio 25, P.R.O.

[23]Thomas Symonds to Graves, 31 August 1781, ADM 1/491, folio 241, P.R.O.

[24]Ibid.

[25]Ewald, *Diary of the American War*, p. 325.

[26]J. G. Shea, ed., *The Operations of the French Fleet under the Count de Grasse in 1781–2, as Described in Two Contemporaneous Journals* (New York: Bradford Club, 1864), p. 66.

[27]Jonathan Trumbull, "Journal at Yorktown," 19 September 1781, Fordham University Library, New York City.

Chapter 4

[1]Sir Henry Clinton to George Germain, 12 September 1781, 30/55, folio 3778 (2), Public Record Office.

[2]Thomas Graves to Philip Stephens, 30 August 1781, French Ensor Chadwick, ed., *The Graves Papers and Other Documents Relating to the Naval Operations of the Yorktown Campaign, July to October, 1781* (New York: Naval History Society, 1916), p. 52.

[3]Clinton to Graves, 2 September 1781, Letterbook no. 3, "Correspondence with Admirals," folio 257, Sir Henry Clinton Papers, William L. Clements Library, Univ. Of Michigan, Ann Arbor.

[4]Graves to Clinton, 9 September 1781, Clinton Papers.

[5]Clinton to Graves, 8 September 1781, Letterbook no. 3, "Correspondence with Admirals," folio 259, Clinton Papers.

[6]Order for and transcript of court martial, ADM 1/5319, folios 517–22, P.R.O.

[7]Graves to Clinton, 15 September 1781, Clinton Papers.

[8]"Minutes of a Council of War held at Head Quarters N. York 14th Septr. 1781," Clinton Papers.

[9]"Order Books, Headquarters, New York," 19 September 1781, Clinton Papers.

[10]Oliver De Lancey to Major Bruen, 3 September 1781, 30/55, folio 3761 (2), Bruen to De Lancey, 3 September 1781, 30/55, folio 3762 (1), P.R.O.

[11]Clinton to Germain, 12 September 1781, 30/55, folio 3778 (4), P.R.O.

[12]"Minutes of a Council of War held at Head Quarters New York, Sept. 17, 1781," Clinton Papers.

[13]Marquis de Lafayette to Allen Jones, 27 August 1781, Allen Jones Letters, Southern Historical Collection, University of North Carolina, Chapel Hill.

[14]James McHenry to Nathanael Greene, 11 September 1781, "Documents Relating to the Siege of Yorktown, 1778–1788," J. Pierpont Morgan Library, New York City.

[15]Lord Cornwallis to Clinton, 16 September 1781, Benjamin Franklin Stevens, ed., *The Campaign in Virginia, 1781*, 2 vols. (London: B. F. Stevens, 1888), 2:157.

[16]John Knox Laughton, ed., *Journal of Rear-Admiral Bartholomew James, 1752–1828* (London: Navy Records Society, 1896), p. 114.

[17]George Washington to Comte de Grasse, 26 September 1781, John C. Fitzpatrick, ed., *The Writings of George Washington from the Original Manuscript Sources, 1745–1799*, 39 vols. (Washington, D.C.: Government Printing Office, 1931–44), 23:136.

[18]"Précis de la campagne de l'armée navalle, aux ordres du Cte. de Grasse," Castellane Family Manuscripts, cahier 5, Clements Library, Univ. of Mich., Ann Arbor.

[19]"General Richard Butler's Journal of the Siege of Yorktown," *Historical Magazine* 8 (1864):104.

[20]"The Doehla Journal, 1781," *William & Mary Quarterly*, 2d ser. 22 (1942):244.

[21]Thomas Symonds to Graves, 8 September 1781, ADM 1/489, folios 454–55, P.R.O.

[22]Ibid.

[23]Symonds to Cornwallis, 29 August 1781, 30/11/6, folio 369, Cornwallis to Symonds, 29 August 1781, 30/11/89, folio 33, P.R.O.

[24]Cornwallis to Thomas Nelson, Jr., 26 September 1781, "Documents Relating to the Siege of Yorktown, 1778–1788."

[25]St. George Tucker, "Diary of the Siege of Yorktown," *William & Mary Quarterly*, 3d ser. 5 (1948):382.

[26]Johann Ewald, *Diary of the American War: A Hessian Journal*, trans. and ed. Joseph P. Tustin (New Haven: Yale Univ. Press, 1979), p. 327.

[27]"Relation of a Commander of a boat taken coming out of the River York," Washington Papers 185, folio 107, Manuscript Division, Library of Congress.

[28]Symonds to Graves, 29 September 1781, Clinton Papers.

[29]Laughton, *Journal of Rear-Admiral Bartholomew James*, p. 117.

[30]Transcript of court martial, ADM 1/5320, folio 278, P.R.O.

[31]Ibid, folio 280.

[32]Symonds to Graves, 29 September 1781 and 4 October 1781, Clinton Papers.

Chapter 5

[1]Thomas Graves to Sir Henry Clinton, 21 September 1781, Letterbook no. 3, "Correspondence with Admirals," folio 269, Sir Henry Clinton Papers, William L. Clements Library, Univ. of Michigan, Ann Arbor.

[2]Edmund Affleck to Board of Admiralty, 14 September 1781, ADM 1/491, folio 247, Public Record Office.

[3]Andrew Snape Hamond to A. J. Douglas, 14 October 1781, Hamond Papers, Letterbook 7, folio 33, University of Virginia Library, Charlottesville.

[4]"Some thoughts on our present situation, September 23, 1781," Newcastle Papers, Department of Manuscripts, Nottingham University, Nottingham, England.

[5]Damer to George Germain, 27 September 1781, George Germain Papers, Clements Library, Univ. Of Mich., Ann Arbor.

[6]Journal of Captain John Peebles, 5 October 1781, Cunninghame of Thornton Papers, 492/12, Scottish Record Office, Edinburgh.

[7]Ibid., 16 October 1781, Cunninghame of Thornton Papers, 492/13, S.R.O.

[8]Samuel Hood to George Jackson, 14 October 1781, French Ensor Chadwick, ed., *The Graves Papers and Other Documents Relating to the Naval Operations of the Yorktown Campaign, July to October, 1781* (New York: Naval History Society, 1916), p. 117.

[9]Order books, Head Quarters, New York, 10 October 1781, Clinton Papers.

[10]Graves to Philip Stephens, 19 October 1781, Main Papers, 25 February 1782, House of Lords Record Office, London.

[11]Journal of Captain John Peebles, 18 October 1781, Cunninghame of Thornton Papers, 492/13, S.R.O.

[12]Clinton to Marriot Arbuthnot, 28 June 1781, Letterbook no. 3, "Correspondence with Admirals," folio 214, Clinton Papers.

[13]Clinton to Lord Cornwallis, 14 October 1781, Benjamin Franklin Stevens, ed., *The Campaign in Virginia, 1781*, 2 vols. (London: B. F. Stevens, 1888), 2:185.

[14]Clinton to unknown, 19 October 1781, Lord Shelburn Papers, 67, folios 167–70, Clements Library, Univ. of Mich., Ann Arbor.

[15]Transcript of Court Martial, ADM 1/5319, folios 508–10, P.R.O.

[16]Ibid.

[17]Ibid.

[18]James Thacher, *A Military Journal during the American Revolutionary War, from 1775 to 1783* (Boston: Cottons & Barnard, 1827), p. 283.

[19]"The Doehla Journal, 1781, *"William & Mary Quarterly*, 2d ser. 22 (1942):251.

[20]Jonathan Trumbull, "Journal at Yorktown," 28 September 1781, Fordham University Library, New York City.

[21]Thomas Nelson, Jr. to Buller Claiborne, 25 September 1781, William P. Palmer, ed., *Calendar of Virginia State Papers and Other Manuscripts Preserved in the Capitol at Richmond*, 11 vols. (Richmond: N.p., 1875–93), 2:491.

[22]George Weedon to George Washington, 3 October 1781, General George Weedon Papers, Ann Mary Brown Library, Brown University, Providence.

[23]Henri Doniol, *Histoire De La Participation De La France A L'Establissement Des Etats-Unis D'Ameriques: Correspondance Diplomatique et Documents*, 5 vols. (Paris: Imprimerie National, 1886–99), 5:557.

[24]Comte de Grasse to Comte de Rochambeau, 5 October 1781, transcript in Herbert H. Vreeland Collection, Swem Library, College of William and Mary, Williamsburg, Va.

[25]Weedon to Washington, 13 October 1781, Washington Papers, 185, folio 121, Manuscript Division, Library of Congress.

[26]"Précis des Evenements qui ont précédé et suivi la jonction de l'Escadre de M. le Cte. de Barras avec cette de M. le Cte. de Grasse dans la baye de Chesapeak en Virginie le 11 7bre, 1781," Fr. N. A., Margry 9420, folios 153, 154, Bibliothèque Nationale, Paris.

[27]Master's Log, H.M.S. *Fowey*, January 1 to October 17, 1781, ADM 52/1748, P.R.O.

[28]Claims for Schooner *Sally*, A. O. 13/5, folder 93, P.R.O.

[29]Johann Ewald, *Diary of the American War: A Hessian Journal*, trans. and ed. Joseph P. Tustin (New Haven: Yale Univ. Press, 1979), p. 336.

[30]Weedon to Washington, 29 September 1781, Weedon Papers.

[31]Circular letter from Weedon, 12 October 1781, Weedon Papers.

[32]Cornwallis to Clinton, 20 October 1781, Clinton Papers.

[33]Banastre Tarleton, *A History of the Campaigns of 1780 and 1781, in the Southern Provinces of North America* (London: T. Cadell, 1787), p. 388.

[34]Cornwallis to Clinton, 20 October 1781, Clinton Papers.

[35]*Military Journal of Major Ebenezer Denny, with an Introductory Memoir* (Philadelphia: Historical Society of Pennsylvania, 1859), p. 248.

[36]Thomas J. Fleming, *Beat the Last Drum: The Siege of Yorktown, 1781* (New York: St. Martin's, 1963), p. 349.

[37]St. George Tucker, "Diary of the Siege of Yorktown," *William & Mary Quarterly*, 3d ser. 5 (1948): 391.

[38]*A Hessian Soldier in the American Revolution: The Diary of Stephen Popp*, trans. Reinhart J. Pope (N.p.: Privately printed, 1953), p. 29.

[39]Cornwallis to Clinton, 15 October 1781, Chadwick, *Graves Papers*, p. 140.

[40]Washington to William Heath, 16 October 1781, Miscellaneous Collections, Heath Papers, Massachusetts Historical Society, Boston.

[41]Germain to William Knox, 4 November 1781, William Knox Papers, Clements Library, Univ. of Mich., Ann Arbor.

[42]Clinton to Germain, 29 October 1781, CO 5/239, folios 253–57, P.R.O.

[43]"Account of What passed in consequence of Lord Cornwallis's surrender brought down to the 17 Jany. 1782 & 1st Feby. 1782," Knox Papers, 10, no. 31.

[44]Germain to Clinton, 2 January 1782, Germain Papers.

[45][Resolutions], Main Papers, 6 March 1782, House of Lords Record Office.

Chapter 6

[1]Worthington C. Ford et al., eds. *Journals of the Continental Congress, 1774–1789*, 34 vols. (Washington, D.C.: Government Printing Office, 1904–37), 21:1082.

[2]John C. Fitzpatrick, ed., *The Writings of George Washington from the Original Manuscript Sources, 1745–1799*, 39 vols. (Washington, D.C.: Government Printing Office, 1931–44), 23:208.

[3]Liberge de Granchain to Martelli Chautard, 20 October 1781, Papers of Joseph-Jacques-François de Martelli Chautard, Collection of Dr. and Mme Pierre Porruchio, Toulon, France.

[4]Ibid.

[5]Granchain to Martelli Chautard, 21 October 1781, Papers of Martelli Chautard.

[6]Ibid.

[7]*Pennsylvania Packet* (Philadelphia), 6 November 1781.

[8]See Charles H. Metzger, *The Prisoner in the American Revolution* (Chicago: Loyola Univ. Press, 1971).

[9]Granchain to Martelli Chautard, 22 October 1781, Papers of Martelli Chautard.

[10]Timothy Pickering to Edward Hand, 22 October 1781, Edward Hand Papers (Force Transcripts) Manuscript Division, Library of Congress.

[11]Comte de Rochambeau to Comte de Grasse, 28 October 1781, Rochambeau Papers, 12, folio 179, Manuscript Division, L.C.

[12]Edward Carrington to unknown, 3 November 1781, Executive Department, Governor's Office Papers, Letters Received, Virginia State Library, Richmond.

[13]De Grasse to Rochambeau, 24 October 1781, Rochambeau Papers, Manuscript Division, L.C.

[14]Thomas J. Fleming, *Beat the Last Drum: The Siege of Yorktown, 1781* (New York: St. Martin's, 1963), p. 348.

[15]Granchain to Martelli Chautard, 21 October 1781, Papers of Martelli Chautard.

[16]"General Richard Butler's Journal of the Siege of Yorktown," *Historical Magazine* 8 (1864):111.

[17]Report of the Court Martial of Capt. Dundas of the *Bonetta*, 16 March 1782, SP 42/57, Public Record Office.

[18]Lord Cornwallis to Philip Stephens, Secretary of the Board of Admiralty, 9 March 1782, Report of the Court Martial of Capt. Dundas of the *Bonetta*, 16 March 1782, SP 42/57, P.R.O.

[19]"Christopher Vail's Journal, 1775–1782," folios 34–35 (Force Transcripts), Manuscript Division, L.C.

[20]"Condemnation of Bonnetta," HCA 32/286, folder 32, P.R.O.

[21]George Washington to de Grasse, 23 October 1781, Washington Papers, ser. 3, subser. D, folio 381, Manuscript Division, L.C.

[22]Washington to Blain and Stewart, 31 October 1781, Washington Papers, series 4, 187, folio 44, Manuscript Division, L.C.

[23]Ibid., folio 94. The names of the persons embarked on board the *Cochrane* may be found in Record Group 93, Miscellaneous Numbered Records, no. 31598, National Archives. Those on board the *Andrew* are listed in the same record group, no. 31601.

[24]Johann Ewald, *Diary of the American War: A Hessian Journal*, trans. and ed. Joseph P. Tustin (New Haven: Yale Univ. Press, 1979), p. 343–44.

[25]Cornwallis to Rochambeau, 25 November 1781, 30/11/92, folio 81, P.R.O.

[26]Journal of Captain John Peebles, 17 December 1781, Cunninghame of Thornton Papers, 492/13, Scottish Record Office, Edinburgh.

[27]"Robt. Carter's proportion of a present to be presented to the Count da Grasse," Robert Carter Collection, Chicago Historical Society, Chicago.

[28]De Grasse to Rochambeau, 29 October 1781, Rochambeau Papers, 12, folio 179, Manuscript Division, L.C.

[29]David Ross to Thomas Nelson, Jr., 17 November 1781, Executive Department, Governor's Office Papers, Letters Received, V.S.L.

[30]Ross to Nelson, 31 October 1781, Executive Department, Governor's Office Papers, Letters Received, V.S.L.

[31]Thomas Symonds to Board of Admiralty, 18 December 1781, ADM 1/2485, P.R.O.

[32]Chevalier de La Villebrune to unknown, 4 May 1782, Archives de la Marine, B4, 185, folio 345, Archives Nationales, Paris (hereafter cited as Archives de la Marine).

[33]Thomas Tonken to Commissioners of His Majesty's Navy, 21 January 1782, ADM 49/2, folio 273, P.R.O.

[34]Symonds to Board of Admiralty, 17 January 1782, ADM 1/2485, Order for court martial, ADM 2/1116, folio 170, Transcript and verdict of court martial, ADM 1/5319, folios 507–10, P.R.O.

[35]Order for court martial, ADM 2/1116, folio 195, Transcript and verdict of court martial, ADM 1/5320, folios 276–83, P.R.O.

[36]La Villebrune to unknown, 30 January 1782, Archives de la Marine, B4, 185, folio 331.

[37]William Reynolds to James Eyma, 30 December 1781, William Reynolds Letterbook, Manuscript Division, L.C.

[38]La Villebrune to unknown, 30 January 1782, Archives de la Marine, B4, 185, folio 331.

[39]Rochambeau to La Villebrune, 24 January 1782, Letterbook 11, Rochambeau Papers, Manuscript Division, L.C.

[40]Rochambeau to La Villebrune, 13 December 1781, Letterbook 11, Rochambeau Papers, Manuscript Division. L.C. This particular cargo, belonging to the *Leendert & Matthy's*, was the source of much debate. As a private Dutch vessel previously captured by a British privateer, restitution was also demanded from the British by the original captor, by the vessel owners, and by the cargo owners HCA 32/387, folder 6, P.R.O.

[41]Papers concerning the Army of the Revolution, vol. 2 (1777–1789), folios 383–94, V.S.L., Richmond.

[42]La Villebrune to unknown, 30 January 1782, Archives de la Marine, B4, 185, folio 337.

[43]La Villebrune to Admiralty, 5 April 1782, ibid., folio 342.

[44]La Villebrune to unknown, 4 May 1782, ibid., folio 348.

[45]La Villebrune to unknown, 4 May 1782, Archives de la Marine, B4, 185, part II, folio 330.

[46]La Villebrune to unknown, 28 May 1782, Archives de la Marine, B4, 185, folio 358.

[47]Account, May 1782, ibid., folio 353.

[48]"Instructions particulieres au Sieur de la Touche," 1 July 1782, Rochambeau Papers, 4, folio 488, Manuscript Division, L.C.

[49]Chevalier de La Vallette to Benjamin Harrison, 9 July 1782, Executive Department, Governor's Office Papers, Letters Received, V.S.L.

[50]Harrison to The Commodore of the French Men of War at York, 16 July 1782, Executive Letterbook, 1 December 1781—30 September 1782, folio 206, Executive Department, V.S.L., Richmond.

[51]Journal of Jean-Baptiste-Antoine de Verger, *The American Campaigns of Rochambeau's Army: 1780, 1781, 1782, 1783*, trans. and ed. Howard C. Rice and Anne S. K. Brown, 2 vols. (Princeton: Princeton Univ. Press, 1972), 1:161.

[52]Rochambeau to La Villebrune, 13 October 1782, Letterbook 11, folio 221, Rochambeau Papers, Manuscript Division, L.C.

Chapter 7

[1]Robert Alexander to Brook Watson, 27 November 1782, WO 60/25, part I, Public Record Office.

[2]Alexander to Watson, 26 November 1782, WO 60/25, part I, P.R.O.

[3]Johann David Schoepf, *Travels in the Confederation*, trans. and ed. Alfred J. Morrison (1911; reprint New York: Bergman, 1968), p. 85.

[4]Edward C. Carter, ed., *The Virginia Journals of Benjamin Henry Latrobe, 1795–1798*, 2 vols. (New Haven: Yale Univ. Press, 1977), 2:489. Other travelers recorded similar decay. See Isaac Weld, Jr., *Travels through the States of North America, and the Provinces of Upper and Lower Canada, during the Years 1795, 1796, and 1797* (London: John Stockdale, 1800), 163–166; Benson J. Lossing, *The Pictorial Field-Book of the Revolution*, 2 vols. (New York: Harper & Brothers, 1851), 1:507–30.

[5]Mary Wiatt Gray, *Gloucester County* (Richmond: Cottrell & Cooke, 1936), p. 84.

[6]Virginia State Library, photostat, Ship's Papers Collection, The Mariners' Museum, Newport News, Va.

[7]*Acts of the General Assembly of Virginia, Passed in 1852, in the Seventy-Sixth Year of the Commonwealth* (Richmond: William F. Ritchie, 1852), p. 312.

[8]Edward Dunning to Mrs. Edward Dunning, 16 February 1851, Mrs. Edward Dunning Papers, Duke University Library, Durham, N.C.

[9]William Lightner Cowan to President, Society of the Sons of the Revolution, State of New York, 22 February 1909, Fraunces Tavern Museum Archives, New York City.

[10]It has proved impossible to locate this cannon and the "stern of the ship" which accompanied it. A Bannerman representative in a telephone conversation of March 1973 stated that the cannon was to be donated to "the Staten Island Museum," the woodwork to South Street Seaport. Inquiries with the Seaport and various Staten Island institutions have produced no results. The cannon is approximately six feet in length and has a hole rusted through the barrel, near the muzzle. It was claimed to have been fully authenticated.

[11]James W. Head, Jr., to B. Floyd Flickinger, 15 May 1934, Colonial National Park Archives, Yorktown, Va.

[12]News release of 23 November 1934, Col. Nat. Hist. Park Arch.

[13]Homer L. Ferguson to William Gatewood, 8 October 1934, The Mariners' Museum Archives, Newport News, Va.

[14]Homer L. Ferguson, "Salvaging Revolutionary Relics from the York River," *William & Mary Quarterly*, 2d ser. 19 (1939):267.

[15]Ralph E. Chapman to Archer M. Huntington, 10 September 1934, Mariners' Museum Arch.; R. G. Skerrett, "Lake Champlain Yields Wreck of 'Royal Savage,' " *Compressed Air Magazine* 40, no. 1 (January 1935):4626–30.

[16]*Daily Press* (Newport News, Va.), 1 November 1934, Clipping File, The Mariners' Museum Library, Newport News, Va.

[17]Ferguson, "Salvaging Revolutionary Relics from the York River," p. 267.

[18]Christopher Ipswich, "Diving at Yorktown," *Richmond Times-Dispatch*, 16 January 1938.

[19]Interview with Harry H. Hamilton, 18 August 1978, Yorktown, Va.

[20]News release, Colonial National Monument, 14 December 1934, The Mariners' Museum Arch.

[21]Interview with Harold S. Sniffen, assistant director of The Mariners' Museum, June 1972, Newport News, Va.

[22]Report of 29 October 1935, Col. Nat. Hist. Park Arch.

[23]Report of 19 November 1935, ibid.

[24]Report of Thor Borreson, 19 March 1937, ibid.

[25]Minutes of staff meeting, 6 November 1934, ibid.

[26]Press release, 23 November 1934, ibid.

[27]Interview with Harry H. Hamilton, photographer for National Park Service in 1935, 18 August 1978, Yorktown, Va.

Chapter 8

[1]Fred Frechette, "Cornwallis Fleet, Ahoy," *Richmond Times-Dispatch*, 2 August 1954, pp. 1–4.

[2]Ibid.

[3]Howard Gibbons, "Army Divers Recover Piece of Vessel Believed British Revolutionary Warship," *Times Herald* (Newport News, Va.), 10 January 1950, p. 4. The analysis of the fragments was undertaken by the Newport News Shipbuilding and Dry Dock Company and the National Bureau of Standards. It was determined that the copper sheathing was separated from the planking by a layer of bedding compound consisting of an oil or tar product with a vegetable fiber filler, probably flax or hemp. Reports of the analysis are in The Mariners' Museum Archives, Newport News, Va.

[4]Walter M. Dotts, Jr., to Curator, 19 April 1953, The Mariners' Museum Arch.

[5]Correspondence, ibid.

[6]George Dufek to Stanley W. Abbott, 30 October 1961 and Memorandum to the Director, 17 November 1961, ibid.

[7]The Mariners' Museum Arch.

[8]Interview with Herndon Jenkins, June 1972, Richmond, regarding artifact identification; Memorandum, J. Paul Hudson to Charles Hatch, 22 May 1968, collection Herndon Jenkins.

[9]Collection of Virginia Historic Landmarks Commission, Richmond.

[10]Ivor Noël Hume, *Here Lies Virginia: An Archaeologist's View of Colonial Life and History* (New York: Knopf, 1968), pp. 180–85.

[11]John O. Sands, "Shipwrecks of the Battle of Yorktown, 1781: A Preliminary Archaeological Study," Master's thesis, Univ. of Delaware, 1973.

[12]John D. Broadwater, John O. Sands, and Gordon P. Watts, Jr., "Report of an Archaeological Survey of Several Shipwreck Sites near Yorktown, Virginia," report submitted 8 December 1975 to Va. Hist. Landmarks Comm.

[13]"The Commonwealth's Ownership and Interest in British Vessels of the Revolutionary War, Sunk at Yorktown, Virginia," memorandum to Va. Hist.

Landmarks Comm., prepared by the office of the Attorney General, Richmond, 7 November 1975.

[14]The details of this excavation are more fully available elsewhere. In particular see George F. Bass, Ivor Noël Hume, John O. Sands, and J. Richard Steffy, "The Cornwallis Cave Shipwreck," report submitted to Va. Hist. Landmarks Comm., 1976; Paul F. Johnston, John O. Sands, and J. Richard Steffy, "The Cornwallis Cave Shipwreck, Yorktown, Virginia: Preliminary Report," *International Journal of Nautical Archaeology and Underwater Exploration* 7, no. 3 (August 1978):205–26.

Chapter 9

[1]Additional details on these surveys may be found in Gordon P. Watts, Jr., "The Location and Identification of the Ironclad USS *Monitor,*" *International Journal of Nautical Archaeology and Underwater Exploration* 4, no. 2 (September 1975):301–29; John D. Broadwater, "A Search for the USS *Monitor,*" *International Journal of Nautical Archaeology and Underwater Exploration* 4, no. 1 (March 1975): 117–21; Edward M. Miller, ed., "Project Cheesebox: A Journey into History," manuscript, U.S. Naval Academy, Annapolis, 1974.

[2]William J. Andahazy, Douglas G. Everstine, and Bruce R. Hood, "Magnetic Search for Shipwrecks from the Battle of Yorktown," *Sea Technology* 17, no. 11 (November 1976):20.

[3]J. Richard Steffy, "The *Charon* Project: A Preliminary Report," 10 August 1980, Texas A&M University, College Station.

Catalogue of Ships

[1]Orders, 25 October 1781, Washington Papers, ser. 4, 186, folio 57, Manuscript Division, Library of Congress.

[2]Audit of Transports, 30/55, folio 3696 (1), (7), Public Record Office.

[3]Order books, Headquarters, New York 13 June 1781, Sir Henry Clinton Papers, William L. Clements Library, Univ. Of Michigan, Ann Arbor; Ship's Muster, 1 January–31 May 1781, ADM 49/6, folio 80, Thomas Symonds to Board of Admiralty, 18 December 1781, ADM 1/2485, P.R.O.; French Ensor Chadwick, ed., *The Graves Papers and Other Documents Relating to The Naval Operations of the Yorktown Campaign, July to October 1781* (New York: Naval History Society, 1916), p. 149; *Lloyd's Register,* 1776, 1779, 1781 (reprint London: Gregg Press, n.d.), not paginated.

[4]Chadwick, *Graves Papers,* p. 149; Ship's Muster, 1 January–31 May 1781, ADM 49/6, folio 67, "A State of the Transports . . . on the Virginia Station, 30 June 1781," 30/11/6, folio 269, P.R.O.; Passport, Washington Papers, Ser. 4, 187, folio 94, Manuscript Division, L.C.

[5]Liberge de Granchain to Martelli Chautard, 21 October 1781, Papers of

Joseph-Jacques-François de Martelli Chautard, Collection of Dr. and Mme Pierre Porruchio, Toulon, France; *Lloyd's Register*, 1780, 1781.

[6]Audit of Transports, 30/55, folio 3696 (1), (7), P.R.O.

[7]Chadwick, *Graves Papers*, p. 149; Order books, Headquarters, New York, 13 June 1781, Clinton Papers; Hugh Robinson to Board of Admiralty, 19 December 1781, ADM 1/2393, William Mathews to Navy Board, 9 April 1778, ADM 106/3525, William Wilkinson to Navy Board, 30 July 1781, Charles Jackson to Navy Board, 17 January 1782, ADM 108 1B, folios 12, 180, Unknown to Commissioners of the Navy, 17 June 1782, ADM 108 1C, folio 102, P.R.O.; *Lloyd's Register*, 1781.

[8]Chadwick, *Graves Papers*, p. 149; Audit of Transports, 30/55, folio 3696 (8), Account of Major Richard England, deputy quartermaster general, 1 January to 31 December 1781, Audit Office, 1/338/1357, P.R.O.

[9]John Charnock, *An History of Marine Architecture*, 3 vols. (London: Nichols & Son, 1800–1802), 3:260; Progress books, ADM 180/9, folio 438, P.R.O.; Ralph Dundas to James Dundas, 2 May 1779, 3 May 1780, GD 35/57/1–17, GD 35/57/9, Scottish Record Office, Edinburgh.

[10]Audit of Transports, 30/55, folio 3696 (1), (7), P.R.O.

[11]John Knox Laughton, ed., *Journal of Rear-Admiral Bartholomew James, 1752–1828* (London: Navy Records Society, 1896), pp. 113–15.

[12]Charnock, *History of Marine Architecture*, 3:254; Progress books, ADM 180/7, folio 218, Stephen Harris to Commissioners of the Navy, 13 August 1780, ADM 49/2, Part I, folio 50, P.R.O.

[13]Log of H.M.S. *Fowey*, 10 November 1780, ADM 51/375, P.R.O.

[14]Alexander Leslie to Lord Cornwallis, 12 July 1781, 30/11/6, folio 284, P.R.O.

[15]Chadwick, *Graves Papers*, p. 104.

[16]Laughton, *Journal of Rear-Admiral Bartholomew James*, pp. 111, 114.

[17]Chadwick, *Graves Papers*, p. 104.

[18]Logbook of the Comte de Grasse, 10 October 1781, Archives de la Marine, B4, 184, Archives Nationales, Paris (hereafter cited as Archives de la Marine).

[19]Laughton, *Journal of Rear-Admiral Bartholomew James*, p. 122.

[20]Requisition for *Danae*, Archives Diplomatiques: Correspondence Politiques, Etats Unis Supplement, 13, folios 226, 227, Archives Nationales, Paris (hereafter cited as Archives Diplomatiques).

[21]U.S. Naval History Division, *Naval Documents of the American Revolution* (Washington, D.C.: Government Printing Office, 1964–), 3:545.

[22]Report, Archives de la Marine, B4, 185, folio 347; Passport, Washington Papers, Ser. 4, 187, folio 94, Manuscript Division, L.C.; List of Officers, War Department Collection of Revolutionary War Records, Record Group 93, Miscellaneous Numbered Records, no. 31598, National Archives; Minutes of the Board of Ordnance, 3 May, 27 May 1782, WO 47/99, folios 329, 398, P.R.O.; *Lloyd's Register*, 1781.

[23]Chadwick, *Graves Papers*, p. 149; Andrew Barkley to Board of Admiralty, 21 March 1781, ADM 1/1501, P.R.O.

[24]Account of Major Richard England, deputy quartermaster general, 1 January to 31 December 1781, AO 1/338/1357, P.R.O.

[25]List of armed vessels, 30/55, folio 3700 (1), P.R.O.; Report, Archives de la Marine, B4, 185, folio 347.

[26]Passport, Washington Papers, ser. 4, 187, folio 94, Manuscript Division, L.C.

[27]"A State of the Transports . . . Virginia, 30 June 1781," 30/11/6, folio 269, "Miscellaneous Lists of Transports, 1776–1782," ADM 7/565, folios 3, 9, Audit of Transports, 30/55, folio 3696 (1), (7), P.R.O.

[28]"Intelligence from Yorktown, James Baillie, October 1781," Clinton Papers.

[29]Chadwick, *Graves Papers*, p. 149; Thomas Carter to Navy Board, 11 February, 1782, ADM 108 1B, folio 210, P.R.O.; *Lloyds Register*, 1781.

[30]Chadwick, *Graves Papers*, p. 149; Archives Diplomatiques: Correspondence Politiques, Etats Unis Supplement, 15, folio 352; Ship's Muster, ADM 49/6, folio 69, P.R.O.

[31]Chadwick, *Graves Papers*, p. 149; Ship's Muster, 1 January–31 May 1781, ADM 49/6, folio 69, Thomas Fisher to Navy Board, 26 February 1782, ADM 108 1B, folios 229, 230, James McHenry to Alexander Ross, n.d., 30/11/270, folio 159, P.R.O.; Archives Diplomatiques: Correspondence Politiques, Etats Unis Supplement, 15, folio 324; *Lloyd's Register*, 1781.

[32]Chadwick, *Graves Papers*, p. 149; Barkley to Board of Admiralty, 21 March 1781, ADM 1/1501, Charles Hudson to Cornwallis, 13 August 1781, 30/11/89, folio 17, P.R.O.

[33]Chevalier de La Villebrune, "Report of Shipping," 4 May 1782, Archives de la Marine, B4, 185, folio 330; Archives Diplomatiques: Correspondence Politiques, Etats Unis Supplement, 15, folio 306; List of armed vessels, 30/55, folio 3700 (1), P.R.O.; Johann Ewald, *Diary of the American War: A Hessian Journal*, trans. and ed. Joseph P. Tustin (New Haven: Yale Univ. Press, 1979), p. 334.

[34]Charnock *History of Marine Architecture*, 3:260; Progress books, ADM 180/3, folio 368, P.R.O.

[35]Master's Log of *Fowey*, ADM 52/1748, Marriot Arbuthnot to Board of Admiralty, 2 June 1781, ADM 1/486, folios 675–76, P.R.O.

[36]Granchain to Martelli Chautard, 21 October 1781, Papers of Martelli Chautard.

[37]"Passport for Flag Ship General de Reidsel," 9 December 1780, Washington Papers, ser. 3, subser. E, folio 189, Capt. H. Gerlach to Washington, 20 October 1781, Washington Papers, ser. 4, 186, folio 52, Manuscript Division, L.C.

[38]Charnock, *History of Marine Architecture*, 3:259.

[39]Hudson to Thomas Graves, 12 August 1781, Chadwick, *Graves Papers*, p. 37.

[40]"Remarks on Board His Majesty's Ship Guadaloupe, 29 August 1781," ADM 1/491, folios 243–44, P.R.O.

[41]Symonds to Graves, 20 October 1781, Chadwick, *Graves Papers*, p. 151.

[42]Symonds to Robinson, 15 October 1781, ADM 1/2393, "Robinson," P.R.O.

[43]St. George Tucker, "Diary of the Siege of Yorktown," *William & Mary Quarterly*, 3d ser. 5 (1948):391.

[44]Archives de la Marine, B4, 288, folio 70.

[45]Archives Diplomatique: Correspondence Politiques, Etats Unis Supplement, 15, folio 70. See also, K. V. Burns, *Plymouth's Ships of War: A History of Naval Vessels Built in Plymouth between 1694 and 1860* (Greenwich, England: National Maritime Museum, 1972), p. 65.

[46]Chadwick, *Graves Papers*, p. 149; Account of Richard England, deputy quartermaster general, 1 January to 31 December 1781, AO 1/338/1357, Audit of Transports, 30/55, folio 3696 (1), Condemnation of *Harlequin*, HCA 32/358, folders 10, 11, 32/359, folder 20, P.R.O.

[47]Chadwick, *Graves Papers*, p. 149; Order books, Headquarters, New York, 13 June 1781, Clinton Papers; Archives de la Marine, B4, 185, folio 330; Ship's Muster, 1 January–31 May 1781, ADM 49/6, folio 78, P.R.O.

[48]Chadwick, *Graves Papers*, p. 149; "A list of Ships freighted . . . as Victuallers or Store Ships, 1 January 1778," Main Papers, 2 February 1778, House of Lords Record Office, London; Captain's Log of *Roebuck*, 22 March 1781, ADM 51/796, "A State of the transports . . . on the Virginia Station, 30 June 1781," 30/11/6, folio 269, Ship's Muster, 1 January–31 May 1781, ADM 49/6, folio 70, P.R.O.; *Lloyd's Register*, 1781.

[49]Chadwick, *Graves Papers*, p. 149; "A State of the transports . . . on the Virginia Station, 30 June 1781," 30/11/6, folio 269, P.R.O.

[50]Audit of Transports, 30/55, folio 3696 (1), (7), P.R.O.

[51]"Affidavit of Protest filed by John Buchanan . . . 1 November 1781," HCA 42/134, P.R.O.; Report, Archives de la Marine, B4, 185, folio 350.

[52]Chadwick, *Graves Papers*, p. 149.

[53]Ibid; Passport, Washington Papers, ser. 4, 187, folio 94, Manuscript Division, L.C.; Benjamin Harrison to Charles Dabney, 2 November 1782, "Executive Letter Book, 3 October 1782 to 28 December 1782," Executive Department, Governor's Office Papers, Virginia State Library, Richmond; Ship's Muster, 1 January–31 May 1781, ADM 49/6, folio 79, Troops Victualled on board Transports, ADM 7/565, folio 249, P.R.O.

[54]Chadwick, *Graves Papers*, p. 149; "An Account of All Transports," ADM 106/3529, P.R.O.

[55]List of armed vessels, 30/55, folio 3700 (1), P.R.O.; Leslie to Sir Henry Clinton, 9 July 1781, Clinton Papers.

[56]Account of Richard England, deputy quartermaster general, 1 January to 31 December 1781, AO 1/338/1357, P.R.O.; Intelligence Report, 25 October 1781, Newcastle Papers, 2:311b, Department of Manuscripts, Nottingham University, Nottingham, England.

[57]Audit of Transports, 30/55, folio 3696 (1), (7), P.R.O.

[58]Chadwick, *Graves Papers*, p. 149; "Returns of Provisions . . . 17 July 1781," Clinton Papers; *Lloyd's Register*, 1781.

[59]Passport, Washington Papers, ser. 4, 187, folio 94, Manuscript Division, L.C.

[60]Chadwick, *Graves Papers*, p. 149; Audit of Transports, 30/55, folio 3696 (8), Report, 30/55, folio 3656 (2), List of armed vessels, 30/55, folio 3700 (1), Condemnation of *Nancy*, HCA 32/414, bundle D, P.R.O.

[61]Chadwick, *Graves Papers*, p. 149; Report, Archives de la Marine, B4, 185, folio 330; John Atkinson to Navy Board, 8 March 1779, ADM 106/280, Ship's Muster, 1 January–31 May 1781, ADM 49/6, folio 79, P.R.O.; *Lloyd's Register*, 1781.

[62]Condemnation of *Nonsuch*, HCA 32/415, bundle A, P.R.O.

[63]Condemnation of *Jolly Tar*, HCA 32/381, folder 17, William Chisholm Petition, 10 October 1785, AO 13/2, folder 36, P.R.O.

[64]Chadwick, *Graves Papers*, p. 149; "Return of Provisions . . . 17 July 1781," Clinton Papers; Report, Archives de la Marine, B4, 185, folio 330; *Lloyd's Register*, 1782.

[65]James Barron, "The Schooner Patriot," *Virginia Historical Register* 1 (1848):129.

[66]William P. Palmer, ed., *Calendar of Virginia State Papers and Other Manuscripts Preserved in the Capitol at Richmond*, 11 vols. (Richmond: N.p., 1875–93), 2:403, 546.

[67]Account of Richard England, deputy quartermaster general, 1 January to 31 December 1781, AO 1/338/1357, P.R.O.

[68]Chadwick, *Graves Papers*, p. 149; "A State of the transports . . . on the Virginia Station, 30 June 1781," 30/11/6, folio 269, John Reed to Navy Board, n.d., ADM 106/280, Parrey to Navy Board, 28 December 1780, ADM 106/3529, Miscellaneous Lists of Transports, 1776–1782, 22 April 1782, ADM 7/565, folios 2, 10, P.R.O.; *Lloyd's Register*, 1782.

[69]Chadwick, *Graves Papers*, p. 149; Account of Richard England, deputy quartermaster general, 1 January to 31 December 1781, Audit Office 1/338/1357, P.R.O.; Log of *Roebuck*, 17 May 1781, ADM/L/R/161, National Maritime Museum, Greenwich, England; *Lloyd's Register*, 1781.

[70]Chadwick, *Graves Papers*, p. 149; Ship's Muster, 1 January–31 May 1781, ADM 49/6, folio 72, "A State of the transports . . . on the Virginia Station, 30 June 1781," 30/11/6, folio 269, P.R.O.; *Lloyd's Register*, 1781.

[71]Chadwick, *Graves Papers*, p. 149; "A State of the transports . . . on the Virginia Station, 30 June 1781," 30/11/6, folio 269, Navy Board Minutes, 8

January 1782, ADM 106/2607, P.R.O.; *Letter-Books and Order-Book of George, Lord Rodney, Admiral of the White Squadron: 1780–1782* (New York: Naval History Society, 1932), p. 765; *Lloyd's Register,* 1781.

[72]List of armed vessels, 30/55, folio 3700 (1); Benedict Arnold to Clinton, 21 January 1781, CO 5/101, folio 249, P.R.O.

[73]Audit of Transports, 30/55, folios 3656 (1), 3696 (1), (7), P.R.O.

[74]Chadwick, *Graves Papers,* p. 149; "A State of the transports . . . on the Virginia Station, 30 June 1781," 30/11/6, folio 269, Wilkinson to Navy Board, 16 January 1779, ADM 106/280, P.R.O.; *Lloyd's Register,* 1781.

[75]Chadwick, *Graves Papers,* p. 149.

[76]Ibid.; Audit of Transports, 30/55, folio 3696 (1), (7), Wilkinson to Navy Board, 30 July 1781, ADM 108 1B, folio 12, John Liddell to Navy Board, 27 February 1782, 6 March 1782, ADM 108 1B, folios 228, 281, Mathews to Navy Board, 9 April 1778, ADM 106/3525, P.R.O.; *Lloyd's Register,* 1781.

[77]Account of Richard England, deputy quartermaster general, 1 January to 31 December 1781, AO 1/338/1357, Claim for damages, AO 13/5, folder 93, P.R.O.

[78]Chadwick, *Graves Papers,* p. 149; "A State of the transports . . . on the Virginia Station, 30 June 1781," 30/11/6, folio 269, Bill of Lading, 2 May 1779, ADM 106/280, P.R.O.; *Lloyd's Register,* 1781.

[79]Report, Archives de la Marine, B4, 185, folio 330; Archives Diplomatiques: Correspondence Politiques, Etats Unis Supplement, 15, folio 306.

[80]Chadwick, *Graves Papers,* p. 149; "A State of the transports . . . on the Virginia Station, 30 June 1781," 30/11/6, folio 269, Ship's Muster, 1 January–31 May 1781, ADM 49/6, folio 72, P.R.O.; *Lloyd's Register,* 1781.

[81]List of armed vessels, 30/55, folio 3700 (1), Claim for Damages, AO 13/5, folder 93, P.R.O.; *Correspondence of General Washington and Comte de Grasse: 1781, 17 August–4 November,* ed. Institut Français de Washington (Washington, D.C.: Government Printing Office, 1931), pp. 123–25.

[82]Chadwick, *Graves Papers,* p. 149; Report, Archives de la Marine, B4, 185, folio 330; *Lloyd's Register,* 1781.

[83]*Correspondence of Washington and de Grasse,* pp. 123–25; Archives de la Marine, B4, 288, folio 44.

[84]List of armed vessels, 30/55, folio 3700 (1), Graves to Board of Admiralty, 26 September 1781, ADM 1/489, folio 447, Account of Richard England, deputy quartermaster general, 1 January to 31 December 1781, AO 1/338/1357, P.R.O.

[85]*Correspondence of Washington and de Grasse,* pp. 123–25; Report, Archives de la Marine, B4, 185, folios 335, 354; William Phillips to William Fyers, 4 April 1781, Letterbook, "Correspondence with Phillips, 10 March–30 April 1781," folio 58, Clinton Papers.

[86]Condemnation of *Three Sisters,* HCA 32/467, bundle D, P.R.O.

[87]Chadwick, *Graves Papers,* p. 149; Symonds to Board of Admiralty, 18

December 1781, ADM 1/2485, "An Account of Transports & Victuallers," ADM 106/3529, "An Account of . . . Beds," Plymouth, 31 December.1780, ADM 106/3526, "An Account of . . . Beds," Portsmouth, 8 January 1781, ADM 106/3526, Hall to Commissioners of the Navy, 29 December 1781, ADM 108 1B, folio 133, P.R.O.; *Lloyd's Register,* 1781; *New Lloyd's List,* no. 1332, 1 February 1782 (reprint Farnborough, England: Gregg International Publishers, 1969).

[88]Charnock, *History of Marine Architecture,* 3:260; "Progress and Dimension Book, 1765–1782," folio 50, photostat in National Maritime Museum, Greenwich, England; Joseph A. Goldenberg, *Shipbuilding in Colonial America* (Charlottesville: Univ. Press of Virginia, 1976), fig. 10.

[89]Laughton, *Journal of Rear-Admiral Bartholomew James,* pp. 117–18; Transcript of court martial, ADM 1/5320, folio 281, P.R.O.

[90]"Sailing and Fighting Instructions for His Majesty's Fleet," ADM 7/205, Navy Board Letterbook, 23 September 1779, ADM 106/3319, folio 58, P.R.O.

[91]Cornwallis to Marquis de Lafayette, 15 September 1781, Lafayette to Cornwallis, 31 October 1781, 30/11/92, folios 55, 73–75, Symonds to Navy Board, 15 August 1782, James Walker et al. to Navy Board, 24 September 1782, ADM 108 1C, folios 143, 174, P.R.O.

[92]"Claims for losses of York County in British Invasion of 1781," folios 25, 35, 56, York County Records, York County Courthouse, Yorktown, Va.; Account of Richard England, deputy quartermaster general, 1 January to 31 December 1781, AO 1/338/1357, P.R.O.

[93]Arnold to Clinton, 23 January 1781, Clinton Papers.

[94]Arnold to Clinton, 25 February 1781, Letterbook, "Clinton/Arnold Correspondence," folio 29, Clinton Papers; Clinton to Cornwallis, 19 June 1781, 28 June 1781, 30/11/68, folios 26, 30, P.R.O.

[95]Leslie to Cornwallis, 10 June 1781, 30/11/6, folio 220, Cornwallis to Hudson, 27 July 1781, 30/11/88, folio 54, P.R.O.; Weedon to Washington, 21 October 1781, Washington Papers, ser. 4, 186, folio 64, Manuscript Division, L.C.; *The Revolutionary Journal of Baron Ludwig Von Closen, 1780–1783,* trans. and ed. Evelyn M. Acomb, (Williamsburg, Va.: Institute of Early American History and Culture, 1958), p. 146.

[96]"Dimensions for two Gondolas to be built at Chamblé," Howard I. Chapelle, *The History of American Sailing Ships* (New York: Norton, 1935), pp. 363–64; John H. Jeffries "Maryland Naval Barges in the Revolutionary War" (Princess Anne, Md.: Privately printed, 1978), p. 21; Arnold to Clinton, 10 August 1781, Clinton Papers; Navy Board Minutes, 1 February 1782, ADM 106/2607, P.R.O.

Bibliographical Essay

Although the war was not to end until two years later, with the signing of the Treaty of Paris, and the country was not to achieve political stability until seven years later, with the ratification of the Constitution, the Battle of Yorktown has long symbolized the end of the American Revolution. It looms in the popular imagination as the terminus of the war and the watershed of the national era. Even while it was being fought, the significance of the event was evident to the participants. In consequence, the battle has had much written about it, both by contemporaries and later historians. Many of the participants wrote journals of the battle or extensive letters home detailing the events in which they had participated; these documents along with the official correspondence, must provide the basis for a study.

Unlike many other events of the colonial period, there is a surfeit of material relating to the battle. Literally thousands of pages of pertinent manuscript material survive, to the extent that its very volume makes the study of the battle difficult. The significant groups of documents have been listed in the bibliography; it may, however, be useful to detail those items which are not listed, either because they were not located or do not survive. The logs of the naval vessels involved in the battle proper do not survive, except in the case of the *Fowey*, because they were destroyed or captured with the ships. The transport service of the British navy was, at best, a confusing and somewhat poorly documented branch of the government at this time. With scattered records and many ships of the same name, it is frequently difficult to distinguish one from another. This problem is compounded by the loss of the records of the New York agent for transports, Thomas Tonken, outlined in chapter 6.

In addition to these general problems, two specific lacunae have been especially irksome. When the *Richmond* sailed from Yorktown on 25 August, she must have escorted some vessels back to New York. A number of the vessels which were recorded in the audit of 17 August 1781 as being present in Virginia receive no further mention in the records. It is probable that at least some of these returned to New York. Unfortunately, lists of convoyed ships generally were kept only by the captain of the naval vessel in charge and sporadically submitted to the fleet admiral. The capture of the *Richmond* in early September seems to have precluded the survival of this document. More surprising is the report submitted by Captain Symonds describing in detail the naval actions of the battle. In his letter to the Admiralty written December 18, 1781, upon his arrival in England, Symonds stated: "I have enclosed for their Lordships perusal a journal of the transactions that happened in York river from the day the command of His Majesty's Ships devolved to me, to the time of the capitulation, also the journal for the passage home, and the original passport delivered to me by the Chev. de la Villebrune."[1] A search of the probable resting places of this journal has not brought it to light. It can only be hoped that someday it will surface to further enlighten us on the details of this battle. Notwithstanding these gaps, there is still abundant material for study.

Though the battle lived in the memories of the populace for a time, it was not written up in any comprehensive sense until 1851. That year Benson J. Lossing published his *Pictorial Field-Book of the Revolution*, the result of a wide-ranging tour during the preceding years. His intention was outlined early in the work:

For many years, as I occasionally saw some field consecrated by revolutionary blood, or building hallowed as a shelter of the heroes of that war, I have felt emotions of shame, such as every American ought to feel, on seeing the plow leveling the breast-works and batteries where our fathers bled, and those edifices, containing the council-chambers of men who planned the attack, the ambuscade, or the retreat, crumbling into utter ruin. . . . To delineate with pen and pencil what is left of the physical features of that period, and thus to rescue from oblivion, before it should be too late, the mementoes which another generation will appreciate, was my employment for several months.[2]

With this lofty goal Lossing set out to visit the sites of the war, and eventually came to view what he termed "the field of humiliation" at Yorktown.[3] Interested as he was in memorializing the heroic deeds of our forefathers, Lossing concentrated largely on the patriots who fought the battle. Though he detailed the history of the event in fairly comprehensive form for the first time, his viewpoint was highly colored by his nationalistic attitude. Others would follow, with a similar approach and limitation, especially at the time of the centennial of the battle, in 1881.

The significance of the naval aspects of the battle, and particularly of the Battle of the Capes, was first fully appreciated in that seminal work by Alfred Thayer Mahan, *The Influence of Sea Power upon History, 1660–1783* (1890). This work first attempted to formulate the various aspects of naval warfare as one concept, that of sea power. Among the many examples cited by the author was that of the Battle of Yorktown and its associated naval actions. He gave considerable attention to the engagement of 16 March 1781 and suggested the parallels that might be drawn between it and the Battle of the Capes on 5 September. Mahan concentrated on the fleet movements that led up to the Battle of the Capes and virtually ignored both the tactical aspects of the battle and the strategic goals that had led the British to the South in the first place. He made amends for his first omission when he expanded this section of the original work in *The Major Operations of the Navies in the War of American Independence* (1913). He gave considerably more detail concerning the tactical details of the sea battle, but he ignored the further ramifications of the siege itself. The implication was that, once the French had control of the bay, the die was cast. Though this was the ultimate result, Mahan ignored the role played by the captive fleet. That he was not unaware of the important interrelationship between coastal fortresses and the fleets they defended was made evident in another of his works, *Naval Strategy Compared and Contrasted with the Principles and Practice of Military Operations on Land* (1911). He observed that "Fortresses, coast or other, defend only in virtue of the offensive power contained behind their walls. A coast fortress defends the nation to which it belongs chiefly by the fleet it shelters."[4] Had he explored that idea he would no doubt have been interested in the fact that Yorktown was chosen to defend an offensive ocean-going fleet and to act as the home base for a riverine police force, thus serving as the focal point of the attempts to reduce Virginia and the South.

Subsequent authors have amplified the theme Mahan first introduced. Comdr. A. H. Miles's "Sea Power and the Yorktown Campaign," published in the *U.S. Naval Institute Proceedings* (1927), went into considerable detail concerning the fleet movements that led up to the Battle of the Capes and the choice of Yorktown as a naval post. He chose to ignore the larger theater of operations, however, as well as the tactical role of the shipping engaged in the battle. Writing in the *Coast Artillery Journal* (1930), Maj. C. W. Jenkins in "Combined Operations, Revolutionary War: Yorktown" covered some of the same territory. Again he ignored the details of the battle, though in this instance he did draw some parallels between this campaign and earlier attempts at cooperation with the French fleet. His observation of similarities to the effort to take Clinton at Philadelphia in 1778, a cooperative venture between Washington and Admiral d'Estaing, is well founded. A similar comparison was made with attacks against New York and Newport the same year. But the choice of Yorktown as a naval base and the role of the shipping in the battle were again overlooked. Perhaps the most comprehensive view of the battle, the way it compared with similar campaigns, and the way it evolved, is given by Comdr. John F. Shafroth, "The Strategy of the Yorktown Campaign, 1781," in the *U.S. Naval Institute Proceedings* (1931). He emphasized the singular importance of cooperation and coordination between the army and the navy in such a campaign. He contrasted it with the 1778 effort against Newport, where d'Estaing abandoned operations against the town to chase a British fleet. He wrote, "While the proper objective of armies and navies is the armed forces of the enemy, the proper immediate naval objective is not always the enemy's fleet. At Yorktown it was most properly the English Army."[5] He further examined the campaign in terms of the grand strategy of the war, discussing the disposition of the fleets and forces, the choice of allies, and the choice of theaters of operations. It was a perspective that in all likelihood, had been inspired by the "Great War" which had just taken place. While Shafroth dealt extensively with the naval aspects, his work was not widely noted. Writing in *William & Mary Quarterly*, Col. John W. Wright ignored the naval aspects of the battle entirely in his "Notes on the Siege of Yorktown in 1781 with Special Reference to the Conduct of a Siege in the Eighteenth Century" (1932). More recent works have dealt extensively with the Battle of the Capes, its importance and its implications, but have once more excluded a consideration of the tactical effect of the captive fleet at Yorktown. Chief among these more recent works is William J. Morgan's "The Pivot upon Which Everything Turned," published in *The Iron Worker* (1958), and the section on the Battle of the Capes included in *Sea Power: A Naval History*, edited by E. B. Potter and Chester W. Nimitz (1960).

Other authors have pursued a similar course of analysis, often with greater emphasis on the actors involved. Rear Adm. W. J. James's *The British Navy in Adversity: A Study of the War of American Independence* (1933) included a treatment of Yorktown and the Battle of the Capes. Like his predecessors, however, he tended to focus rather narrowly on the events and those who were directly involved in them. Charles Lee Lewis, in *Admiral De Grasse and American Independence* (1945), went into considerable detail not only about the subject of the biography but the critical role his fleet played in the victory at Yorktown. Emphasis is not given to the siege itself, however, nor to the shipping involved. A similar presentation, more readable and accurate, is given in *Decision at the Chesapeake* (1964), by Harold A. Larrabee. Dudley W. Knox, in *The Naval Genius of George Washington* (1932), gave full credit for the victory to Washington and his coordination of the disparate forces involved. He properly gave Washington credit for his good timing, for persuading de Grasse to remain in the Chesapeake rather than cruising off the Capes, and for promoting the idea of sending ships up the river to control the navigation of the York above Yorktown. He oversimplified the picture, however, by not mentioning the shipping at Yorktown, by not grasping the reasons for delay of the relief expedition under Graves, and by overlooking the strategic reasons for the British presence in the South. Piers Mackesy, in *The War for America, 1775–1783* (1964), laid primary emphasis on the military aspects of the battle, though he did attempt to paint the larger picture by bringing the ministerial directives from England into the discussion. He seems to have overlooked the letter from Germain to Clinton which virtually ordered Clinton to leave Cornwallis in Virginia and which was therefore instrumental in the final defeat.

Don Higginbotham in *The War of American Independence* (1971) explored the strategic decisions that led the British to concentrate their attentions on the South. He correctly recognized the critical role the navy played in the South. With forces dispersed and requiring supplies, and a blockade of trade to be undertaken, naval forces were vital. Higginbotham observed that the abandonment of North Carolina and the decision to take post at Yorktown was at odds with the strategic goal of gathering and supporting the loyalists. In contrast to his attention to the causes and goals of the campaign, however, Higginbotham paid little more than lip service to the actual details of the battle itself.

While the strategy and tactics of the war were of considerable importance and have received rather extensive treatment in consequence, the importance of logistical support has not been so widely recognized. In a war fought overseas, in a hostile countryside, the British faced massive problems with the continuing supply of their forces. Robert G. Albion observed in his *Forests and Sea Power: The Timber Problem of the Royal Navy, 1652–1862* (1926), the critical effect of a lack of timber on the British navy. He suggested that the delay Graves experienced in sailing to relieve Cornwallis was directly attributable to a lack of timber, particularly masts. The importance of logistics was explored by Piers Mackesy in "British Strategy in the War of American Independence," in *The Yale Review* (1963). He made the point, quite correctly, that the British lost the war in spite of winning the battles. By the avoidance of decisive defeat and the attrition of British resources, the Americans were able to wear down the enemy. Mackesy observed that the basic reasons for the strategic decision to blockade the coast from a few naval strongholds were essentially logistical. The problem of transporting and supplying the British army in North America was of such proportions that it necessarily dictated the type of offensive which could be launched. Obviously, the defeat at Yorktown was the result not only of strategy but of logistics as well. The shipping Cornwallis had at Yorktown was essentially logistical, and the large number of ships is some indication of the scope of the problem he faced. The attempts the British made throughout the war to come to grips with this massive new problem were outlined by David Syrett in *Shipping and the American War, 1775–83: A Study of British Transport Organization* (1970). Notwithstanding continued efforts to supply their North American forces properly, the British never provided adequate support during the war. The problem was only compounded when the strategic decision to disperse forces throughout the South was made.

Two popular histories tell the most comprehensive story of the Battle of Yorktown and its naval aspects. *The Campaign That Won America: The Story of Yorktown,* by Burke Davis (1970), and *Beat the Last Drum: The Siege of Yorktown, 1781,* by Thomas J. Fleming (1963), both chronicle the history of the siege in detail. Neither author attempted to set the stage from either a strategic or a logistical point of view, and neither dealt in detail with the history of the captive fleet. In an area in which there is no shortage of literature, however, it must be said that these two books present the most readable and the clearest view of what was, at best, a complex and confusing campaign.

Notes

[1] Thomas Symonds to Board of Admiralty, 18 December 1781, ADM 1/2485, Public Record Office.

[2] Benson J. Lossing, *The Pictorial Field-Book of the Revolution,* 2 vols. (New York: Harper & Brothers, 1851), 1:34.

[3] Ibid., p. 530.

[4] Alfred Thayer Mahan, *Naval Strategy Compared and Contrasted with the Principles and Practice of Military Operations on Land* (London: Sampson Low, Marston, 1911), p. 433.

[5] John J. Shafroth, "The Strategy of the Yorktown Campaign, 1781," *U.S. Naval Institute Proceedings* 57, no. 6 (June 1931):736.

Bibliography

~~~~~~~~~~~~~

Primary Sources
Published Works and Interviews

Acts of the General Assembly of Virginia, Passed in 1852, in the Seventy-Sixth Year of the Commonwealth. Richmond: William F. Ritchie, 1852.

Barron, James. "The Schooner Patriot." *Virginia Historical Register* 1 (1848):127–31.

[Butler, Richard]. "General Richard Butler's Journal of the Siege of Yorktown." *Historical Magazine* 8 (1864):102–12.

Carter, Edward C., ed. *The Virginia Journals of Benjamin Henry Latrobe, 1795–1798.* 2 vols. New Haven: Yale Univ. Press, 1977.

Chadwick, French Ensor, ed. *The Graves Papers and Other Documents Relating to The Naval Operations of the Yorktown Campaign, July to October 1781.* New York: Naval History Society, 1916.

[Closen, Ludwig, Baron Von]. *The Revolutionary Journal of Baron Ludwig Von Closen, 1780–1783.* Translated and edited by Evelyn M. Acomb. Williamsburg, Va: Institute of Early American History and Culture, 1958.

[Denny, Ebenezer]. *Military Journal of Major Ebenezer Denny, with an Introductory Memoir.* Philadelphia: Historical Society of Pennsylvania, 1859.

[Doehla, Johann Conrad]. "The Doehla Journal, 1781." *William & Mary Quarterly,* 2d ser., 22 (1942):229–74.

Doniol, Henri. *Histoire De La Participation De La France A L'Establissement Des Etats-Unis D'Ameriques: Correspondence Diplomatique et Documents.* 5 vols. Paris: Imprimerie Nationale, 1886–99.

[Duncan, James]. "Diary of Capt. James Duncan of Colonel Moses Hazen's Regiment in the Yorktown Campaign, 1781." *Pennsylvania Archives,* 2d ser. 15 (1893):743–52.

Ewald, Johann. *Diary of the American War: A Hessian Journal.* Translated and edited by Joseph P. Tustin. New Haven: Yale Univ. Press, 1979.

[Feltman, William]. "The Journal of Lt. William Feltman, of the First Penna. Regiment, 1781–1782." *Pennsylvania Archives,* 2d ser. 11 (1891):709–62.

Fitzpatrick, John C., ed. *The Diaries of George Washington, 1748–1799.* 4 vols. Boston: Houghton Mifflin, 1925.

————. *The Writings of George Washington from the Original Manuscript Sources, 1745–1799.* 39 vols. Washington, D.C.: Government Printing Office, 1931–44.

Ford, Worthington C., et al., eds. *Journals of the Continental Congress, 1774–1789.* 34 vols. Washington, D.C.: Government Printing Office, 1904–37.

Gottschalk, Louis, ed. *The Letters of Lafayette to Washington, 1777–1799.* New York: Privately printed, 1944.

Hamilton, Harry H. Yorktown, Va. Interview, 18 August 1978.

Institut Français de Washington, ed. *Correspondence of General Washington and Comte de Grasse: 1781, August 17–November 4.* Washington, D.C.: Government Printing Office, 1931.

Jenkins, Herndon. Richmond, Va. Interview, June 1972.

Journal of the Siege of Yorktown as recorded in the hand of Gaspard de Gallatin and translated by the French Department of the College of William and Mary. Washington, D.C.: Government Printing Office, 1931.

[Lafayette, Marquis de]. *Memoirs, Correspondence and Manuscripts of General Lafayette, Published by His Family.* London: Saunders and Otley, [1837].

Laughton, John Knox, ed. *Journal of Rear-Admiral Bartholomew James.* London: Navy Records Society, 1896.

Lloyd's Register, 1776–1782. Reprint ed. London: Gregg Press, n.d.

New Lloyd's List. Reprint ed. Farnborough, England: Gregg International Publishers, 1969.

Palmer, William P., ed. *Calendar of Virginia State Papers and Other Manuscripts Preserved in the Capitol at Richmond.* 11 vols. Richmond: N.p., 1875–93.

Pennsylvania Packet. Philadelphia: September–December 1781.

[Popp, Stephen]. *A Hessian Soldier in the American Revolution: The Diary of Stephen Popp.* Translated by Reinhart J. Pope. N.p.: Privately printed, 1953.

Rice, Howard C., and Brown, Anne S. K., translators and editors. *The American Campaigns of Rochambeau's Army: 1780, 1781, 1782, 1783.* 2 vols. Princeton: Princeton Univ. Press, 1972.

[Rodney, George, Lord]. *Letter-Books and Order-Book of George, Lord Rodney, Admiral of the White Squadron: 1780–1782.* New York: Naval History Society, 1932.

Ross, Charles, ed. *Correspondence of Charles, First Marquis Cornwallis.* London: John Murray, 1859.

Schoepf, Johann David. *Travels in the Confederation.* Translated and edited by Alfred J. Morrison. Reprint ed. New York: Bergman, 1968.

Shea, J. G., ed. *The Operations of the French Fleet under the Count de Grasse in 1781–2, as Described in Two Contemporaneous Journals.* New York: Bradford Club, 1864.

Sniffen, Harold S. The Mariners' Museum, Newport News, Va. Interview, June 1972.

Stevens, Benjamin Franklin. *Facsimiles of Manuscripts in European Archives Relating to America: 1773–1783*. London: Chadwick Press, 1898.

———— ed. *The Campaign in Virginia, 1781*. 2 vols. London: B. F. Stevens, 1888.

Tarleton, Banastre. *A History of the Campaigns of 1780 and 1781, in the Southern Provinces of North America*. London: T. Cadell, 1787.

Thacher, James. *A Military Journal during the American Revolutionary War, from 1775–1783*. Boston: Cottons & Barnard, 1827.

[Tucker, St. George]. "Diary of the Siege of Yorktown." *William & Mary Quarterly*, 3d ser. 5 (1948):375–95.

U.S. Naval History Division. *Naval Documents of the American Revolution*. Washington, D.C.: Government Printing Office, 1964–.

Weld, Isaac, Jr. *Travels through the States of North America, and the Provinces of Upper and Lower Canada, during the Years 1795, 1796, and 1797*. 2 vols. London: John Stockdale, 1800.

Manuscripts

Ann Arbor, Mich. William L. Clements Library, University of Michigan. Castellane Family Manuscripts. Sir Henry Clinton Papers. George Germain Papers. William Knox Papers. Lord Shelburn Papers. Richard Oswald, "General Observations Relative to the Present State of the War, London, August 9, 1779"; "Thoughts on the War between Great Britain and America wrote in Septr. and October 1776 and Thoughts on the Same Subject wrote Feby., 1778."

Boston. Massachusetts Historical Society. Miscellaneous Collections. Heath Papers.

Chapel Hill, N.C. University of North Carolina. Southern Historical Collection. Allen Jones Letters.

Charlottesville. University of Virginia Library. Hammond Papers.

Chicago. Chicago Historical Society. Robert Carter Collection.

Durham, N.C. Duke University Library. Mrs. Edward Dunning Papers. John Page Papers.

Edinburgh, Scottish Record Office. Cunninghame of Thornton Papers. GD 35/57—Dundas Muniments.

Fort Eustis, Va. U.S. Army Transportation Museum. Historical Files.

Greenwich, England: National Maritime Museum. Admiralty Logbooks. "Progress and Dimension Book, 1765–1782" (photostat).

London. House of Lords Record Office. Main Papers, February–March 1782, February 1778.

————. Public Record Office. Admiralty 1/486–491, 1501, 1839, 2393–2485, 5319–5320; 2/1116; 7/205, 565; 49/2–6; 51/375, 796; 52/1748; 106/280, 2607, 3319, 3525–29; 108/1; 180/3–9. Audit Office 1/338/1357; 13/2–5. Colonial Office 5/95–102; 5/239. High Court of Admiralty 32/286–467; 42/134. State Papers 42/57. War Office 47/99; 60/25. 30/11 Cornwallis

Papers. 30/55 Headquarters Papers of the British Army in North America.

Morristown, N.J. Morristown National Historical Park. Lloyd W. Smith Collection.

New York City. Fordham University Library. Jonathan Trumbull, "Journal at Yorktown."

———. Fraunces Tavern Museum Archives. Society of the Sons of the Revolution, State of New York.

———. J. Pierpont Morgan Library. "Documents Relating to the Siege of Yorktown, 1778–1788."

Newport News, Va. The Mariners' Museum. Archives. Ship's Papers Collection. Clipping File.

Nottingham, England. Nottingham University. Department of Manuscripts. Charles Mellish of Hodstock Papers. Newcastle Papers (Clinton Letters).

Paris. Archives Nationales. Archives de la Marine, B4, 184–225. Archives Diplomatiques. Correspondence Politiques, Etats Unis Supplement.

———. Bibliothèque Nationale. Fr. N. A. Margry.

Providence. Brown University. Ann Mary Brown Library. General George Weedon Papers.

Richmond. Office of the Attorney General. "The Commonwealth's Ownership and Interest in British Vessels of the Revolutionary War, Sunk at Yorktown, Virginia." Memorandum to Virginia Historic Landmarks Commission, November 7, 1975.

———. Virginia State Library. Executive Department. Governor's Office Papers. Papers concerning the Army of the Revolution.

Toulon, France. Collection of Dr. and Mme Pierre Porruchio. Papers of Joseph-Jacques-François de Martelli Chautard.

Washington D.C. Library of Congress. Geography and Map Division. Rochambeau Collection. Yorktown Campaign Collection. Manuscript Division. "Diary of French Naval Operations in America, 5 January 1779 to 2 September 1782." Edward Hand Papers (Force Transcripts). William Reynolds Letterbook. Rochambeau Papers. "Christopher Vail's Journal, 1775–1782" (Force Transcripts). Washington Papers.

———. National Archives. Record Group 93. Miscellaneous Numbered Records.

Williamsburg, Va. College of William and Mary. Swem Library. Herbert H. Vreeland Collection.

———. Colonial Williamsburg Foundation. Department of Research and Record. Simcoe Papers.

Yorktown, Va. Colonial National Historical Park. Park Archives. Ensign Dennis Orderly Book (photostat).

———. York County Courthouse. York County Records. "Claims for Losses of York County in British Invasion of 1781."

Secondary Sources

Albion, Robert Greenhalgh. *Forests and Sea Power: The Timber Problem of the Royal Navy, 1652–1862.* Cambridge, Mass: Harvard Univ. Press, 1926.

Andahazy, William J.; Everstine, Douglas G.; and Hood, Bruce R. "Magnetic Search for Shipwrecks from the Battle of Yorktown." *Sea Technology* 17, no. 11 (November 1976):19–22.

Bass, George F.; Noël Hume, Ivor; Sands, John O.; and Steffy, J. Richard. "The Cornwallis Cave Shipwreck." Report submitted to Virginia Historic Landmarks Commission, 1976.

Broadwater, John D. "A Search for the USS *Monitor.*" *International Journal of Nautical Archaeology and Underwater Exploration* 4, no. 1 (March 1975):117–21.

———; Sands, John O.; and Watts, Gordon P., Jr. "Report of an Archaeological Survey of Several Shipwreck Sites near Yorktown, Virginia." Report submitted to Virginia Historic Landmarks Commission, 8 December 1975.

Burns, K. V. *Plymouth's Ships of War: A History of Naval Vessels Built in Plymouth between 1694 and 1860.* Greenwich, England: National Maritime Museum, 1972.

Carson, Jane. *Travelers in Tidewater Virginia 1700–1800: A Bibliography.* Williamsburg, Va: Colonial Williamsburg, 1969.

Chapelle, Howard I. *The History of American Sailing Ships.* New York: Norton, 1935.

Charnock, John. *A History of Marine Architecture.* 3 vols. London: Nichols & Son, 1800–1802.

Clos, Jean Henri. *The Glory of Yorktown.* Yorktown, Va.: Yorktown Historical Society, 1924.

Colonial National Monument. "A Bibliography of the Virginia Campaign and Siege of Yorktown, 1781." Yorktown, Va: U.S. National Park Service, 1941.

Davis, Burke. *The Campaign That Won America: The Story of Yorktown.* New York: Dial, 1970.

Etat Sommaire Des Archives De La Marine Antérieures A La Révolution. Paris: Librairie Militaire de L. Baudoin, 1898.

Ferguson, Homer L. "Salvaging Revolutionary Relics from the York River." *William & Mary Quarterly,* 2d ser. 19 (1939):257–71.

Fleming, Thomas J. *Beat the Last Drum: The Siege of Yorktown, 1781.* New York: St. Martin's 1963.

Frechette, Fred. "Cornwallis Fleet, Ahoy." *Richmond Times-Dispatch,* 2 August 1954, p. 144.

Gibbons, Howard. "Army Divers Recover Piece of Vessel Believed British Revolutionary Warship." *Times Herald* (Newport News, Va.), 10 January 1950, p. 4.

Goldenberg, Joseph A. *Shipbuilding in Colonial America*. Charlottesville: Univ. Press of Virginia, 1976.

Gray, Mary Wiatt. *Gloucester County*. Richmond: Cottrell & Cooke, 1936.

Greene, Jack P. "The Reappraisal of the American Revolution in Recent Historical Literature." Baltimore: American Historical Association Service Center for Teachers of History, Publication no. 68, 1967.

Higginbotham, Don. "American Historians and the Military History of the American Revolution." *American Historical Review* 70 (1964):18–34.

———. *The War of American Independence: Military Attitudes, Policies, and Practice, 1763–1789*. New York: Macmillan, 1971.

Inventaire Des Archives De La Marine: Séries B, Service General. Paris: Librairie de L. Baudoin and Archives Nationales, 1885–1963.

Ipswich, Christopher. "Diving at Yorktown." *Richmond Times-Dispatch*, January 16, 1938.

James, W. M. *The British Navy in Adversity: A Study of the War of American Independence*. London: Longmans, Green, 1933.

Jeffries, John H. "Maryland Naval Barges in the Revolutionary War." Princess Anne, Md.: Privately printed, 1978.

Jenkins, C. W. "Combined Operations, Revolutionary War: Yorktown." *Coast Artillery Journal* 72 (April 1930):315–33.

Johnston, Paul F.; Sands, John O.; and Steffy, J. Richard. "The Cornwallis Cave Shipwreck, Yorktown, Virginia: Preliminary Report." *International Journal of Nautical Archaeology and Underwater Exploration* 7, no. 3 (August 1978):205–26.

Knox, Dudley W. *The Naval Genius of George Washington*. Boston: Houghton Mifflin, 1932.

Larrabee, Harold A. *Decision at the Chesapeake*. New York: Clarkson N. Potter, 1964.

Lewis, Charles Lee. *Admiral De Grasse and American Independence*. Annapolis: U.S. Naval Institute, 1945.

Lossing, Benson J. *The Pictorial Field-Book of the Revolution*. 2 vols. New York: Harper & Brothers, 1851.

Lynch, Barbara A. *The War at Sea: France and the American Revolution, a Bibliography*. Washington, D.C.: Government Printing Office, 1976.

Mackesy, Piers. "British Strategy in the War of American Independence." *Yale Review* 52, no. 4 (June 1963):539–57.

———. *The War for America, 1775–1783*. Cambridge, Mass.: Harvard Univ. Press, 1964.

Mahan, Alfred Thayer. *Naval Strategy Compared and Contrasted with the Principles and Practice of Military Operations on Land*. London: Sampson Low, Marston, 1911.

———. *The Influence of Sea Power upon History, 1660–1783*. Boston: Little, Brown, 1898.

————. *The Major Operations of the Navies in the War of American Independence.* London: Sampson Low, Marston, 1913.

Metzger, Charles H. *The Prisoner in the American Revolution.* Chicago: Loyola Univ. Press, 1971.

Miles, A. H. "Sea Power and the Yorktown Campaign." *U.S. Naval Institute Proceedings* 53, no. 11 (November 1927): 1169–84.

Miller, Edward M., ed. "Project Cheesebox: A Journey into History." U.S. Naval Academy, Annapolis, Md., 1974.

Morgan, William J. "The Pivot upon Which Everything Turned." *Iron Worker,* Spring 1958.

Noël Hume, Ivor. *Here Lies Virginia: An Archaeologist's View of Colonial Life and History.* New York: Knopf, 1968.

Potter, E. B., and Nimitz, Chester W. *Sea Power: A Naval History.* Englewood Cliffs, N.J.: Prentice-Hall, 1960.

Sands, John O. "Sea Power at Yorktown: The Archaeology of the Captive Fleet." Diss., George Washington Univ. 1980.

————. "Shipwrecks of the Battle of Yorktown, 1781: A Preliminary Archaeological Study." Master's thesis, Univ. of Delaware, 1973.

Shafroth, John F. "The Strategy of the Yorktown Campaign, 1781." *U.S. Naval Institute Proceedings* 57, no. 6 (June 1931):721–36.

Skerrett, R. G. "Lake Champlain Yields Wreck of 'Royal Savage.' " *Compressed Air Magazine* 40, no. 1 (January 1935):4626–30.

Steffy, J. Richard, "The *Charon* Project: A Preliminary Report." Unpublished report, 10 August 1980, Texas A & M University, College Station, Tex.

Stewart, Robert Armistead. *The History of Virginia's Navy of the Revolution.* Richmond: R. A. Stewart, 1933.

Syrett, David. *Shipping and the American War, 1775–83: A Study of British Transport Organization.* London: Athlone, 1970.

Verner, Coolie. "Maps of the Yorktown Campaign 1780–1781: A Preliminary Checklist of Printed and Manuscript Maps Prior to 1800." *Map Collector's Circle* 18 (1965):1–64.

Watts, Gordon P., Jr. "The Location and Identification of the Ironclad USS *Monitor.*" *International Journal of Nautical Archaeology and Underwater Exploration* 4, no. 2 (September 1975):301–29.

Wickwire, Franklin, and Wickwire, Mary. *Cornwallis: The American Adventure.* Boston: Houghton Mifflin, 1970.

Willcox, William B. "The British Road to Yorktown: A Study in Divided Command." *American Historical Review* 52, no. 1 (October 1946):1–35.

————. *Portrait of a General: Sir Henry Clinton in the War of Independence.* New York: Knopf, 1964.

Wright, John W. "Notes on the Siege of Yorktown in 1781 with Special Reference to the Conduct of a Siege in the Eighteenth Century." *William & Mary Quarterly* 2d ser. 12 (1932):229–52.

Index

Page numbers in *italics* refer to illustrations.